Goldsmiths
University of London

GO[illegible]H

an antholog[illegible]ing from
Goldsmiths

EDITOR
Sara Grant

EDITORIAL TEAM
Peter Carter
Lara Frankena
Elizabeth Mercereau
Helena Michaelson
Alex Mitchell

Goldsmiths
University of London
Masters in Creative and Life Writing
New Cross
London SE14 6NW

ISBN 1-904158-66-8
First published in Great Britain 2006 by
Goldsmiths, University of London, New Cross, London SE14 6NW

Visit Goldsmiths online magazine of creative and life writing at www.goldfish.gold.ac.uk

Additional copies of this publication are available from:
English and Comparative Literature
Goldsmiths
University of London
New Cross
London SE14 6NW

Price £6.99
Cheques made payable to Goldsmiths College
should be sent with the order.

Designed and printed by the Reprographic Unit, Goldsmiths.

CONTENTS

INTRODUCTION

This volume gathers together a selection of work by some of the students who have graduated from the first five years of the Masters in Creative and Life Writing at Goldsmiths College. The selection has been made largely by course tutors, but the students themselves took charge of the editing and production of the anthology, in collaboration with the College's Reprographic Unit.

The decision to take a Masters in Creative Writing is sometimes hard won. Our students are of all ages and backgrounds, and have often struggled to find the time and the money to study. What motivates them is the knowledge that for them writing is not an indulgence or a hobby but a serious and profound force in their lives. Often they have been writing in spare moments and in isolation for several years, then reach the point where they feel ready for the discipline of a formalised programme – and are receptive to the guidance of other practitioners.

We are fortunate at Goldsmiths in the range of writers we have been able to draw upon. Among those who have acted as tutors and mentors are Lavinia Greenlaw and Stephen Knight (both members of staff here), as well as Romesh Gunesekera, Richard Skinner, Emily Perkins, Joan Anim-Addo, Maggie Gee, Maurice Riordan, Pamela Johnson and Susan Elderkin. Many other writers have also come to the College to share their insights into the craft, during specially arranged sessions with our Masters students . . . among them Kazuo Ishiguro, Helen Simpson, Jackie Kay, Andrew O'Hagan, James Kelman and Aminatta Forna.

For most people the first association with the name Goldsmiths' will be a stream of talent in the visual arts. That stream includes Turner Prize winners Damien Hirst, Gillian Wearing and Antony Gormley. There are others, like Sam Taylor-Wood or Fiona Banner, whose presence in and beyond the arts world has been stimulating and influential. But there is also excellent and noteworthy work in every other department of this creative arts college. Although the Masters in Creative and Life Writing is still young, as the promise of this volume shows it is beginning to make its mark. Several of our students have been taken on by major publishers and agents. We hope some of the other names to be found here, new to a reader now, will become familiar, established even, in a few years' time.

Maura Dooley & Blake Morrison

ABOUT GOLDSMITHS

Founded in 1891 and located in South-east London, Goldsmiths has been part of the University of London since 1904. It aims to be pre-eminent in the study and practice of creative, cognitive, cultural and social processes. Fifteen academic departments – together with smaller centres and units – interact to provide a unique approach to creativity.

Currently in its sixth year, Goldsmiths' Masters in Creative and Life Writing is designed to meet the needs of students who are interested in exploring and exploiting their own possibilities as writers.

GREENFLY!

by Tom Lee

During the time when B and I first started telling each other we were in love, one of the conversations we used to have was about how injured, disabled, disfigured or otherwise debilitated we would have to be to make the other fall out of love. I said we should draw up a document which specified what level of injury to one of us released the other from the obligations of being in love. B said he'd still push me around if I lost both my legs. I said I'd empty his colostomy bag if he had to have one. B said he'd feel justified leaving me if I had 90 percent or more burns but anything else was fine. I said I didn't care if he was burnt to a crisp as long as his dick could still stand up.

I noticed the greenfly problem on a Friday night. B was watching TV, a documentary I think, and I was playing backgammon on the computer. The adverts came on and B said: 'Martin's coming over to dinner next week. He's thinking of buying a place round here. OK with you?'

'I can hardly stop him.'

'I meant about dinner.'

'I knew what you meant,' I said.

'His girlfriend's coming too. She works in TV. You'll like her.' The adverts finished – the final freeze frame seemed to last forever – and B's programme came back on. I carried on at the computer and had just brought my last counter home, winning the game narrowly, when something broke my concentration; perhaps the light flickered or there was some slight noise. I looked away from the screen and up at the ceiling. Spreading out from around the light fitting were lots of little specks, too many to count, each with their own little shadow. I stood on a chair to get a closer look.

'Molly?' said B.

'We've been invaded by greenfly,' I said.

'You're blocking the light.'

I got down from the chair and went into the kitchen. The greenfly were swarming over the ceiling there too. I went into the bathroom, the bedroom, then the spare bedroom. It was the same thing. I stood in the doorway of the living room.

'We're infested.'

'Hold on a minute, Molly I just want to see this.'

A few minutes later the programme finished. B turned off the TV and stood up. He stretched and looked at his watch. He flinched when he saw me and then tried to look like he hadn't.

'I'm off to bed,' he said. 'Big day tomorrow.'

'Every day's a big day,' I said, putting on the American drawl we sometimes used.

'Sure is, baby,' said B, smiling, and speaking in the same accent. 'So that's OK about dinner?'

I nodded. 'Great,' he said. 'It'll be fun.'

B went to bed and I looked up at the ceiling. A funny time of year for insects, I thought, standing there. I shut all the windows, turned out the lights and went to bed in the spare room.

As usual, I slept badly. When I got up I looked into the bedroom, but B had already gone to work, even though it was Saturday. The greenfly were everywhere. Too little light or not enough air, either way, they were all dead. Everywhere. Greenfly on the bed, along windowsills, on the floor, on kitchen surfaces, on the top of cupboards and picture frames, the TV and the computer. There were green specks in the sugar, in plant pots, on dirty plates and bowls. Thousands of little deaths, all delicately rigid and contorted.

I began to clean up. There was something satisfying about the way they covered every upturned surface. I wondered if they all died at the same time and fell throughout the flat, a sudden, thick green rain. Or if they dropped one by one when they ran out of light, or air, or whatever it was they needed. Did they die and then fall, or perhaps weaken, lose their grip, the unlucky ones drowning, flailing, in the toilet bowl or a half drunk cup of coffee? The possibilities were endless. Maybe they only lived for a day anyway – some insects were like that, I knew.

It took me until about midday to clean up. After lunch I went over the surfaces with bleach, because it seemed like the right thing to do. There was a stale smell that may or may not have had anything to do with the greenfly massacre; 'the smell of death,' I said dramatically, flinging the windows open to let in some air. After that I showered and washed my hair. A few little bodies spun around the plughole before darting down.

B phoned at six to say that he and 'Marty' were going for a beer and maybe some food. 'I won't be late,' he said.

After dinner I switched on the computer and played a few games of backgammon. At level five I won about half and the computer won about half. The technique I use is to move the counters up slowly, keeping them close together and evenly spread, until I can block out the whole final quarter. Then, with at least one of their counters out of play, my opponent is unable to take their go until I release a space. At this point I can take my time rolling, bringing up my other counters and cleaning up any of the other player's stray pieces. This strategy gives the most consistently good results, and has the added advantage of attacking your opponent psychologically. Frustrated, trapped, unable to even roll, they invariably end up doing something reckless. This was the technique I used to beat B when he and I played – when we first lived together and on holiday. 'Passive-aggressive,' he called it, and he may have been right. About a year ago B said he found the game boring. I said: 'Always losing *is* boring. But spare a thought for me. Always winning is boring too.'

At some point I must have fallen asleep. Normally I take a nap in the afternoon, to make up for not sleeping so well at night, but I had been preoccupied with the cleaning and forgot. I woke up in the computer chair, my hand still on the mouse. The screen saver was scrolling around and around: 'All play and no work makes Molly a dull girl. All play and no work . . . ' The first time B saw it he laughed, but that was months ago. The windows were black and still open and the greenfly had returned. Their shadows wavered slightly in the breeze, like tiny flames.

I swore aloud, more for effect than out of feeling. It was careless, I thought, falling asleep like that. It made me smile, though, when I thought of the girl slumbering at her computer like some fairytale ogre, while the greenfly rushed through the open window, attracted to the homely glow. I considered turning the lights off and leaving the window open. Perhaps they would leave of their own accord. But perhaps more would come. I didn't want to risk it. The thought of them floating down on me in the night was unsettling, and on top of that I had no wish to spend my Sunday cleaning.

I closed the windows and got the vacuum cleaner out. It was quite awkward and I felt a little ridiculous. I was glad there was no one else to see me doing it, standing on a chair, vacuuming the ceiling. I did the same in each room.

Before going to bed I wrote a note: 'Don't open windows or leave lights on. GREENFLY!'

In the morning I was pleased to see there were no signs of the invaders. I hadn't heard B come in, so I supposed it must have been late. He got up at lunchtime, made some toast and put on the TV. There was an old film on, the one where Kirk Douglas has his eye pecked out by an eagle.

In an advert break B said: 'Martin's invited us away for a weekend. His parents own a cottage on the coast.' Martin is one of B's work-people. I hadn't met him but I pictured him to be quite handsome, better looking than B anyway. Since Martin joined B's firm, B can't stop talking about him. Men are just like children when they make a new friend.

'Why don't you go on your own?'

'Sophie will be there as well. It'd be odd if you didn't go.'

'Would it?'

B didn't say anything. I said: 'Did you see my note about the greenfly?' B pointed at the screen. The film had come back on and a great Viking feast was in progress. I went back to the backgammon, winning one game and losing two.

After a while the adverts came on again.

'What were you saying?' said B.

'Could you hold on?' I said. 'I just want to see this ad. I'm particularly interested in this product.'

B sighed. 'Molly, you've got to stop living your life from behind a hedge.' B's company spends a fortune sending him on courses where they teach him to say things like that.

'I think they're coming up from the canal.'

'What?' said B.

'The greenfly. They're probably attracted to stagnant water.'

'Give it a rest, Molly. I've been non-stop all week. I don't want to spend my day off talking about fucking bugs.'

'Greenfly,' I said.

I went and lay on the bed in the spare room. A few minutes later the phone rang. B answered it and I heard his voice brighten, though I couldn't hear the words. I heard him put the phone down and start whistling quietly to himself. It was a new thing, this whistling. Then he knocked at the door and came in. He stood in the doorway, fidgeting.

'I'm sorry,' he said. 'It's just – if you didn't have so much time on your hands, maybe you wouldn't get so – ' He paused and looked at his palms, pretending to search for the appropriate word. I propped my head up on my hand to listen. 'So obsessive about things. Have you thought about going back to work?' He paused again. 'Sometimes it's not good to think too much.'

'Thanks for the advice,' I said. They should put that last comment on his gravestone.

'Anyway, that was Marty. We're going to shoot some pool at a bar he knows. We'll talk about things tomorrow, OK?'

I heard B come in later, but it was after midnight and I was already in bed, trying to sleep. In the morning there were greenfly everywhere, dead again. It was as if I had never cleared them up the first time and had just been ignoring their presence. But of course this was a whole other batch, a new generation in all likelihood. In the bedroom a window was open.

Using a broom and a dust pan and brush I swept the greenfly into about ten little heaps. Then, out of curiosity, I gathered them all together and made a pile about as big as my fist. There must have been thousands of them. All balanced on top of each other it looked like some complicated molecular structure from a science book.

I was just about to flush the whole lot down the toilet when the phone rang. It was B.

'I've fixed up for a guy to come round and finish the tiling. Will you be in?'

'There's every possibility.'

'It'd be nice to have the apartment finished for dinner tomorrow.' B paused, perhaps waiting for me to speak. I was confused for a second when he said 'apartment' but then I realised he meant our flat. 'Any thoughts about our conversation yesterday?' he went on. I listened to the grey hum of office noise coming over the line: voices, air conditioning, electronics. 'Molly, have you – '

'What conversation?' I said.

'About going back to work.'

'I haven't had time. I've been non-stop. Clearing up all the greenfly you let in when you opened your window.'

'For christsake Molly.' B lowered his voice; I imagined people in his office looking over. 'Forget about the damn bugs. Get over it. The builder's coming at three.'

'Greenfly,' I said. But he had already hung up.

Sweeping the pile into the dustpan I went into the bedroom and drew back the duvet. 'The devil makes work for idle hands,' I murmured, shaking the greenfly out over the sheets.

The builder buzzed just after three. I looked at his face bobbing on the monitor and then let him in. I could see he was impressed by the flat. It is quite impressive, though sometimes I have to be reminded of that. It is situated in a sought-after block in a desirable location, as the estate agent put it. The building is a converted textile factory and that was one of the things B said he liked about it, the sense of history. We are on the fifth floor, overlooking the canal, and there is a good view across the city. It was the last available flat in the block and up until we moved in it was used as the 'show home' and temporary offices of the estate agent. As a result it was expensively done out in up-to-the-minute interior decoration – reclaimed wood floors in the living room and bedrooms, slate floors in the hall and kitchen, designer kitchen units, bathroom suite and furniture. When we bought the flat they threw in all these interiors at a knock-down price. Of course they had little bits of damage: floors marked by all the shoes that had traipsed through, greasy stains from where endless anonymous hands had fingered things, but nothing you'd notice if you weren't actively looking for it. Nevertheless, it was a stretch for us – and if my salary were stopped then I don't know what we'll do – but once B saw it he had his heart set on it. I said I could take it or leave it, we could carry on looking. That annoyed B. He said: 'We're moving for your benefit, remember,' which was debatable, though what he meant was that it was close to the school. It is all very tasteful and modern but often I am reminded that it is someone else's idea of perfect living.

While the builder worked away in the bathroom I looked up some things on the internet. When he was finished he came into the living room and I wrote him a cheque.

'Nice place,' he said.

'It has its disadvantages.'

'Oh?'

'Bit of an insect problem at the moment.'

'Funny time of year for them.'

'Greenfly. We've never had them before.'

'You would've thought you'd be safe from them up here.'

'You would have thought.'

'Perhaps they're attracted by the tropical climate.'

'Perhaps,' I said, and smiled at his joke.

The builder had nodded at the back wall of the living room which was papered with a vast photograph of a jungle scene. The trees were heavy with brightly coloured fruits and parrots and a frothing waterfall tumbled through the middle, the image of a bountiful paradise. This was the one significant addition we had made to the flat, the stamp of our personality. Or B's anyway. It was his idea, I think he'd seen it in a bar he drank in with work-people. I came home late one evening soon after we moved in, when I was still working, and B intercepted me at the door.

'Close your eyes,' he had said, leading me into the living room. 'OK.'

'Wow,' I said.

'It's kitsch,' B said triumphantly.

'Does that mean the same as ugly?' He looked downcast. 'Joke,' I said.

'Funny,' said B.

That night we took off our clothes and photographed ourselves posing in front of the new addition, draped in garlands of plastic flowers left over from a party. I said I felt like I was in an Elvis movie. B said this was the Garden of Eden and that he had an appetite for some of Eve's forbidden fruit.

By eleven B wasn't home. I went to bed but was still awake when he came in just after twelve. From the amount of noise he was making it was obvious he was drunk. I didn't call out and when he pushed the door of the spare room open I pretended to be asleep. I listened as he clumsily took off his clothes and dropped them on the floor. He got into bed and moved against me.

'Can I stay in here tonight?' he whispered. 'I'm sorry about before, on the phone. I'm under a lot of pressure.' His penis was pushing against my buttock. 'Molly?' He smoothed my hair away from my face. 'Molly?' I lay still. He began to rub gently against me, my back, my buttocks and my thighs, his breaths coming quicker, shallower. His body tensed suddenly, briefly, and he came into the small of my back.

I lay awake listening to B's breathing even out, deepen. When it seemed likely he was asleep I got out of bed, put on my dressing gown and went to the bathroom to shower. Afterwards I went into the kitchen. I drank a glass of water and looked up at the ceiling. It was thick with greenfly. I switched on the light in the living room and saw the same thing. I turned on the computer and waited whilst it booted up.

I concentrated on the computer screen. I won three games at level five, a good result. My head felt clearer and I shut the computer down and stood up. Standing in the doorway, about to switch off the light, I looked up at the greenfly and had the curious thought that they had been waiting for me, that they were there for my benefit. When I thought of this I felt, I suppose, comforted, as if we shared a secret. I even felt a twinge of guilt for vacuuming them up that time.

In the bedroom I slid under the duvet. I couldn't feel them but I knew all against my skin were the greenfly I had deposited there earlier. Still, there were worse things to spend the night with and I wasn't about to put on new sheets at this time.

I woke to the sound of B slamming the door on his way out to work. I got up and checked each room but there were no open windows so it was really a mystery how the greenfly had got in in the night. Nevertheless, the evidence was there, all around, a snowfall of little green bodies. I began the clean-up straightaway, still wearing my dressing gown. I hadn't been doing it long when the phone went. It was B, calling from work.

'You haven't forgotten about tonight?' he said. He sounded fragile. 'I'll be home early to cook. Could you,' he said tentatively, 'Could you make sure the place is clean?'

'You mean get rid of the greenfly?' There was a pause.

'Sorry, Molly? someone was speaking to me.'

'I said I'm doing it as we speak.'

'Great. I'll see you later.' He hung up.

Martin and Sophie arrived promptly at eight, with a bottle of wine. B had been back for a couple of hours and done all the cooking. At about half past seven he had put the lasagne in the oven and gone into the bedroom to change. When he came out he looked at me and said: 'What are you wearing?' I cocked my head, pretending not to understand. 'Make an effort, Molly,' he said, 'for me?'

'Well, if you put it like that,' I said. In the bedroom I took off the comfortable tracksuit bottoms and T-shirt and debated. Finally I put on a skirt and a tight top that B once said was 'whorish, but in a good way'.

B asked me to open the wine whilst he gave Martin and Sophie 'the tour'. They went out onto the balcony and Martin gave a low whistle when B pointed out how far you could see across the city. In the living room I heard them laugh and when I went in with the wine they were looking at the jungle scene on the back wall. B was grinning inanely, like a proud father. I poured the wine and handed it round.

'Finally, the famous apartment,' said Martin. 'And the famous Molly.'

'The infamous Martin,' I said.

'I love your apartment,' said Sophie.

'I tend to think of it as a flat really,' I said.

'Flat, apartment, what's the difference?' said Martin, smiling.

'I've no idea,' I said. 'Perhaps you can tell us,' I said, turning to B.

'Sit, sit,' said B. 'The food's nearly ready.' We all sat down around the glass coffee table. I was surprised at how similar Martin and Sophie were to how I had expected. She had long blonde hair and I could see she was pretty, in the unimaginative way men find attractive. Martin was reasonably good looking, as predicted, with what is probably known as a good jaw. He had a cleft in his chin that was like the one Kirk Douglas – and later Michael – has, though the resemblance ended there. B and I often used to talk about couples we knew or who we saw in the street and judge which was the better looking of the pair. Based on the degree of difference we would estimate how long the relationship would last. B and I were usually in agreement. The striking thing about Martin and Sophie was that there was nothing to choose between them; they were exactly as attractive as each other. I wondered if it had occurred to B.

'We're thinking of buying a place round here,' said Sophie, addressing me.

'So I gather,' I said.

'It's very up-and-coming, isn't it? Such a mixture of cultures. I love all that. Is it dangerous?'

'Only on the fifth floor,' I said and everyone laughed.

'Martin,' said B, 'come and give me a hand with the food.' B and Martin went into the kitchen.

'Smells amazing,' said Sophie, pronouncing amazing as if it were a very long word.

'More wine?' I said, and filled her glass.

'Martin can just about manage cheese on toast, under supervision. It must be wonderful having a man that can cook.'

'Yes, I'm so lucky,' I said. Sophie got up and walked around the living room, pausing in front of things, touching them. B and Martin came in, each carrying two plates of food.

'Here it is folks,' said Martin.

'The famous lasagne,' I said.

'Dig in,' said B. We sat down around the dining table and there was no conversation for a while, just the sound of Martin and Sophie murmuring satisfied noises as they ate.

'B says you're a teacher,' Martin said, taking a sip of wine. I nodded. 'I think you people are amazing saints. I could never do it.'

'It's a tough school too,' said B. 'I wouldn't send my kids there.'

'He doesn't mind sending his girlfriend there,' I said, putting a forkful of lasagne into my mouth. Martin chuckled.

'You're not working at the moment though?' said Sophie. I shook my head.

'She's thinking of going back in the new year,' said B.

'What do you do with all the time?' said Sophie. 'I'd go crazy.' I made a crazy face and Martin and Sophie laughed. B looked uneasy.

'Cheer up,' I said to him, 'the food's not that bad.' Martin and Sophie laughed again. Martin was laughing so much I thought he might slide off his chair, or throw up the lasagne.

'She's priceless, isn't she,' said Martin when he had more or less stopped laughing. 'I was told you had a great sense of humour.'

'Were you?' I looked at B. 'Well I suppose that's one way of putting it.'

'Sophie works in TV,' said B hastily.

'It's funny,' I said. 'I'm always hearing about people who work in TV. Personally I prefer the adverts – more imaginative. Tell me, what do you do in TV?'

'Well, at the moment I'm working on a documentary,' said Sophie. 'Very gritty. Inner city kids, no prospects, crack addiction and the rest. Give them their own cameras, let them tell their own story.'

'Sounds depressing,' I said.

'You'd be surprised,' said Sophie, 'it's actually great TV.'

'Speaking of TV,' I said, 'I read a story in the paper about a woman who always had the box on at full volume because she was deaf. Eventually it drove her husband mad and he strangled her with the aerial lead.' Martin and Sophie looked at each other. B was looking at his food but not eating it. Martin started laughing first, then Sophie. After that B joined in.

'It worries me how often she tells that story,' said B. It was hard to know what he was talking about because I only just made it up.

Sophie looked around the room. 'I just adore this place. You've done such nice things with it.'

'Oh, that wasn't us,' I said. 'It was all already here. We bought it knock-down from the estate agents. They were only going to trash it otherwise.'

'Please, Martin, can we get one just like it,' she said.

'It's a bit like being trapped in someone else's life,' I said. 'Do you know what I mean?'

'It must be lovely being so close to the water, the canal.'

'Except for the greenfly,' I said.

'Greenfly?' said Sophie.

'Molly seems to think we've been invaded by bugs,' said B.

'Greenfly,' I said. 'They appear every night on the ceiling. In the morning they're dead and Molly clears them up. Then, at night, they come back. We're infested.'

'Funny time of year for them,' said Martin.

'Isn't it,' I said.

'No sign of them now,' said Sophie, looking up and around.

'Stage-fright,' said B, idiotically. 'Molly does like to exaggerate things.'

'Yes,' I said, 'She's always making out things are worse than they are.'

B stood up. 'Molly, come and help me with the dessert.' B and I went into the kitchen and he took some raspberries out of the fridge. He turned towards me and looked like he was about to say something.

'How long do you give them?' I said, before he could speak.

'What?'

'Who's better looking?'

'Molly!' said B 'They're our guests.'

We went back in with the dessert. It was a pavlova, the other thing B cooked. The meringue was soft in the middle because it hadn't been in the oven for long enough. I had a few mouthfuls and then put my spoon down.

When everyone had finished eating B cleared the plates away and we moved onto the sofa and comfy chairs. Martin said: 'So who'd like a little after-dinner pick-me-up,' and spilled a small mound of cocaine onto the glass table. B said he wouldn't mind at all and Sophie said just a small one for her.

'Molly?' said Martin. B gave me a wary look.

'It doesn't agree with me, Martin,' I said, looking at B. 'Makes me prone to exaggeration.'

After that B, Martin and Sophie talked about their work and people they worked with. Martin said how he already had more money than he knew what to do with and if it kept on like this he could retire in five years. B said he'd been told it would be a miracle if he didn't get a promotion by Christmas. Sophie said how vital she felt her work was because it let people know what was going on beyond their front doors and garden fences. They all agreed with each other very strongly about everything.

I was distracted. I kept looking up at the ceiling. 'Molly,' said Martin, 'it looks like we've lost you. We're telling funny stories about people at work. Tell us something from the world of teaching.' The three of them turned towards me.

'I'm not sure if this counts,' I said, after thinking for a second. 'There was a man I used to teach with. One of his classes locked him in a stationery cupboard. He wept for two hours until someone let him out. His wife had just left him. Three days later I found him hanging from the ceiling of one of the prefabricated classrooms.' B, Martin and Sophie all looked blank, as if I had suddenly started speaking in a foreign language.

'How about some coffee?' said B.

'I'll give you a hand,' said Martin, and they got up and went into the kitchen.

When they had gone Sophie started smiling a funny, half smile, like she had a guilty secret. 'The reason we want a new place,' she said, 'is that we're having a baby. We've known for a little while but we wanted to wait and see if everything was alright. I came from the doctor this evening. You're the first person I've told.'

'You know,' I said, leaning across the table to Sophie, 'B doesn't even believe the greenfly exist.'

B and Martin came back in carrying the coffee and some cups. They were both smiling.

'Martin told me the wonderful news,' B said. He went over to Sophie and kissed her on the cheek. 'Congratulations.'

'You don't mind do you, baby?' said Martin. Sophie shook her head happily.

'They're having a baby,' B said to me.

'Also known as Plant Louse or Ant Cow, they are a species of sap-sucking, soft-bodied insects with tube-like projections known as cornicles on the abdomen. Wingless females produce living young without fertilization. It can be a serious pest. And yes, it is a funny time of year. I'm guessing global warming has disorientated them. Sudden alterations to a creature's environment can make them act unpredictably or erratically.' B had poured the coffee. He and Sophie were watching Martin divide up three more lines of cocaine. 'If we'd taken the problem seriously to begin with it wouldn't be an issue now,' I went on. 'Still, benefit of hindsight and all that. Of course B doesn't notice much that's going on around him, he's so focussed, obsessive you might say, about his work. Unfortunately poor Molly doesn't have that luxury.' B leaned over the table and snorted the cocaine through a rolled note.

'What was all that, Molly?' he said. Martin and Sophie took their turn leaning over the glass. For a while they talked about what it would be like to have a baby and they all agreed about how exciting it was. Martin mentioned someone at work who had just had a baby and they carried on talking about work-people, new bars in town, and a holiday Martin and Sophie had taken in the Maldives. They were talking quickly and were very enthusiastic about everything that was said. At about midnight they got their coats and B walked them to the door.

'I told you it'd be fun.' B had come back into the living room and was massaging my shoulders. His hands felt very rigid and it was quite uncomfortable. 'You were a real hit with them. Martin's suggesting we go down to the cottage the weekend after next.' B stopped massaging, sat down on the sofa and flicked on the TV. 'You know,' he said, not taking his eyes off the screen, 'If I get this promotion you wouldn't have to go back to work at all. You could stay here and have babies.'

I crossed the room and switched on the computer. When it had booted up I played a few games of backgammon. After a while B stood up.

'Right, I'm off to bed,' he said.

'Big day tomorrow?' I said.

'That's it, baby,' said B.

After B had gone I shut down the computer and looked up. It seemed completely normal to see the greenfly there, exposed on the white ceiling, expectant, vigilant, as if they weren't anywhere they shouldn't have been, their shadows flickering in the breeze from the open window.

GRANDMA CLARICE

by Amy Hanson

'Can you make the lunch?' my mother asks.

'Why can't *you?*' I want to know. 'I'm trying to work!'

'I'm *also* trying to work but Grandma has crapped herself and I'm cleaning her up. What would you rather do? The choice is yours – clean up crap or make lunch?'

I make lunch.

Mum doesn't want to eat because she has been cleaning up crap. Grandma doesn't want to eat because she's upset that she crapped herself. I don't want to eat because I can smell disinfectant and everyone is talking about crap.

We put Grandma back into bed all clean. The TV is on loudly. We both go back to working on our computers. Grandma does nothing. She stares at the TV. Crapping herself must have been the most exciting part of her day.

I go into her room and sit on the end of the bed.

'How are you feeling?' I ask.

'Ufol,' she replies in a slurred voice.

I start to recount a story, about trying to buy a football top for my boyfriend; she smiles. Her eyes are watery and glazed, like an old pug's.

'Is she going to die? Is this it?' I ask my mother in the kitchen, after the crapping and cleaning and cooking saga, which happens in a slightly different way every day.

'I don't know. When she moved in I thought she'd last a week, a year at the most.'

My grandmother, my mother's mother, moved in with us over a decade ago, when she was eighty-eight. At first this was good. She was funny, bossy, animated, emotional, loud, cross. Then two years ago she had a stroke. Now she is quiet and sad and waiting to die. My mother and I are waiting too. We know that she is waiting and she knows that we are waiting. You could call it a waiting game but there is nothing fun or game-like about it. The only game it makes me think of is a really long and drawn-out game of Monopoly when you've had to mortgage everything, you're in jail, you've got no money, the person next to you has Mayfair and you just want it to be over.

*

Before the stroke my mother didn't like to leave her alone in the house much, *in case something happened.* On the one night she did go out – something happened.

I'm sitting upstairs in my room. We've had dinner together and Grandma has been talking about her friends cheating at bridge. Then she told me a story she tells on a regular basis about Grandpa and how she met him at a dance, where she had been wearing a backless dress. She 'sensed' him watching her, turned around and they fell in love, but really, she felt, it was the dress that did it.

For some reason I feel like I should really go and talk to her again, before bed. I don't know why, I don't have anything to say, I know she'll bend my ear with the same old stories but I go anyway. Maybe I sense that this could be my last chance.

As I walk into her room she immediately starts talking from where she left off earlier:

'And then I saw the old bugger looking at Cynthia's cards. Well, I think, I'm not having that, I gave Cynthia a kick under the table and then I said to Martha, I said, "Your husband's a bloody cheat!" Ooh I tell you, she didn't like that, couldn't believe it, but I saw it! "He's not," she says. "I'm not," he says, but I know what I saw and so I just got up and I said to Cynthia, "You can stay but I'll be damned if I'm having my game of bridge ruined by a pair of bloody cheats." Oooh you should have seen their faces …'

'Are you watching this?' I ask, pointing at the telly.

'No, don't turn over. I'm waiting for Graham Norton, oooh he's so funny! So rude! Always talking about willies! Did you see it last week when …'

'Grandma!'

I look at her and she is staring in a vacant way in the direction of the telly.

'Grandma?'

One side of her face looks funny. It's all droopy and there is a tear rolling down the other side.

'Grandma! Grandma!'

She doesn't blink. The corner of the left side of her mouth is right down her chin, her cheek sagging, her left eye lower than her right. When I wave my hand across her face, she doesn't react. I shake her gently by the shoulder. She flops to the side.

'Grandma, are you all right?'

She doesn't move.

'Grandma please say something.'

Tears start to fall down my cheeks. Tears of fear – fear of something that has happened, fear of something that can't be stopped, tears that fall fast. I'm not making a noise. This is not the sort of crying when you have noise and snot and tears, just the tears on their own. Tears that know they don't need to be concealed because the person they are for does not know what is going on. She is still. She has stopped. That is why her face has flopped. I do not know why I am crying, but something in me realises before I do that this is Grandma dying.

I watch in fast-forward through rain as the ambulance men come. They are frightened of the dog. They put Grandma on a stretcher and cover her with a red blanket. I remember my mum saying, 'If anything happens, don't take her to the Whittington Hospital'.

They take her to the Whittington Hospital.

I sit with her on a stretcher in a corridor for hours. Nobody looks at her. Nobody rushes her anywhere. No handsome doctor comes and says not to worry she'll be all right. We just wait in the corridor.

'What's your name?' says a patronising nurse.

'Clarice,' I say, 'She can't say her name, look at her!'

'Ahh,' says the nurse.

'She can't say her name because she's had a bloody stroke!' My voice starts to rise and become shrill.

'How long has she been like this?'

'Just tonight, she's just had *a stroke*. Where is the fucking doctor?'

'Please don't swear.'

One nurse goes, another comes and goes, and they all ask the same questions and every time I try to explain that this is not my grandma, that my grandma is very different from this normally, that this is very bad, that she is normally very talkative, that this is an emergency, they look at me as if I'm mad, that I'm deluded, that this is an old dying lady and I can't accept it.

'How old did you say she is?' asks another nurse.

'Ninety-six.'

'Ahh,' she says in a 'that explains it' kind of voice.

'But she's not usually like this, I know she's old but seriously she's usually very, you know, awake!'

The nurse puts her head on one side and smiles at me sympathetically.

She does not believe me. I want to slap her, but instead I say, 'Where is the doctor?'

'He'll be round soon, lots of emergencies tonight.'

'This *is* an emergency!'

She smiles and walks away.

After four hours a twelve-year-old looking doctor arrives and I tell him what is wrong with her. Why did I let them bring her to the Whittington? I think. I start to cry and then to my great relief my mum arrives.

My grandma spends the next two days on a ward where no one seems to do anything. My mother and I take it in turns to visit every couple of hours. We find her waiting in her own wee, waiting in her own shit, falling out of the bed, unable to sit up. This is not the place for her to recover. This is a place where nurses with fat arses walk up and down kissing their teeth at old women and showing them no respect or love. This is the Whittington Hospital and it is a joke.

For these first couple of days she cannot talk at all, she can only sign or point at things she wants. I make her a sign on a piece of cardboard that says 'I NEED TO GO TO THE TOILET PLEASE', which she can hold up as the nurses idle by.

'She won't be able to talk again,' says one doctor.

'She may be able to talk again,' says another.

'She will probably be able to say a few words,' says a third. 'But at her age she probably won't live long enough to regain her vocabulary in time.'

'Balls,' says Grandma after two days. It's a miracle. We jump up and down and hug her, we are so proud.

'Say it again,' says my mother.

'Balls,' says Grandma smiling.

'Again,' I say.

'Balls,' she says loudly. My mother and I are thrilled and tell everyone that asks after her the amazing news: 'Grandma said Balls!'

When it is time to leave the ward of uncaring nurses and kleptomaniac patients, one of whom keeps stealing Grandma's slippers, she stands up ready to go and as we get to the door she turns round to the ward and the nurses, raises two fingers and says, 'Balls to ya all,' and if that is not enough, she follows this with what is undeniably the word 'Bollocks!' We clap and cheer and laugh all the way home.

'Balls to you all ... bollocks,' we chant, and she joins in.

A week passes and Grandma can say shit and crap too. We get her to repeat all the swear words as often as possible and then we try to teach her names. We print out a piece of paper with the names of family and friends on it in large letters. My mother Michele becomes Misle, I become Illy instead of Amy, as does my dog, whose name is Lily. Hazel, my mum's best friend is Izle: though she can say 'Hay' and 'Zel' separately, she cannot put them together. She cannot say Martin, my mum's boyfriend. But one day as we are practising words, she tries to tell me something. She's in a bit of a bate – someone has annoyed her.

'Who are you talking about?' I ask.

'Imma.'

'Who?'

'IMMA.'

'I don't know who that is, can you point to the name?'

She bashes her finger into the word 'Martin'.

'Martin? Are you cross with Martin?' I ask.

'Yes,' she replies, 'Parasite.'

'Parasite?'

'Parasite,' she repeats.

'Wonderful!' I cry. 'Say it again.'

Then I call up the stairs to Mum, 'Something wonderful has happened! Grandma called Martin a parasite!'

'Wonderful!' my mother replies.

The GP says that all this swearing is quite normal. Swear words are the easiest to say after a stroke. Names are difficult because they only stand for one thing, a person. We sit with her for hours asking her to repeat words, breaking them into syllables. But it's not single words she wants to say. She wants to talk, non-stop. Some things come out quite clearly and other things make no sense. Yes and No are frequently confused as is shaking and nodding her head. We listen hard. Every exchange of words becomes a game of charades. She looks exasperated when she can't say what she wants. Sometimes she just says complete nonsense and if she realises I don't know what she is saying, she gives up and shouts 'Balls!'

I am looking after Grandma this evening.

'What would you like for dinner?'

Grandma shrugs her shoulders and looks depressed.

'Chops?' I say cheerfully, knowing she likes them.

She nods.

'With which vegetables?' I continue in my most cheery singsong voice.

She shrugs her shoulders.

'Broccoli?'

Shrug.

'Mashed potatoes!'

Nod.

'Courgettes?'

Shrug.

'What then?'

She moves her finger up and down.

'A long vegetable?'

She nods.

'Leeks?'

She shakes her head.

'Carrots?'

She shakes her head.

'Celery?'

She shakes her head and says, 'White.'

'It's a white vegetable!' I cry as if she has given me the password to a safe full of gold.

She nods and smiles.

'Cabbage?'

She shakes her head.

'Definitely *not* leeks?'

She shakes her head.

'Swede?'

She shakes her head.

'Can you draw the mystery vegetable?'

She nods. I give her a pencil and the back of a bank statement to draw on. She starts reading the statement.

'Draw the vegetable.' I point at the plain side of the paper. She looks at the plain paper blankly, turns it round and starts to read the numbers on the statement. I turn the paper round, replace the pencil in her fingers at a better angle and give her a book to lean on.

'Can you draw the white vegetable?'

'Yes,' she says and nods. Then she turns the paper over and reads the bank statement again.

I turn it around again, touch the hand clasping the pencil and point at the paper.

'Draw the vegetable,' I say in my most enthusiastic voice.

She draws a parsnip. The parsnip is perfectly in proportion and very neat. This morning she could not hold her spoon at breakfast. She can barely write anything. Every number she says is zero or seven. When she says phone numbers she says zero or seven in a different voice eleven times to make a phone number. But she has drawn a perfect parsnip on the back of a Barclays Bank statement.

'Parsnip!' I shriek. She smiles. I am so pleased and it took only fifteen minutes!

Over the last two years she has learnt more words. But these days she hardly gets out of bed. She's too tired even to try and speak.

It's late and I'm working. I make a coffee.

'Got a biscuit?' I ask Mum.

'Grandma's room,' she calls up the stairs.

The three generations of women in our family all live in the same house on separate floors. Grandma is on the first floor with a Stannah stair lift from the ground floor to her room, strategically placed next to the bathroom. The middle floor is my mother's room and the top floor is where I hide/dwell.

I pass my mother's room, down the next flight, past the bathroom. The walls of the corridor here are cramped with outsized oil paintings of bouquets of flowers and bowls of fruit that my grandmother painted when she could hold a brush. We call this corridor 'The Gallery'.

Sitting half up in bed, her mouth open, her eyes closed, her skin more grey than I've seen it before, is Grandma. The only way I can think to describe the way she looks is dead. I take one step into the room. On my right is a small dresser with the box of biscuits on it. Across the far wall is her bed, under the window, which looks out onto the back garden. Her head is in the right hand corner opposite the dresser. I reach into the box and take a biscuit. Quietly. I take a step back from the dresser. She is dead, I think. I take another step back; I'm now in the doorway. She's dead. I'm going to leave this room with this chocolate biscuit and let my mum find her. Mum will be up in five minutes. If Grandma's dead it makes no difference, except I don't want to be the one to discover her. No sooner have I thought this than I take a step forward. I can't take a chocolate biscuit from my dead Grandma, I think. I can't believe that my first reaction was to leave her. What is wrong with me? I go over to the bed and put my face close to her. A faint breath from her lips touches my cheek and I leave the room, with a great sense of relief and a biscuit.

Grandma's full name is Clarice Queenie Hanson and she used to talk, a lot. She is the most talkative person I have ever met, in fact, but now she can barely talk at all.

Her parents were Jews who came to England from Latvia. They were middle class and arranged a marriage for her to an older, rich man with epilepsy. At eighteen the fits frightened her and when he wasn't ill she didn't like him. At twenty-two she ran away and met my grandpa. He was a poor Jew from Camden Town with nine siblings and together mother and he eloped to Ruislip.

When she could talk she told me that she drove a motor bike, that she was the first woman in Manchester to wear trousers, that she owned a cake shop when she was in her twenties, that her family were the first in the street to have a bath, that she loved to dance, that she had a brother called Cyril and a sister called Cissy and she loved Cyril and hated Cissy and that she was much prettier than her sister.

She was the oldest and used to baby-sit her younger brother and sister just as I baby-sit her now.

My grandma was, at one point in my life, the person I loved more than any other living thing on earth. I loved her more than my mother, father, grandfather and siblings. I loved to cuddle her, to smell her, to sit with her, talk to her, cook with her, walk with her. I loved to be close to her. She would spend hours playing with me in the garden, making me fairy costumes and flower garlands out of convolvulus. She once made me a pinafore out of purple fabric, with eight pockets, one for each of my guinea pigs, with their names embroidered in pink onto each pocket. Dressing up was an important part of our relationship. We would be different characters and she would bring stories to life. It wasn't one-sided either, she too would dress up. I remember her doing the dance of the seven veils in the living room of her flat in Hove, to attract the attention of my grandpa who had his hearing aid turned off and his sight tuned in to the horse racing on television. Both of us wore eight layers and then danced around flinging different coloured fabrics at my grandpa's bald head.

Now she is the baby, I am in another room from her. Actually I am in the room which is furthest away from hers.

I am late for work this morning and even though she can't say my name properly any more, I know that's what she's saying as I close the door. I return in the late afternoon feeling guilty. I am tired because I've been busy but I know the day has been longer for her. All she has done is lie in her bed watching the birds out of her window through little binoculars. It's lonely in her bed with only the birds to look at. And company is the one thing I can give her, though I find it hard to give it to her all the time and that's what makes me feel guilty.

'I'm home,' I call up the stairs cheerfully, 'Up in a minute,' and go down the stairs to the kitchen. I get out her special flowery tray and place her matching teacups with saucers on it. Then a little plate with cheese on crackers and biscuits, arranged in the shape of a flower, knowing she'll like it and lessening my guilt.

I take up the tray and she smiles and slurs what is probably, 'How was your day?' I spread a towel under the tray on her lap and a napkin round her neck. She tries to eat the crackers but I look round and the cheese is mixed with spit and dribbling down her chin, the cracker is sticking out of her mouth at a strange angle, at which point I realise that her false teeth have come out and I have to turn away. Watching her is making me feel sick. I feel angry that it makes me feel sick and guilty all over again. I wipe her chin and pop her teeth back in but concentrate on the telly.

'Stop talking till you've eaten it,' I say as the teeth come out again and the cheese drops everywhere and bits of cracker spill all over the bed. She looks down, sad, embarrassed. I feel horrible and look away. I start to write in my diary. I can't eat because every mouthful I take reminds me of what is chewed up and falling from hers.

'Ya've gat larvely andwriting,' she whispers sounding like a drunk. 'Better van ya mammy's.' She can't read it; she can just see the shape of the words.

Behind her glazed eyes I think I can see pride. I feel like a bitch.

'All the boys liked me the best!' Grandma used to exclaim, 'More than Cissy, I was their favourite, she was jealous rotten when I married Daddy.'

Grandma is not keen on many men and has been known to behave like a battle-axe. However there have been men who made her blush. A dashing Irish friend of mine, for instance, who used to kiss her hand when he dropped round after college. *He* never got *his* ciggies confiscated. And anyone else who complimented her appearance or cooking made this strong, witty, loud old lady seem to turn to jelly.

As I say good-bye to her today, the sun is shining through her window.

'Would you like some sunglasses?' I ask. She nods and I fetch her some comedy Elvis glasses I have from a party. I put the enormous gold Elvis glasses over my Grandma's old watery eyes on her wrinkly face and she smiles. Then I take a photo of her with my phone.

'Ohh, Oooh,' she says pointing at the phone and turning it around.

'It's got a camera on it,' I explain.

'Oooohhh,' she says in amazement.

I turn the phone round so she can see herself as a ninety-eight-year-old Elvis and we both laugh.

'Sam wore these at the party,' I explain 'with a football top, a wig and a moustache!'

'Lord!' she exclaims.

I lean down to kiss her good bye.

'Ya luk im?' she asks

'I do like him.'

'I wanna shee im.'

'You want to meet him?'

She nods.

'Well next time he's round, I'll bring him up to say hello, OK? You can meet him.'

She nods her head and smiles.

That day she has her hair done. She wants her hair looking nice and a new nightie on because she has a new, young, Australian carer called Wes who is very 'amshom' and wears beads and jeans, she tells me, smiling and going pink.

The following evening I have a girlie night with my friends and we are sitting upstairs drinking pink wine, watching *Sex and The City* and gorging ourselves on Milk Tray, when my mother comes up.

'Grandma's trying to tell me something and I don't know what she's talking about,' she says, 'She thinks she's meeting Sam tonight, she won't go to bed or put her hair net on until she's seen him with her hair done. Did you tell her he was coming to meet her?'

'I did, but he's not coming till tomorrow.'

'What a relief, I thought she'd lost it.'

I go downstairs and explain that she isn't going to meet him tonight.

'But would you like the girls to see your hair?' I ask.

'Naaa, no bova,' she puts her navy hair net on over her newly set white hair and goes to sleep.

The next night I go out with Sam and get drunk. We tumble in around midnight. That's odd I think, the house is in darkness apart from a light coming from Grandma's room.

'Oh no, she's waited up to meet you!'

'Meet me?'

'I promised she could see you today.'

'Now?'

'Now!'

I run up the stairs and find her sitting upright in bed dozing.

'Are you awake?' I whisper.

She nods.

'Were you waiting up to meet him?' I ask.

She nods.

'Well he's downstairs, you're not too tired?' She shakes her head.

I lift her up into a better position, a receiving visitors position, and we remove her hair net to reveal her still very neat white hair.

'Come in,' I call, and Sam comes in.

She smiles and instantly goes pink.

He says everything right.

'Hello, lovely to meet you!' He shakes her hand. 'Your hair looks nice. Are you feeling all right?' She nods and smiles.

'Yesh, ank oo. Hallo.'

'So lovely to meet you properly. I met you before but very briefly, on my way upstairs, but it's good to meet you in person!'

She gazes up at him and then looks at me and then at him.

'She's good,' she says.

'I know,' he replies, 'I think so.'

She smiles and says 'Good nat.'

'Good night.'

'Good night, Grandma.'

'Fank oo,' she whispers as I lean down to kiss her forehead.

I think of her all alone in the dark, waiting, waiting to meet my boyfriend, keeping her hair nice, remembering, for two days, while I forgot and whizzed about being twenty-five.

'She's got all her marbles,' says Sam. 'My grandma's much worse and she's not that old.'

It's hard to remember what she was. It is hard for people to meet her now and have any idea of the person she was inside this old body. But, unlike the nurses, Sam saw her, just a glimmer, a spark of Clarice Queenie my Grandma. That is the Grandma I will always try to remember.

I didn't know whether to laugh or cry as I passed her room today. Through the gap in the door I saw this old lady, sitting on the commode, big white knickers drooping round her knees, staring blankly at the wall. She cannot read any more so the mobile library brings her these story tapes. I can hear one now. It interrupts my sad thoughts. The whole house can hear it. A middle aged female narrator booming from Grandma's stereo.

' "It's sort of like that. Wow, I'm dizzy," Nell said, breathless now. "I felt a tingling inside, not unpleasant. Almost like you do when you're thinking – really thinking – about sex." '

And I'd thought she was sitting there thinking about death.

STARLING SONG

They stipple the spreading head of the tree
in pearls of oil, alert as leaves.

They string their speech through branches
in a peal of fervent bodies.

Their circular breathing, drawn through reeds,
calls the sky with its whistle.

They loop their notes like radar
round all their sounds can wrap.

They make a memory-cloud in song,
of fooling hawks in swirling flocks.

Their beaks push holes through the earth like awls
for a thread of the air to stitch.

They tune the tree until its tines
ring in the bow of infinity.

HEREDITY

Beside a sheaf of primrose, picked fresh the day
before she died, I guessed, I found a box
the size of a head. Its casing had cracked
like leather in the sun. A deep lid held it tight.
Written in a hand that looped like a waltz,
Great-Grandmother. I lifted the lid
like a face for a kiss and it let go its years,
a box of held breath sighing to the air.
A scent sprang out like a breeze charged with pollen,
opening the curtains on a window of summer.

The box was filled with soft dark light.
A cushion of curls, soft dark coils of hair
at rest across each other, a bed of eyeless snakes.
Streaks of a sheen the colour of brandy
curved through the mass, lifting like a smoke.
I ran my fingers through its depth like a lover,
washing my hands in its gentle weight,
in the proud black hair of the adulteress, severed clean.
I wanted somehow to bear that crime. But of course, I did.
The kissing curls that shone. A lust that glinted in the sun.

THE CALL

A rabbit's scream like the one
that woke me as a child
blared in the green.

I saw a weasel
streak its sine-wave
over the grass

and pinch the neck
of the wide-eyed
victim twice its size,

tumble, wrapped
like a twist of wire
around its body,

splitting the nerve
with needle-teeth,
squeezing out

the stare of the rabbit.
As if I were there
to collect the dripping life

with the hands that fit the foxglove.

LONDONARIUM

Crossing the bridge
over the river, South Bank to Embankment,
you step into the dead of London. Stop in its crystal dome.
Let everything centre, the universe turn
on the sixpence of your eye.

The pivoting fact
is the setting sun of October. Light
and dark split open, court each other across the sphere,
burning bullion in the western sky,
a curve of slate in the east.

Opposing hands
paint the egg-shell from within:
the sun reveals a silhouette city in the west,
builds in geometric fire to the east.
You are an axis in between.

In the topaz roof
lapis lazuli soaks through the ozone.
A marbling of cirrus in pastel red drapes through.
Aeroplanes cruise the liquid glass
as if they had never known land.

Beneath you, the river
is rising, a glacial cobalt, tides
flowing from out of this world, through and beyond it,
a Nile-flood of specular influence
taking the place of the sun.

Beneath the Thames
the other, buried half of this luminous globe
is the sediment of its clarity, interred by the weight of experience:
the dark solution of a drop of water
distilled by a filter of light.

6 JUNE 1944

We knew something was up
when they cancelled our leave.
I sneaked a letter out to Evelyn
before they stopped that too.
When they gave us beer
vouchers and French francs –
two hundred to the pound –
we were sure it was on.
We left hidden in a tide
of ships. We didn't know
our own secret. Thousands
of us, and even God
was in the dark that night.
We crossed the tar-black sea
like a floating constellation
out of synch with the sky.
We lurched on the waves
like drunks, navy-strength
rum warming our bellies,
adding its fire to ours.
Some never got their sea-legs
and coughed their breakfast
into the drink with a curse.
We heard the fleet open up
to knock seven shades
out of the enemy's sleeping
defences. Some of the lads
smiled. I kept my head down.
We blurred out of the English
horizon, crept up on France
behind the breakers and I thought,
Why Juno? Where did she
come into this? Why here?
Why now? Was this her doing?
And the bullets broke across

the boat, its bow opened,
a one-way ticket to the cross-
fire. A mine lifted two men
into the air and put them back
all wrong. A pit-prop
left to trip the tanks up
was booby-trapped and blew out
the sergeant like a candle.
I ran headlong up a road
made by my own roar.
The earth burst open
here and there and I could smell
the sea, cordite, a dew
of blood. I heard the wounded
boys cheer us on,
and I saw the grey hoods
of bunkers shooting glances
from the slits of their eyes,
and I stared them out, shot
and bombed and stared them out.
Slowly, we emptied ourselves,
soaked into the beaches,
washed between each blade of grass.

THE DEPARTED

A country road I had driven for years
drawing me into its green lane
bent my car around a corner
and saved my life. I felt a tangent
leave my centre and travel straight on
into the waiting trees, a heartbeat escaping me.

Later, this flicker of life forgotten,
a word spoken miles away
sat me up in the middle of the night.
My mother told me my great aunt had written
to say she was sure it was me she had seen
crossing a bridge at dawn in New Zealand
while I was asleep in England.

A friend called to say she could swear
it was me she noticed late one evening
leaving a bar in the company of strangers,
laughing, joking in fluent Portuguese.
She said I looked different, but familiar enough
for her to believe I had learnt a new language.

I was introduced to a friend of a friend
at a party, who stared to the back of my skull
with forested eyes. A bottle of wine
later she whispered, when we were alone,
'You've got a nerve, *du schlecter Mann,*' and smiled
a secret, as if I knew what to do
with the number she folded into my hand.

I began to fear the morning post.
Letters arrived addressed to me
requesting that I repeat the miracle
they had seen my hands perform,
to hear me speak the words again
that healed the sick, enriched the poor.

All this led me to this afternoon,
a séance in a mirror, face to face.
My hands are pressed to the cooling glass
in concentration, my eyes are closed
in the circle of arms. Two minutes' silence
adapts my eyes to darkness. I see
what the part of me that died has seen.

FIFTH OF NOVEMBER

Is that Parliament I can hear going up?
There are people hurrying through the streets
as if they were late for a good party.
I stay in my room and count the bangs.

What does it look like from an aeroplane?
An entire city in a huge bonfire?
No doubt the pilots will tell their stories
in due course, saying *I remember*

that happy day, the fifth of November,
London went up like a Roman Candle.
I can hear the sound of thunder above
and below. A rocket lands nearby.

Who would have thought good old Wernher
von Braun would end up working for us,
putting men on the moon for Uncle Sam?
He was only following orders, right?

A blown-up Parliament, the end
of speaking, assumes that someone is listening.
But while the custom of playing with fire
remains, I'll drink to the English heresy,

celebrate its lack of a Final Solution,
and won't fear the knock on the door, each
fifth of November, that I half-expect:
'Open up! Don't you know there's a war going on?'

AMERICAN SYCAMORE

by Karen Herman

SUGARVILLE

I have yet to see a bear walk in the woods.

I have not seen anybody struck by lightning or drown in the river. But these things happen. They always do and they always will and Billy Sycamore, who is two years older, two foot taller, and too good a fisherman to notice, got a little funny.

The great cities of the world have built themselves upon the great rivers of the world. People need the rivers, not vice versa. People forget that.

Some rivers criss-cross each other, roar along steady and strong or disappear. Some come from snows high-up or springs underground. They all have various beginnings.

I have been thinking a lot about my old river, the Susquehanna, with its rivulets and hundreds of tributaries spread across parts of New York, Pennsylvania, and Maryland. I am lonely for this river.

The house with black shutters and large-winged crows. Red geraniums in summer and horse chestnuts in the fall. The abandoned old house by the creek.

The fish in the woods that walked to the river.

OLD LADY WAGNER

I remember an electrical storm that blew the geography teacher's roof off.

I was ten years old and she lived in a tin-clad house close to the Susquehanna River. There were lightning rods jutting from the roof in various odd angles and directions, much like the hair that sprung out of old lady Wagner's head.

Mrs Wagner was our seventh grade geography teacher. Her eyeglasses were cat-shaped, and she hated the North Vietnamese. She despised them in the same way a televangelist rages on about Satan. On the other hand, she seemed to like Richard Nixon and Germany was pretty big on her list too. She made us learn the days of the week in German. Then she'd tell us the North Vietnamese were going into South Vietnam to kill all those poor people.

She made it sound pretty dire, old Mrs Wagner. Next she'd have us write on a piece of paper if we were for the North Vietnamese or the South Vietnamese. After a manipulative speech like that, who in their right mind is going to write down 'North Vietnam' unless their father is a tenured professor at Berkeley, who's growing pot in the backyard?

Nobody in our seventh-grade class, to my knowledge, had any more enlightened parental types than we had – upper middleclass drunks – who voted for Richard Nixon, twice.

I remember glancing up from my desk to see Mrs Wagner unfold each piece of paper and nod her head with the satisfaction of a mongoose. And I remember when she asked me if Billy Sycamore was my brother. 'Are you related to Billy Sycamore?' she asked.

'Yes. He's my older brother, my only brother.'

'Well that's odd,' she said, 'when I asked if you were his sister, he said, 'Why, Mrs Wagner, we aren't related at all.'

YELLOW BREECHES CREEK

Billy Sycamore wore a vest with 97 pockets.

It was regulation khaki and he kept all sorts of things in there. Bait and tackle, a can of Pepsi, a .38 caliber pistol, his math homework. He saved up a lot of birthday money to buy the gun.

The Santorini sisters, identical twins who would one day grow into the well-deserved titles "Herpes I" and "Herpes II" liked to hang around the river. They tried to seem adept at bait and tackle. They tried to seem knowledgeable about the Fathead Minnow and the Rainbow Smelt. They did all of this fishing fabrication to impress Billy because Billy was most handsome. He had blonde hair that grew into a wild curly haze. His eyes were sea green with black lashes. His smile brilliant and uneven; he had removed his braces with a wrench.

On his thirteenth birthday the twins gave Billy a lighter. It was well-polished brass with a flint lock and tiny wheel. They shoplifted it.

Billy liked the sisters and he liked the lighter known as the *Dwight D. Eisenhower* of Zippo Lighters. Billy used the *Dwight* to ignite the many joints and bongs he smoked to keep him prepared for the final one, he said, should he ever have to face a firing squad.

There are no firing squads in south-central Pennsylvania, so Billy used the lighter to set the field behind the house on fire. A great whirl of flame, wheat, and dried summer grass rose into the sky.

It became a very good thing Billy spent time by the river. Not because the twins sat either side of him, mostly without their clothes on. It was the waist-deep waters of Yellow Breeches Creek and the cool, fast-flowing current that tugged at his heart and fishing line. He stood barefoot in the cold mountain stream. He could adapt to the stream, the creek, the river. He became clear-eyed, truer to the curve of his own life with a fishing rod than what was to come.

Sometimes he dead-drifted a Hare's Ear Nymph, and when water levels ran high from heavy spring rains, he'd dry-fly fish using Woolly Buggers. When he was out of flies and streamers he used pieces of Velveeta Cheese.

He did a lot of dry-fly fishing in August, when the trout feed on top of the creek. He mostly fished the upper end of the creek, by the Route 223 Bridge where the stream widens to just twenty feet in spots. The river gains in size of course, when it flows eastward, and at Boiling Springs a shot of cold water flows there from nearby Boiling Springs Lake.

Sometimes his best friend Juan Goldstein came along. He was like the Ludwig Wittgenstein of our little town. Juan could relate to Billy in parallelograms. His IQ ranked up there with the best thinkers of his time and place and he was philosophical from an early age. When his grandparents were killed during an earthquake in Mexico City (a building fell on them), he said, 'Ah, yes. But they were old.' He'd cast his fishing rod and say:

Nuestras vidas son los rios
que van a dar en el mar

Billy held the unwavering respect of Juan, for both his original way of seeing reality and for never failing to have, on hand, a reliable source of energy.

Our lives are the river
that run into the sea…

Sometimes Billy started to smell like lighter fluid. The Zippo was invented in the state of Pennsylvania. The fact that we live in this state and the Zippo factory produces eighty thousand lighters per day caused him to begin thinking laterally, which is not a very good thing for somebody who walks into a room and says, 'I'm going to kill myself today, and what are you doing?'

que es el morir…

I have never found any sort of tie, mystical or otherwise, between my life and the invention of the Zippo Lighter.

Try as I might, I could not see the conjunction between butane and one's own soul except when Billy and Juan tried to set me on fire.

which is death…

To compensate, Billy would offer an insufficient yet brotherly bit of advice: 'Anything you don't understand is just trying to fuck with you,' and then we'd go fishing. Along that part of the river that flowed nearest to our house.

GENERAL LEE

My name is Alice Sycamore. I do not have a nickname.

'Hey, Alice,' people say.

'Hey,' I say.

My middle name is Lee. My father says we are related to General Robert E Lee which is a huge and ridiculous lie. We are about as related to Robert E Lee as we are to a walrus.

Now I can stay with one thing, but I have to change rivers. I change rivers like I change a pair of shoes. I move to different major bodies of water and their tributaries and streams because, as the Homecoming Queen once said along the Susquehanna River, (and the Homecoming Queen knows), 'Your family are sick.'

The Homecoming Queen can go fuck herself (I mean that in the nicest way of course) and I like to think of the Sycamores as rugged individualists: We and Theodore Roosevelt. This makes my dad, William Mathias Sycamore, as happy as a worm in a Tequila bottle.

'You're a rugged individualist,' I tell him. 'You and Teddy Roosevelt.'

'Indeed!' he says, 'Let's go pick pineapples!'

There are no pineapple plantations in south-central Pennsylvania and the Homecoming Queen's brother will eventually move to Hawaii, but before that, he will have a pet monkey.

I liked to go to the Homecoming Queen's house to see the monkey. It lived in a large wire cage in the basement. It was all alone down there.

I've read 99.9% of pet monkeys are mentally disturbed. I know a lot of people who are 99.9% disturbed. This monkey chirped like a tiny sparrow. He rubbed his tiny black hands together like a neurotic French sea captain.

The monkey's name was Kanebridge. In retrospect, I think it was "Cambridge" and not "Kanebridge", although I prefer "Kanebridge", and after a while, like about a month, the monkey's novelty wore off. The Homecoming Queen's brother tried to shoot it with a water pistol. The only friendly face was the cleaning lady. She'd scream: HELLO, MONKEY! Then she'd wring out her mop.

The Homecoming Queen's house had a triangular roof made out of flat, dark shingles. It had a white painted door with a brass knocker. The interior was white. Everything was white. The walls, the ceiling, the couch, the ashtrays were white. It was like living inside a very strange version of an igloo, their house.

One day the house will be demolished by river water. The house will fill with the rising muddy tide flooding the land from the great spring rains that make the Susquehanna River swell. People will clamber onto rooftops and wait for a rescue boat. The boat will run over submerged cars and mailboxes, heading uptown towards Millers' Auto Supply and the Food Fair.

This happened during the summer of 1972. The President of the United States nearly got impeached for monkey business of his own and he flew over to see just what mischief a river can get up to. He had an aerial view of the destruction and power of water. His helicopter landed on the flat-topped roof of a local high school. People couldn't believe it. It could just as well be a visitor from Mars.

He got out and grinned at the people. He waved at the people. Then he got back into his helicopter and flew off.

One day the Homecoming Queen's monkey managed to escape from the basement. It climbed through a high-cut window and ran up the thick trunk of a buttonwood tree, also known as a plane or sycamore tree, and this tree was as good and familiar as anything it had ever swung around in the

Ecuadorian jungle. Its whole mental outlook improved as it pulled off the one-inch brown balls and started to throw them.

It threw them at the sidewalk. It threw them at both parked and moving cars. It hurtled them down on the small crowd gathering. One hit a man on the head. Another struck a woman in the face. The monkey was absorbed. It did not notice the squirrel observing all the commotion from another branch. It saw the monkey, as unlikely a visitor in a buttonwood tree as Richard Nixon was on the roof of the high school.

One day Billy Sycamore sat in the top of a buttonwood tree. He felt the sharpness of the winter cold and the undefined sound of wind streaming through branches and dead leaves that won't let go, but he stayed up there a long time anyway, watching the snow stop falling and the stars come out.

He followed with his beautiful, dark green eyes the confluence of the muddy river. He saw the small islands scattered in the river and the souls of the dead lighting fires. He watched French troops in blue uniforms and the English soldiers in red.

He saw black slaves with impossible irons around their ankles and throats running towards Philadelphia. He saw the fish in the river: the rock bass and pickerel, walleye and trout.

He saw the half-naked Susquehannock people walking barefoot along the river.

They walked along the same path the joggers will use and street performers and kids with handguns. Then they turned away from the river, the Indian people, and walked into the wooded hills. They passed by the Sugarville Country Club, Pumpkin World USA, Gail's Nail Mart, the Bullet Barn and sixteen thousand different churches. They continued along to a concrete dam. Then they very kindly left a couple of arrowheads for Billy and me to find 3,000 years later.[1]

Billy rowed the boat along in the ever drifting memory bank of his mind. He tried to forget and he tried to remember. He saw a man from the Six Nations with a boiled wool jacket and brass buttons. The man, a full-blooded Indian, said, 'You can journey with the dead only so far then you must turn back. Do you understand?'

'No,' said Billy, 'I don't.'

---

[1]One day the white man will buy all the land from the Indian people. The Indian chief who signs the papers will have a heavy heart. He will say: The perfumed flowers are our sisters, the rivers are our brothers. It is a strange concept to buy the sky.

THE REAL PEOPLE

By the Susquehanna River we have the ancient bones of Indian chiefs buried in fetal positions along with strings of beads, a couple of spears and a few clay pots.

We have a spring thaw. If it melts too much snow on the Blue Ridge Mountains, it traps whitetail deer or black bear on chunks of ice in the Susquehanna River, flowing fast. For quite some time, the bears have been lumbering into town, across the State Street Bridge, along Front Street, and into the backyards of houses higher on the hilltops in search of food for themselves and their cubs.

A friend of my mother watched a black bear grab trays of peanut butter cookies she had left to cool on her screened-in porch. The bear stood seven feet tall and ripped through the woven mesh. It sat down on an Oriental rug and ate four dozen cookies. The bear did a huge crap in the center of the rug and went home.

My great-great-grandfather ran like hell when he saw a black bear. He migrated to North America from Wales in 1790. He drank too much, he spoke Welsh when he drank too much, and he arrived with a cane fishing rod and hand-tied flies. He told anybody who would listen the Spanish were not the first explorers to set foot in the new world, it was the Welsh.

He fished the streams feeding the Susquehanna River, flowing east to the sea, those tributaries on the western side running downstream. He caught shad, walleye and trout. For bait he used worms, streamers and nymphs. He could spend a whole lifetime on the river. He met Cherokee people there. He spoke to them in the Welsh national language and they gave him chewing gum. Star-shaped leaves, winged twigs and spiny seed balls. Sweet gum sap.

The Cherokee must have liked my great-great-grandfather. He was friendly and he liked to fish. He was mildly schizophrenic too, but the Cherokee people migrating south along the Blue Ridge Mountains towards eastern Kentucky and Tennessee would not necessarily have detected that.

He might have mentioned Billy. How Billy will get a job at the 7-11 and let his friends come in and steal everything. Billy will give them a shopping bag. 'Take this,' he'll say, 'you can carry more tuna.'

But he didn't have that sort of vision, our great-great-grandfather. He could have said to the Cherokee: 'See this stream? One day it won't meander through the mayflower and dogwood and pine. It's going to shift and the water won't act right anymore. It will be put upon. When things are put upon, they don't act right. But he would not have said that. He wasn't that sort of person. His vision was simpler, specific, relegated to the moment, to the creeks and streams that flowed merrily along in front of him, and filled with wild brown trout.

The Cherokee people told my great-great-grandfather they were called the "Ani-Yunwiya", or the "Real People". My grandfather told them his name was Mathias Sycamore, which means "Mathias Sycamore".

The Cherokee people liked my great-great-grandfather. He wore rakish hats and a coat with brass buttons. He wore shiny shoes with silver buckles.

He had pinned the tail feather of an eagle to his heart.

WHERE YOU LIE SLEEPING

by Patrick Hobbs

ONE: FORGETTING

I was in the plaza when they brought the gringos down. It was an evening late in September, the driest September we had known for years. They came in a dented white Toyota pick-up along the road that led out past the maize fields and up to the cordillera. A bow-wave of dust span out from the wheels and washed against the walls of the adobe buildings that ran along the street, the driver pulling up in front of the church, as if this was the only right place to bring the dead.

Everyone entering our small town paused somewhere in the plaza; it was a place where people came to sit, to talk, to mourn, to watch the evening fall, or simply to know that life continued and they were not as alone as they felt. It was little more than a large square of dirt, a dozen trees around it, their boles once painted white in an attempt to stop vehicles colliding with them on the nights when the four street lights were not working, which was most of the year. The street ran round all four sides, and around the edge stood a bar, a shop and our few public buildings, the church in pride of place, its doors always catching the late sun as it sank towards the ocean.

I had been sitting on the cracked bench, watching the football, some twenty boys in T-shirts and fraying tracksuit bottoms weaving patterns through the dust, their shifts in direction a response to the movements of the player on the ball, as if he were a magnet passing through them. I saw my great-nephew shimmy and swerve his way to goal, the ball curving into the space where a net should have been. In the past I had come here with his grandfather, my brother, to see him play in the evenings, wondering how long it would be before the scouts from Trujillo found him and took him away to the city on the coast. It would be a great sadness, but I did not want to see him stay here. He was sixteen, a young star in a small sky, and he knew it. The girls would slip away from their mothers' kitchens to watch him. Already there were rumours, and I did not want to hear of a visit to the old woman by the river with her scouring herbs, or meet a young girl in the street holding a baby whose father had disappeared. He had that light on him as if God or the Devil or the Virgin had touched him. He might bring crowds to their feet one day, perhaps make grown men weep, but he would break a hundred hearts and never see his grandchildren.

He was eclipsed that evening. Perhaps the twilight birds suddenly fell silent or the scent of death rolled in through the streets. I was not aware of either, but the game stopped, and one last boy chasing alone after the ball turned to see his friends looking towards the church. Behind the pick-up the huge khaki jeep of the Guardia Republicana was blasting its horn, but the driver in front took no notice, as though the horn had merely replaced the church bell which should have been tolling over the dead. The Guardia's reputation was fierce; most knew the whispered stories of what had happened behind Don Ignacio's farm, but we knew these men, their families, their drinking habits, their whores, and even the Guardia could not hold back a curious town.

Carlito, a little urchin with the speed of a vizcacha, and not much bigger, was the first to reach the back of the Toyota, and before anyone could stop him he yanked at the tarpaulin that covered the back. He did not have the strength to drag it off at the first attempt, but two other boys joined him and long before I had hobbled over the two corpses were exposed. I had seen bodies before and thought I had no desire to see another, but death has a strange attraction and I leaned through the throng to see two young men, no older than their early twenties, lying face up on the metal deck. One was mangled, his right arm at an angle that made my stomach turn, his head and his face broken open, his blonde hair stiff and muddied black from the wound. The other was dark, his face bruised almost the colour of his hair, but I could not see much sign of other injury, just the drying trickle of blood from the corner of his mouth. Flies were gathering, a loose column of them already twisting above the back of the truck.

The Guardia were out of the jeep now, two officers with revolvers dancing at their hips, waving their arms at the small crowd swelling around the pick-up. They shouted us away, one of them climbing into the cab, ordering the pious driver to swing his vehicle round to the tiny barracks. I looked at the jeep behind. In the back I saw a third soldier, and beside him a girl, long fair hair tied back, her hand held across her chest, her face leaning against the window, staring down at the dust of the football pitch.

I crossed the plaza as the convoy moved round to the Guardia's own building. The boys were ordered back to the football but lingered in the street. The priest overtook me, hurrying from his house behind the church. I followed him in behind the men in uniform, uninvited. I did not have the authority of the cassock, but my age, education and twenty-eight years spent in the capital had combined to gain me a vague respect here. More than this, during my years in Lima I had worked with the father of the officer in command, and when I returned to the North had the sad honour of knowing Don Ignacio's children. I had levers, and, besides, the scene was too chaotic, too desperate, to hold back for formalities.

'So, Hugo, tell me what happened.'

'Wait five minutes,' the officer answered brusquely, turning to give orders to his men who were carrying in the bodies, and gathering some papers from a shelf beside the door.

The girl was sitting in a chair in the corner, her hands in metal cuffs. Hugo ushered her gently into the care of a subordinate who took her out of sight into a back room. Then he led me into his office. There were bars on the windows. I could see the football teams outside and huddles of people I recognised. Behind them two of the street lamps had begun to glow, and night was falling from banks of purple cloud bedding down on the sierras.

Hugo looked across at me, then out of the window. After a long pause and a sigh he began, as usual, to give me an edited version of the truth as far as he knew it.

'A taxi came off the road coming down from Bambamarca. There were three English tourists, one in front, two in the back. The two boys are dead; the girl is cut, but she survived and she's here. The driver's in a bad way. He's in the hospital at Caracayo and the Guardia there will question him.'

'I know the road to Bambamarca; I've driven it a few times, years ago. A car or a truck goes over the edge every month, but you're holding a girl in handcuffs.'

'She attacked one of my men. We had to protect ourselves.'

I laughed.

'What? She attacked the Guardia Republicana? What did she attack you with, Hugo?'

'With her hands.' He looked at his desk, profoundly embarrassed, then up at me, and I could see from the light in his eyes that he wanted to laugh too. There were moments when I almost liked this man, when I saw some of the same boyish sense of the ridiculous that I had loved in his father, something the job and the uniform had not yet suffocated. The laughter faded and he continued, 'Listen, Indians die in the mountains, terrorists die in the mountains, sometimes soldiers die in the mountains. Europeans don't die here. If they do, we have to know why, there has to be a report. I need your help. My English isn't good, and yours is perfect. I have to ask her some questions, not now but maybe tomorrow. Will you help?'

'You need to be very gentle, Hugo. She looks as though she's only held together by her clothes. She's in shock.'

'We won't be taking off her clothes. We'll be gentle. Will you help?'

'Yes, but I have one condition. She can't stay here. I want you to let her come to my house. I have a good spare room, and Isabel will look after her. If she needs the doctor, he can come to us. I'll be answerable for her, and you know I'm not going anywhere.'

I opened the front door a little before eleven. Isabel was waiting up, alerted by a neighbour who had been at the plaza. Isabel was my housekeeper, but she had long since refused any payment beyond the meals she ate in my kitchen or sometimes sharing my table at evening. She had the loyalty of a guardian angel, and the tongue of a demon, though she rarely used it on me. I had given up trying to understand why she continued to look after me as she did. Perhaps she knew some happy secret about me that I had forgotten. We lived in a place where almost everyone treasured some special knowledge, something dark or shining in the memory. Sometimes she seemed to treat me like a younger brother, though I was nearly twenty years older than her; sometimes like a beloved old horse; sometimes like a lord. She always called me Don Alberto, and though I hated the title at first it had become a note of intimacy, and it would have cut me to hear her drop it.

I had insisted on walking home, not wanting to ride in the Guardia jeep. Hugo arrived a few minutes later, and brought in the English girl. There were no handcuffs now.

'Are you sure you're safe, Hugo?' I smiled.

He scowled at me, but the look from the girl was more troubled. She clearly understood some Spanish. Hugo looked round the small house, not for the first time, and checked the guest room. He was trying to appear officious.

'I want you to keep the window shuttered, do you understand?'

'Yes, yes, I understand. She didn't kill anyone, Hugo.'

'I know. There might be other questions. If you help me, you help her. Take good care of her.' He gave me a knowing look and walked out into the headlights of his jeep.

'Good night.' I closed the door slowly. Isabel had already taken the girl into her wide hands. I did not see her again till late the next morning.

For twenty-seven years I drove taxis in Lima. It was not the career I had hoped for, but I was lucky, finding myself on some good runs – Miraflores, the

Sheraton Hotel and the drag out to the airport. I studied English at San Marcos University and it brought me extra money. Many foreigners were nervous amid the poverty, the lack of things they took for granted, and grateful for someone who could speak an international language. I worked at it, learning to distinguish the different accents – the English from the American, the Australian twang and the strange transatlantic tone used by the Germans, the French and the Scandinavians. I remember once, not long before I left, I carried another taxi driver, a man from London with his wife. He showed me a picture of him with his vehicle – a hunchback thing, like a black armadillo with a snub nose. I refused to charge him.

It was on the long runs to the planes that I got used to listening to the stories, asking questions at the right moments, leaving pauses which the passengers could run into like the boys dribbling the ball in the plaza. I learned to remember. I would go to my home at night carrying echoes of other lives, some of them true, some like myths I could store up alongside the tales from the sierras that my grandmother used to tell me. I would take them to bed, sometimes retelling them to my wife before we fell asleep, sometimes pushing them under the pillow. I left them there while I turned to her and lifted the hem of her night-dress, forgetting every other destination. There are still nights when I reach over to my left, trying to find that edge of cotton, the border where her skin began.

I was one of the first at the bakery in the morning. At seventy there is a simple choice: to get up early or not at all, and I thought it did me good to push my old legs at the beginning of the day. The doctor had not appeared the evening before and I was still angry at his absence, but in the shop I learned why he had not responded to the call from the Guardia. He had gone out in the morning to a farmer in the foothills who had been pulled from under his overturned tractor, and on his way back to town his car had broken down. I also heard that a white van had left the plaza a little after midnight, taking the bodies of the two young men on the first leg of their journey back to England.

The vegetables needed some weeding, and after breakfast I went out into the garden behind the house. I was hoeing slowly between the beans when I heard Isabel talking to the girl inside. I came in to find her sitting at the table sipping coffee. I sat down opposite her and smiled.

'I'm Alberto. Please forgive me for not welcoming you properly last night.' I spoke in English.

'That's OK.' She smiled faintly back at me.

'What's your name?' Hugo had given me 'Katherine', but I did not want to appear presumptuous, I wanted her to tell me.

'Kathy. Or Kat.'

She had few words, even in her own language, and I was not going to push her. I sat with her for some minutes, speaking as warmly and as gently as I knew how. I explained the doctor would soon come, then left her with Isabel and went back out to the beans.

When Doctor Marín finally arrived he was in high spirits. He had always wanted to be a film director and enjoyed drama of any kind, especially when he felt he could ride to the rescue. I resisted the temptation to tell him how late he was. There was a long gash in the girl's arm where she must have raised it to shield her face from the impact of the crash, and though Isabel had cleaned and bandaged her wounds, he took time to use all the tweezers and antiseptics in his armoury.

He put in a perfect row of stitches, pretending not to notice when Isabel whistled in admiration, then he took Kat's chin in his hand and studied her bruised face as if he were considering her for a part in his next romantic epic. I watched over his shoulder, wondering if he saw the likeness that had struck me the moment I had first seen her the day before. It was clearest when her head was turned down to the right as it was now. Perhaps it was only my fancy, the flotsam of a haunted mind, but it had been strong enough for me to know I could not let the Guardia detain her. I turned and saw my housekeeper looking at me. She mouthed something that I was glad not to hear and walked away into the kitchen, a look of disgust on her face.

Hugo appeared as I was finishing lunch. Kat had said she wanted nothing to eat and was sitting in the garden looking out over the tin roofs towards the Andes, the mountains slowly fading in the rising warmth of the day. Hugo was carrying a book, which he laid on the table.

'This is why she attacked my sergeant. He found this in the car and she didn't want him to take it. She said it was hers.'

I gestured to the chair and let him continue while I swallowed the last of my meal.

'The Guardia at Cajamarca called them in for questioning last week. It was only routine, ten minutes. They thought they might be journalists. The tourists don't normally come this far north in the cordillera – Arequipa, Cuzco,

Huancayo, but not here. Anyway, Cajamarca were happy with them, but they wouldn't have liked the book.'

I looked at the cover. I said nothing. I had not seen anything by Neruda since I left Lima.

'I've made enquiries and I'm not going to do anything, Alberto. Her friends are dead, and there's no sign of a crime. I'll just report a road accident. We've spoken to the embassy, and if she wants to call anyone she can use the phone in my office. Just bring her round for a chat tomorrow, and then we'll put her on the bus for Lima. We need to get her back to her family. Oh, and make sure she takes the book with her. I don't want to see it here.'

'Thank you, Hugo. Tell me, why are you so frightened by a dead poet?'

'He's a communist, Alberto, a communist. He's dead, so he's a better communist than most, but he's still a fucking communist.'

'They're love poems. You should read them. You could memorize them for your wife.'

The man in uniform was human enough to know when he was being teased and professional enough not to rise to every provocation. His tone softened.

'I know; I read some of them. There are more love poems in the back. Please give them to her as well.' He rose to leave.

I picked up the book and saw that folded inside the back cover were several loose pieces of white paper.

'I don't think you had any right to look at those.'

'I was doing my job.' He paused. 'She's alright, isn't she? Doctor Marín said her injuries were slight.'

'Yes, she's alright. I think she's still in some pain, but he gave her his pills. She's sitting outside now.'

'Good. I'll see you tomorrow.' He walked to the door.

'Hugo.'

'Yes?'

'Thank you.'

He nodded and left.

I picked up my stick and went outside to find Kat sitting in the sun, her eyes closed. She opened them as I approached and looked up.

'I think this is yours,' I said, holding the book out to her. '*Los versos del capitán*. I know it. It's very beautiful. I don't think it was written by our captain here, but he asked me to return it to you.'

'Thank you.' She took the book in both hands, slipping one thumb inside the back cover and checking the loose pages were still there. I could see blue handwriting looping across them. 'It's very important to me. Thanks for looking after me here. You're very kind.'

'It's nothing. Tomorrow we'll try to get you back to Lima, but today you must rest, and you must eat. You must eat.'

'Maybe later.' There was a quiver in her voice, a sudden sadness like a chasm opening. She was looking down at the book. I wanted to sit down beside her then, and take her in my arms, but I saw that if I so much as touched her she would break and weep, and I would not know how to stop that weeping. She was my guest. I did not want to embarrass her, or myself. It had been a long time since I had held a grieving woman.

'It's time for my rest now. Perhaps you should sleep too?'

'Yes, I think you're right.' Her voice was like a taut thread.

I turned and left her alone again, gazing out towards the high ridges still visible in the distance.

Bernarda. For years after she died I could not go to my bed without thinking of her. Even when the memory of her began to break into fragments that spread out into the distance of life without her, one image always lingered – her smoothing the sheet over the mattress on our wedding night, pushing the corners further underneath to pull the white surface flat and perfect, while I watched, breathless with anticipation. Until my knee gave out and left me unsteady on my legs I would make the bed with my eyes closed.

She grew up in Miraflores, the wealthy end of the capital, where the houses drip bougainvillea and even in the forties a few had swimming pools. She loved the flowers, the luxury of their colour in a city built on a desert, but hated the anxiety that framed them, the bars on windows, the unspoken fear that one day the poor might come to visit. She found me on the floor at a party underneath one of those barred windows. It was a few weeks after I had finished my studies at the university. I had slipped while trying to dance and she helped me to my feet. I noticed her hands first, the sinewy strength in them, the way the pads at the ends of her fingers were harder and flatter than those of other girls.

She was a dressmaker. The word limits her, but I cannot think of a better one; she was never abstract enough to call herself a designer. She had received no training, had never formally studied fashion, but from the age of twelve she had been making clothes for herself, then for her sister, her mother, her aunt. Schoolfriends began to ask for versions of the dresses she wore, and before long the ladies of the suburb were bringing their daughters to the front door, often coming back alone with their own personal orders, adding their names to a waiting list. She could copy any style in the magazines, but rarely did so, always looking instead for the line that would flatter and add a touch of grace or spirit. In those days the models would be static, wearing fashions standing still, as though the clothes had only two dimensions. She always designed for movement, alert to how the fabric shifted on the body, how like waves it caught the light, how the hem might dance.

Dance was her passion. I had been watching her during that first party, mesmerised by the joyous freedom with which she moved. The miraculous looks easy, and when I tried to compete with her partner that night I soon found myself on the floor. I think that in her dreams she might have preferred a tall musician from Buenos Aires, expert in the tango, and she knew from the moment when she grasped my hand to rescue me from the heels flying around me that I could never be more than her pupil. She spent the rest of her life trying to educate my feet, coaxing them into magical patterns they could never have found on their own.

I dreamt of Bernarda that afternoon, while Kat rested in the garden or slept in the bed next door. I woke with the bedclothes twisted to one side. Perhaps I had been dancing.

HAVING HER CLOSE

by Kellie Jackson

At first I wonder if it is my son Rhett, dropping in to pick up the spare keys. Then the record stops playing and I hear them outside, gabbing like a flock of galahs. I stop packing, peep through the blinds and see that the tall kid, the funny looking one, has a stick. He's giving something in the shrubs a good prod. The others squat down beside him, like they're 'round a campfire, except for the squirt, Lindy Murphy, from over the road. She looks in need of a feed and a bath. She's standing behind them, on my rose bed.

I'm out on my verandah so fast; I shock the flies off the screen door. 'Clear off you little mongrels.' They look at me as though I'm talking a foreign language.

They know who I am. I clean their new school. It's only been open a year. The kids usually give me a wide berth.

'G'arn, the lot of ya. Buzz off. Go and tear up your own bloody front yard.'

They scatter like marbles, except for Lindy, who's too frightened to move.

'Come here, ' I say.

She glances behind to her house. A billy-cart lies abandoned in her drive. Mail sticks out of the letterbox. On the front steps, in full sun, sit half a dozen bottles of milk.

'Come on. I'm not going to eat you.' She moves off the flowerbed onto the grass and stalls.

'For cryin' out loud. Get a wiggle on.'

Barefoot, head down, she walks quickly up the drive. Lindy stops at the stairs, finding the last bit of shade from the house. Her bottom lip wobbles. She's closer to being a baby than a child.

'What are youse' doing under my hibiscus?'

'Nothink.'

'Nothing? Look here.' Her eyes flicker up to mine.

'There's a dead baby cat there,' she says quietly, about to cry.

'What are you poking it with a stick for then?'

A fat tear rolls down her cheek.

'To check it's really dead.'

'That won't do it any good, love.'

'It's got a hole in its guts.'

'Jesus. Well, something's got at it. A dog maybe?' Probably that big kid more like. I'm sure he's got a bolt loose but I keep it to myself.

'Was it yours?' she asks.

'No bloody fear. Hate cats. Doing their business all over the garden and killing the birds.'

'I think Peter Blamey hurt it.'

'He's that big boy isn't he? You should keep away from him. His eyes are too close together.'

'I am staying away from him but he made me and my brothers come and look.' She sniffs, swallows and wipes her eyes and nose with the back of her hand. It leaves dirty streaks across her cheeks, like a matchbox car has run across her face. Then she says, 'Why are you in your swimmers? Are you going swimming?'

'You're a bit of a sticky beak, aren't you Lindy Murphy?' She flinches. I never see this kid smiling. 'We're off on our cruise tomorrow. This is my new cossie,' I put my hands on my hips, leg out, toe pointed. 'Not bad for an old girl, eh? I bet I'd give Betty Grable a run for her money.'

She shrugs and makes a sort of grunt. I could tell she was still thinking about the kitten because she looks down at the hibiscus as though expecting the creature to totter out. 'Are you gonna' bury it, Mrs Koz?'

'No, I'm too busy packing.'

'But what if that dog comes back? Or Peter Blamey even?'

'Mr Koz will take care of it later, love. He's got to run the mower over the lawn after his shift this arvo. Can't go off to Sydney tomorrow without giving the garden a good seeing to. Don't worry about it.'

The sun hits her eyes as she squints at me. The street is quiet, no kids or cars; the men are all at work and the women inside. Lindy stays put.

'That kitten'll be all right. You get yourself home. I'm busy now.'

'Its eyes are all milky. Don't you want to see it?'

'No.'

'I've only seen little dead things before, worms and insect thingies. 'Cept for a rat, at school, behind the wash sheds.'

'You need to wash your hands before you do too much else today.' I still have to dye my hair to get rid of the greys, so I surprise myself when I say, 'You can come in here and give them a wash.'

She sucks a strand of dirty blonde hair, 'I'm not allowed to go in people's houses unless I ask my mum first.'

'She won't mind.' Fern, her mother, has been taken down a peg or two lately with this fifth baby on the way. She did a year at a music college when she was a girl and fancies herself a step ahead of the rest of us. I think of my new things on the bed, the cruise and the islands. Fern and Gerry's lot look like they're dressed by the Salvo's. That Gerry Murphy might be a good lookin' bloke, but he's a useless so-and-so. If Fern didn't look down her nose at me so much, I might almost feel sorry for her.

'I got a heap of nectarines off my tree this morning from down the back. Do you think your mum would like a few? And how about a cold drink for you?'

'Dunno. I don't want to get the wooden spoon. She always tellin' me, "Don't disappear. I don't want to have to come lookin' for you".'

'What's your mum doing now?'

'Having a rest.' Lindy winds her finger around the stretchy fabric of her orange shorts. She wears a seersucker, halter-neck top, homemade. Her bony shoulders are golden without a single freckle.

'Not long till the baby comes then?'

'Nah, not long. Wish it would hurry up. We have to be quiet all the time.'

'Is that why you're all running half-tame 'round the neighbourhood?'

'Dunno.'

'Dunno much, do ya?'

She grins showing the gap where she's lost two bottom baby teeth.

'So are you coming in, Lindy?'

Lindy follows me into the lounge room, then the bathroom. I help her turn on the hot tap. I get the nailbrush going on her grubby nails, 'You shouldn't bite them,' I say.

'You bite yours.'

'Don't be cheeky. Righto, go wait in the lounge.' She plonks herself down on the tan leather recliner, legs dangling.

'You can listen to this.' I put 'Bula Bula – Memories of Fiji' on the stereo and turn up the volume. I have to raise my voice, 'This music comes from the islands where Mr Koz and I are going on holiday.' She nods and looks at me from head to foot, not at all shy now. I should feel like a clown trying to please this tiny lick of a kid but I don't. She better not stop here too long though.

'Stay parked, I'll be back in a mo.'

'Alright.' I leave her swinging her legs in the air as she leans over the chair to fiddle with the footrest lever.

'And mind your fingers.'

I find a brown paper bag from under the laundry sink and fill it with a dozen ripe nectarines. A wasp flies out of the end of one of them and I chase it with a fly swat into the kitchen.

When I come back with her lemon squash and the fruit, she's not where I left her.

'Lindy?' I look for her through the screen door where the flies have settled again. I half expect her to be crossing the road home. The street is empty.

'Lindy?'

'I'm here,' she says from the hall. She's looking at the framed photos of Rhett as a schoolboy on the wall. She doesn't recognise the uniform.

'I had to put him on the bus for school. We had to walk half a mile to that bus. You're a lucky girl to just wander down the hill to your new primary.'

'I'm still in infants.'

She gulps her cordial and then is full of questions about my missing front tooth; knocked out by my first husband Len, a nasty piece of work. 'I don't bother wearing my bridge while I'm working around the house. It rubs me gums raw,' I say.

Then she's on to my tattoo, a lovebird for Len, or what's left of it on my wrist. She wants to know why I have white claw marks over the blue inked bird. When he did me a favour and finally shot through, I scraped it off myself, almost.

'That's shut you up,' I say, but it's not for long. I don't mind her prattle and go into my room and put the bag of fruit on the dressing table. I want to finish packing and open the sliding doors of the built-in wardrobe. I've filled one small suitcase with Erek's gear and the other case is half done on the floor.

'Careful where you put your drink down.'

'It's all gone.'

Lindy stands in the doorway, watching as I work my long hair into a single plait and pin it into a coil at the base of my neck.

'My dad says only boongs and barmaids have hair that black but I like your hair, Mrs Koz.'

'I beg your pardon. Does he?'

'Yep.'

'I was a barmaid once. You can tell him that. And you can tell him my parents were born here just as his were. What else does he say?'

'Nothin'. But Mum says you mustn't ruin your skin in the sun or you'll look like an old boot but I think you look nice all brown. And anyway my Dad's really brown too from being a builder. He doesn't have wrinkles around his belly button like you do though.'

'Do your dad and mum ever tell you it's rude to make remarks about people?'

'Sometimes.' Then as if to say sorry for something she senses rather than understands she says, 'You should see my mum's stomach. It's all scrunchy and saggy.' She shakes her head as though she's tasted something bad.

I have to laugh. 'Well, that's what a mob of kids will do to your figure. Now it's time for you to take those nectarines and troop home. Your mum will be wondering where you are.'

'Is that Rhett's picture of when he was a baby?' She points to the frame on my dressing table.

'Yeah.'

'Why did you only have one baby?'

'Do you like babies?'

She nods, smiles, 'They're all little. Their hands and things.'

'I'll show you something.'

I go to the hall and bring back the photo album. We sit on the bed. 'Here's Erek and me on our wedding day at Wollongong town hall. He was a boiler-maker at the steel works down there. He used to come up and see me when-ever he had a break. We met at the pub when he was passing through Sydney, visiting a pal of his from the refugee camp.'

Lindy's mouth is open, as if listening to a secret.

'What's a referee camp?'

'It's Ref – u – gee,' I say the word slowly. 'Well, they were people who came here after the war, some of them stayed in a refugee camp until they found a home. Mr Koz was one of them. He lost all his people overseas in Poland and thought he could make a new life here.'

'That's why he talks funny.'

'I s'pose you could say that but it might hurt his feelings. He's a nice man, Mr Koz, no oil painting but he's a grafter. No one gives it to you on a plate.'

'What's a grafter?'

'Ask your father.' I turn the page. There's Rhett, at nine, all spruced up at our reception. It was a small do. It didn't take too much persuading to leave Sydney behind. We shifted up to Newcastle for Erek's new job. 'When we bought this block of land, there was nothing here but bush until we built this place.'

Then I have second thoughts and close the album.

'That's enough.'

'Come on Mrs Koz, can I see the rest? Please?'

Lindy moves nearer. Her body feels warm against mine.

'Oh, please?' I let her lean over and re-open the book. She finds the page where I'm expecting and giving Rhett a cuddle. His arms stop short around my swollen waist.

'This is outside the new house. No front garden yet.'

I look chubby in the face, healthy. We were alone for a long time, Rhett and me. It took him a while to get used to Erek. But Erek helped him soup up his first bike, took him to footy training and went to all the matches. He was better than a father.

Lindy turns the page.

'Who's that little baby?'

'Maree. This was taken right after she was born.'

'She's asleep?'

'No, love, she's not.'

'Why are her eyes shut then?'

I hadn't thought about her properly in such a long while. My daughter. She looks beautiful. Plump and fully developed as you could wish for. Normal.

'She was born dead.'

'That's sad.'

'It was very, very sad, love. Still is.'

I wanted a picture of her even if it was all we had. Just so I could remember that we hadn't made her up. The nurse, she was kind enough but I think she thought we were morbid, for doing that. She said as much. Erek understood though. He had seen things during the war to make your hair curl. They had to prise her out of my arms. I wasn't too well after. Erek took care of things for a long while.

Without meaning to, I sigh.

'What's wrong Mrs Koz?'

'She's up there.'

'In heaven?'

I get up and point to the varnished wooden box on the top shelf of the wardrobe, where I keep my winter jumpers. I can just reach to trace my fingers over her name, engraved in brass, Maree. Paulina. Kozlowski. Erek wanted to scatter her ashes under something nice we planted in the garden, between the nectarine and mulberry trees. I couldn't do it, all the flipping wildlife around here. Then he wanted to let her go off the rocks near the ocean baths at Merewether. He said a baby could rest in the ocean, that it wasn't right keeping her in a cupboard. But I like having her close where I can keep an eye on her.

Lindy's back to twiddling the hem of her shorts and looks ready to bolt.

'Oh no love,' I say making a little joke in my voice, 'there's not a baby in there. It's just a sort of memory box. She *is* in heaven.'

'I think I better go home now.'

'OK, love, maybe you better.'

Lindy leaves the bag of nectarines behind and forgets to close the screen door on the way out. I spend the whole afternoon spraying the bloody blowflies that came in.

Later, with the suitcases packed and locked, I have a shower. I run a 'midnight black' permanent through my hair. Wrapped in a towel, I sit on the bed opposite the window while the dye takes. The blinds are now open to the evening sky. A streak of cloud is lit up over the horizon and turns from red to orange. Then it goes mauve and blue. I can't help feeling flat which is silly when first thing in the morning we're off.

Galahs and cockatoos squawk in the gum trees of the school grounds beyond, as though having it out for the day's final word. Fern comes out, with a toddler on her hip, another young fella hanging on to her shift dress and a belly big as a sack full of rabbits. She is taking in the billy-cart and toys. I wonder where Lindy and her other brother are. They should help their mother. Gerry's ute pulls up in their drive, he nearly runs into a scooter. He's had a few. He listens to his wife for about ten seconds, turns his back on her and goes inside. The little ones follow him. Fern glances around the street and then stands with her head up, like she's listening to something the birds are saying.

Erek is out the front; he's mowed the lawn and done the edges. He still wears his bottle green work overalls but has unbuttoned the top part, rolled them down and tied them around his waist. His navy blue singlet is dark with sweat; silver chest hairs curl over the top. He has one last job to do before knocking off for the night. Fern looks over as Erek shovels up the kitten. He holds the shovel at a right angle, and nods g'day to Fern, who gives a lame wave back. It wouldn't kill her to smile. She pads down her drive, into her place. Erek takes the kitten around the side, out of my sight, to the back yard. I know where he's going to bury it.

NOVEMBER
by Joel Mellou

The cold darkens our living room windows a flat convent grey. Josepha's shadow sits at her pink desk doing her homework. Her back curves into the window light. 'Move,' Maman says, nudging Josepha's chair.

'But, Maman Delphine, I'm doing my homework.'

'I've had enough running from room to room.' Maman leans over Josepha, picks up her books and slings them onto the sofa.

'What are you doing?' Josepha leaps off her chair, grabs her pens and stares at Maman. 'I've got exams.'

'As if you've passed exams before.' Maman scoffs and drags Josepha's school desk across the living room.

Josepha's mouth stays open and her face reddens.

'There,' Maman sighs and leaves Josepha's desk by the door.

'But, it's in the doorway, Maman Delphine.'

'There.' Maman pushes it against the wall.

'But, there's no light there, how can I read?'

'What comes first – your reading or my children?'

Maman's bare feet stomp to the bedroom. I copy her.

Clothes, towels and sheets fly onto the big bed as Maman empties the enormous wardrobe. She rolls up her sleeves, puffs her chest out, scoops Pierre off the floor and drops him onto the bed, grinning, 'We'll get the playpen out for you, my duck.' Pierre bounces, laughing and paddling amongst the heaps of clothes. His face flashes big grins at me.

Maman yanks me out of the way. 'Watch out,' she huffs, bends her legs and heaves one end of the enormous wardrobe. Maman turns it, pushes, lifts and, turning with it, she drags it out of the bedroom. With each step, the wardrobe swings past the kitchen door, across the little hallway, past the shoe cupboard in the entrance, then through the living room doorway. Josepha is not helping.

I run to the kitchen door.

Papa's shadow is washing under its arms through the glass pane.

I peep into the living room.

Josepha is carrying her desk back near the doorway and Maman waddles the wardrobe towards the window. The sofa, the table, the wood burner,

Josepha's bed and the walls shrink. The wardrobe drinks all the light. 'There,' Maman sighs, and leaves the enormous wardrobe in the middle of the room. Josepha yanks her desk against the wall, drops on her chair and squints at her book. She's pretending nothing is happening.

'We'll get some peace now, my hen.' Maman grins at me, then yells, 'Louis! Come and help, will you.'

'H' Donoi! What are you doing to my home, woman?' Papa shouts from the doorway. He squeezes past Josepha, wiping his face with a teacloth. 'What's this?'

'Pierre needs room to crawl about in the bedroom.' Maman shouts back at him. Papa frowns at Maman, then looks around him. His vest glares white, browning his arms. Josepha says nothing. The baby's gurgling floats out of his cot, against the wardrobe.

'But, Delphine, this wardrobe is made of walnut wood and has been in my bedroom since my family moved in. It is precious.'

A patch of soap foam slides down his neck.

'Well, since you won't have our Jesus sleep in our bedroom and you'll only have *your* family in *your* bedroom, what can I do? I can't have Pierre crawling in here and waking *our* baby at all hours.'

'Por Dios! What about Josepha? Why don't you leave things as they are, woman?' Papa shakes his head, then his voice trembles against the wardrobes. 'How can my daughter do her schoolwork sitting in the doorway?'

'It's not as if she's top of her class, is it?'

'I can see. Papico.' Josepha quickly stands, flicking a smile at him.

'Electric light is bad for your eyes, Señorita.'

'Who says? She's telling you she can read, and this baby needs his sleep. What about *his* eyes?' Maman stares at Papa.

'My daughter needs God's light to study, Delphine.' Papa slings the tea-cloth over his shoulder, and his large hands push the wardrobe away from one window towards the other. Our living room sways into shadows with each push. 'Basta,' he sighs. 'Before you move anything else, Delphine – tell me. Have you taken your medicine, today?' Papa asks, his hand on his hips like Maman.

'What are you, a nurse?'

'I'll read in the bedroom, Papico.' Josepha sweeps her books and pens off her desk and stomps out. I copy her.

Maman has new words when she goes out, she says, 'I am going to be a small hour, won't be long. Now that you're big, you can be patient. It's only two tiny quarters of an hour and a little half hour.' She looks at her wrist, pretending to wear a watch like Papa. Her new words loom above my head, 'I'll be a short hour or so.' Maman is getting ready to go out this afternoon. 'Josepha's in the bedroom keeping Pierre quiet. Don't disturb them. I'm off shopping.' I follow her legs to the baby's cot. Her little Jesus is fat with sleep. 'You can play on the sofa.' She widens her eyes, pours an angry look into mine, hangs a smacking hand in the air, and waits. I let go of her skirt. Her face softens. 'You can be a little Maman to our baby while I'm out, hmm?'

In the hallway, she pulls Papa's waistcoat over her dress. 'His wife did a good job knitting this, fits me perfect.' She mutters, stretching it from button to button, over her large breasts, hips and stomach. On the last button she smiles, 'He never wears it, same with his wedding ring. You'd think he would've bought me a ring by now.' She knots her scarf over her head and keeps her slippers on. Maman looks like Raymonde. I trail after her back to the baby's cot. Her lighter and cigarettes peep out of her breasts as she leans over the baby and rocks him. 'Yes, my little Jesus, you have a big sleep.' She purrs, then looks over her shoulder to the window. 'Right, I'm off. It looks like snow.' Pulls a chair to the cot, and drops me onto it. 'Just rock him like this, gently, until I am gone.' Her hand rests on mine, we rock her baby.

'You're his little Maman now,' she whispers.

'And I'm good too.'

'So far. But remember, little Maman, Josepha is studying. Don't go in the bedroom.' She smiles, 'You've changed him, haven't you?' I smile back, we're good at pretending together. 'You've left his bottle on the stove, and if he wakes, you knock quietly on the bedroom door, tell Josepha. Don't wake Pierre.' She lifts her hand off mine. I rock our baby by myself. She kisses me. I don't hold onto her neck. 'I'll be back in one tiny hour. I'll get you a surprise.' She glances at her wrist again, 'Oh, god, I'm late.' Stepping backwards, she follows the edge of the table, and picks up her basket. I'm about to run after her, when she hisses, 'Don't you dare move from that chair!' Her eyes pin me to the cot. Opening the flat door, she blows me a kiss and leaves.

As soon as I hear her steps in the staircase the living room becomes darker. I push the chair close to the window.

'Look Maman!' I say to the new Maman inside me.

'Yes,' says my grown-up voice.

'You don't know what I can do, do you?'

'No.' I climb on the chair, twist the window handle open, get off the chair, open the window wide, push the chair back inside the window and climb back onto it. My hands too work like grown-up hands. The street is way below my feet, I'm so tall. I lean over the railing. A whimper scratches the air behind me. It's the baby.

'You'd better see to your new baby, Julienne.' Just when I pretend to be Maman I see her cross the street.

'Maman, Maman! Hello!'

Maman looks up, furious.

'Shut that window! I'm coming back up and you'll see what you'll get.' She yells and turns back.

'Close the window, quick. And watch over our baby before she comes in.' I undo all the work I have done to open the window. I shut the window and stand on the chair, rocking the baby, my eyes fixed to the door. I wait. All is quiet. She is not coming back.

'She's tricked me again!' I sneer like Maman.

The baby lets out small cries. I unhook the side bar of his cot and push his dummy into his mouth, then tap his back. Every time I stop rocking him, he cries.

'Grow up! Stop being stupid! Stop sucking my Maman's tits!' I snatch his dummy and throw it across the room. He cries louder. I slap him.

'You'll see what you'll get if you don't stop crying.' I slap him harder. Josepha runs in, lifts the baby over her shoulder.

'Oh! There! There! You must not smack him, Julienne.'

'But I am in charge, Josepha!'

'Shush … He is only a baby.' Josepha's voice is soft and flows into my chest.

'But he never gets smacked. When Pierre cries he gets smacked and I do.'

'When you were tiny babies no one smacked you.' She strokes my hair and I forget about the Maman inside me.

Josepha lays the baby down. We rock him together, he closes his eyes again.

'Tell you what,' she whispers, taking me into her arms. Her kiss numbs me. All at once I'm her baby. I poke my finger to her dimpled chin. 'I will lend you my tea set and my two saucepans.' Her thick black hair tickles my face as she carries me to the hallway. We open the shoe cupboard and she lowers me to the floor with a kiss. From the top shelf, she drags out a large square box, then beams a smile.

'You're so tall, Josepha.'

'You'll be tall like me when you're seventeen.'

'Oh … the tea set!' She's not allowed to lend it. Papa says it's special.

'You must not break it. It's a present to me from my own mother,' Josepha warns me. Josepha has two Mamans, that's why her smile dimples her face and mine doesn't.

'I won't break it because I need it for my baby.'

She carries the box to the living room and the two saucepans with scarlet wooden handles. I trot after Josepha's swaying skirt.

Placing everything on the floor, she kneels down, pushes the two tiny hooks and opens the box. Inside, it's padded like a mattress. The spoons sparkle like Maman's earrings. Strawberry perfume rises from the tea set.

'This is real antique porcelain. See.'

Honey pink roses swirl from inside each cup.

'Play with me, Josepha.' She nudges two cups and saucers out of the shiny lining. A sky-high chime rings through the air as she places the cake plate under my nose.

'I have to study for my exams.' A three-dimple smile fattens her face. She ruffles my hair. 'Don't break them. Remember,' she warns me, unslotting the coffee pot and tea pot.

'And the sugar bowl,' I say, before she closes the box.

My kitchen is underneath Papa's wardrobe. It's big and strong on the outside. But underneath tiny wormholes eat its wooden legs. It bleeds ham-pink on the inside.

Josepha is out of sight and I am so happy to be alone with the tea set that I feel a wee coming. I just have time to take the lids off the tea and coffee pots. I pull my knickers down and I fill the pots as well as each cup and saucer, keeping an eye under my legs to aim well.

'Julienne, look what you've done.' Maman's voice is back inside me. I run to the hallway, get the newspaper and lay it to soak up the rest of my wee from the floor.

'I've made a table cloth for you, Maman.' My stomach twists. It's too late. A brown creamy lump is coming out. 'Here's some dinner too.' I hold the two saucepans and drop one lump in each pan. They steam. A pea sticks out.

'Nice hot onion smell.' I stay, squatting with my bottom in the air. The ceiling swoops through my legs. So big that it pulls my eyes to every corner.

'Everything is so much better upside down, Maman.'

'This is your living room sky, Julienne.' And a hot black cloud crashes down from the ceiling. I pick the lump up with my knickers, squash it in the sugar bowl. It is sand soft and warm. Earth brown, the colour of Papa's suit. Holding my knickers as a glove, I can press two eyes and a mouth inside the sugar bowl, and in the sauce pans, then pinch a nose in the centre. Three brown faces stare at me from the floor. This is better than drawing with crayons. Their eyes glisten with wet and big smiles dimple their skin.

'Look, Maman, Papa and me. Hmm, good stew.'

'Your knickers are dirty, Julienne.' Maman's words run through my head. I get up quickly and stuff my smelly knickers between the seats in the middle of the sofa. Turning back, I call out to the baby, 'Dinner's ready. Let's put the lids on before it gets cold. Hurry, go and get the knife to cut bread up, our baby is hungry.'

I run to the kitchen, get the bread knife with the help of a chair, and as I climb down, Josepha comes in. I hide the knife behind my back.

'What's that smell?' she asks, screwing a funny look on her face.

'It's you! You're the smelly one.'

'Do you need to go to the potty?'

'No!' I pull my skirt down, dropping the knife.

'What are you doing?' She picks up the knife.

'Give it to me! I must have a big knife to cut my dinner.'

'Shush … Here, you can have this knife, it's safe.' Josepha gives me a proper dinner knife. She plays for real. 'Are you going to give me some of your dinner?' She chuckles.

'No. Not now. Later, because you are a big girl. So you can wait a small hour or two, or three little hours. And, you have to look after Pierre. And you must shut all the doors so that you don't wake my baby.' I run out of the kitchen. Josepha doesn't run after me, catch me, or scoop me into the air with tickles. This time she is good at pretending.

'Ah! There you are at last!' Maman shouts out of me. 'I was just about to leave. Quick, have you got the knife? Hurry I have to go shopping.'

'Yes Maman.'

'Have you closed the door behind you?'

'Yes Maman.'

'Get his plate out then.'

'Done it.'

'Put his dinner on his plate, but first, take his drink to the table. He can drink after he has eaten.'

I place a cup of wee on the edge of the table close to the cot without spilling it, a plate of dinner, next the knife.

'Done it.' I clap my hands.

'Hurry, bring two chairs.'

I make a bridge with the chairs between the cot and the table. I climb, grab the plate and place it at my feet near the cot.

'And the knife, Julienne?' My hands smell bad. No time to stop. I stick the knife in the dinner, it stays on the plate. There's a photograph of an old woman smiling like Papa, on the mantle piece. A vase and a paper flower.

'Let's get you up, my little Jesus.'

The baby's eyes are wide open. With his ginger tuft and his pointed nose he stares at me like a toy rabbit. I unhook the bar of his cot, pull him up, he flops back. Squeezing him against the bars, I hold him with one arm, cut his dinner with the other. He's heavy, his white body slides downward. His head knocks against the cot-bars with a cry. I am slipping with his weight, the knife in one hand and his collar in the other.

'Shut up! This dinner is better than Maman's milk.' I smack him.

A large hand touches my back.

'What is going on?' It's Josepha's bossy voice. I didn't hear her come in.

'No! Let me!' I cry out, holding back the knife from her grip. 'I am his Maman, you're not! I must cut his dinner.'

Josepha ignores me and heaves the baby into her arms.

'Well . . . I wonder what Maman Delphine will say when she comes back?' She looks into my eyes. And I see the hiding I will get. 'Shall we put your dinner away?' Josepha asks. She's not angry with me.

'Let me smack him first. He was naughty. You didn't see it.'

Josepha keeps the baby in her arms and shakes her head at her tea set and says, 'Better to do a big one in something rather than nothing.'

We clear and wash everything. 'We'll leave some poo in the potty, so that Maman can see how good you've been.' Josepha pours my wee in it too. 'Here, play with this and stay in the hallway, where I can see you.' She gives me my red cardboard suitcase.

'Oh! What a smell!' Maman cheers as she comes through the front door. Her face is wet. Snow melts on her scarf and slippers.

'That's a good girl.' Maman peeps at the pot. Josepha picks it up.

'I'll empty it.'

'It is very kind of you, Josepha.' Maman smiles at me like she does with her baby, undoes her scarf and switches on the light in the living room. All at once the wardrobe is huge, the table bloats, piles of nappies sit on chairs and my dirty knickers flash a grin as they stick a brown tongue out, between two cushions. Maman doesn't see them.

'Who's my beautiful little sausage!' she chuckles, darts to the cot, scoops her baby up into her arms, sweeps dancing feet across the room and with his head wobbling side to side, she drops herself in the middle of the sofa. Her bottom squeezes my knickers against her skirt. 'You're a smelly sausage, today!' She sniffs, leans back, puts her feet up. I stay by the shoe cupboard, sit on the floor, open my cardboard suitcase and crouch behind its lid.

Josepha comes in from the half landing toilet, places a clean potty behind me with a wink. 'Shall I start peeling the vegetables?' she asks, and picks up the shopping.

'You're being very helpful today,' Maman nods.

Just as Papa comes through the door Josepha steps into the hallway with Pierre in her arms, and we're all splashed in yellow as he flicks the hallway light on.

'Happy is the man with all his children behind his front door!' Papa laughs. He keeps the door open, shakes snow off his hat, his overcoat and shoes. Icy air runs up my legs.

'Julienne is potty-trained today, Papico.'

Cold bites my bare bottom.

'Good, listening to your Papa, kranoon.'

'She'll do nothing with me on purpose. What's wrong with me, hey Julienne?' Maman grunts.

My knickers glare at me under her skirt.

'Growing up, at last.' Papa pats my head and takes Pierre from Josepha.

Everyone goes to the kitchen. Roars of laughter bellow to the hallway. The toys in my suitcase blush brighter. On his way out, Papa says 'It's so good to laugh like old times.' Papa steps over me, smiling, 'Quelle culloto! What a rascal you are. Ah! I can see she's stretched my waist-coat again.'

'Come back Papa!'

'Just off to buy cigarettes.' As soon as his footsteps fade into the corridor the kitchen door slams. Josepha leaps out, runs past me, her thick black hair hiding her face. She drops in her chair, leans over her desk, kicking the living room door shut. She is crying. Maman comes, running after her, the baby in her arms and Pierre at her feet. She kicks the living room door open. With her free arm, Maman slaps the back of Josepha's head. 'Doing your homework? Dirty liar! That's what you are!' she curses into Josepha's hair. Pierre clings to me, letting out a long cry.

'You did this on purpose!' Maman shrieks over Pierre and the baby's cries. 'That's right; pretend to do your schoolwork! Write the truth for a change!' Josepha writes with one hand, the other covers her face. Her back shakes with crying. She clutches her pen and paper and writes without taking her pen off the paper.

'Write! Go on, write like a mad woman!' Maman shrieks. Josepha writes faster and faster through her tears, spilling her words over the paper and onto her desk. Her desk, her chair, her pen, her paper tremble with her hand. Bent in half, she is breaking.

'I shall tell you what to write!' Maman shouts a rasping voice. Tight burning tears are inside her too. 'Write! "I'm my Papa's favourite child because I can speak his language here!" Write this, "I am jealous of my little sister. I want her to hate her Catholic Maman! I believe that we are the best, the rest are imbeciles!"' Pierre grips my neck. His teeth grow crooked. Maman's voice twists higher and higher against the walls and windows, splintering the air and shaking the wardrobe. 'Write again, "I am superior. I make the law here. I deliberately put those shitty knickers on the sofa to show my father how Delphine is a stinking French peasant. Delphine doesn't know how to care for her children but I know best because this is my mother's home."' Maman speaks without stopping, spitting over her baby's head. 'And write this! "I am a slut! An idiot, a dirty, ungrateful jealous liar!"' Her words splinter our faces. '"Spiteful, devious, vicious, selfish! I want Delphine out of my home!"' For an instant Maman gasps for air, the living room bulges out. Yellow light flares against the pink desk and our clothes. Then, with a deep voice Maman plunges her words into Josepha's back. 'You know that he loves me. Yes, me! You're so jealous, aren't you? And you know your mother will never come back. She's dead, Josepha.' Write that.' Josepha's body shudders over her pen, digging it into her desk. 'Write faster! "I hate my little sister. I hate my little brothers. I hate those who love me. I shall betray those who trust me because it gives me pleasure to hurt them. I am a coward, a cheat, a thief, a spy, a mean, selfish dirty Judas!"'

Maman stops; her lips, wet with her spit, quiver; her eyes squint. She stares all around her, then she leaps into the hallway. Thick smoke is coming out of the kitchen. The baby still in her arms, she swings the hallway door open and darts into the smoke.

Josepha jumps up. Her tears glisten. Avoiding my eyes, she snatches her coat above my head, shoves pen and paper in her pocket and slams the flat door.

I push Pierre off me. He bawls into my face. 'What's the matter with him?' Maman yells. I try to lift him up, but drop him. I sit with him. 'Look!' I swing my suitcase under his eyes. 'Look! See these funny things . . .' Pierre frowns at my tiny eggcup, my story book, then sulks. 'Shut up!' I hiss, then grin. 'Look a dolly.' I wave Claudette at him. He makes to grab her. I pull her back. 'You're only meant to look!' I shout, and he bites me.

CHARLIE
by Alex Pheby

Charlie, it's the end son. I tell you. At last. Me the poor fuck. The lights are going out my baby boy. The lights are going out. After all these years. I'm sorry boy. That's it for me. No more. A poor fuck. Charlie, they won't let me be. The babies. Me lying out in the street and God, at their mercy. Hard in the back, the little shites. And in the face. It hurts Charlie, son. And I know I deserve it all, but it's no way for a man to go. The little fucking dogs. Like flies round shite and me not even moving. Where's the game in that? God, if I could only get up and hammer the little bastards. But the drink. Let me get up God, let me hammer the little shites why not? God, you're a cruel bastard, with a man so low and I'll tell you that to your face. Look at me. Look and do nothing. You're a cruel bastard to a sad fuck and I know. Right Charlie? Right so but you're dead with him too and I'm on my way. God wait and I'll tell you. God wait. To hell. God look at me. So low. Jesus. I'm a bad man, Charlie, though you know. If anyone knows. You know me, son, like a boy never knew his da, looking down on him from above for all these years. Watching him fall, to die, like you Charlie, like I let you fall, every day a little further and now we're here, Charlie my boy. And God must have told you I'm a bad man. And baby fucking Jesus and all the saints must have told you. A bad man from a bad place. That bitch, Charlie. That bitch. God knows there's a place for a woman and I know, but that bitch. My mother. My dirty ma. Thirty years dead and she still does for me in the end, setting me to drink. You won't laugh, Charlie, you won't – the bitch whore. Set me on the road to my last as sure as if she'd pushed the drink down me herself. God Jesus she was the whore of it all. Those men – all of them. And me to watch and me to fetch for the lot of them. All night and her the whore. My dirty ma. Six days from seven and try to live that shame down, from a boy. With them all pointing and God knows the fathers of them in and out at all hours and the mothers' eyes like bricks at my little head and the whore of my mother to blame for it all. And no father, not that would stand up and claim me, their boy. Drove me to the drink. And the drink. The fucking drink. One's not enough neither's ten. Neither's fifty. And my guts. And my legs. So I can't get up and God so the little shites are in on me, having their fun and me on the way to my maker at last. Choking on it all. Choking on the small ones first and then the ones for the road and then the ones I can't even bring to mind that I drank when I was drunk and fuck won't they all choke you in the end, they'll all trip you up and keep you down and God won't want to know you. I know. Charlie. Charlie my little sweet baby boy. Dead to fuck and I'm the one. I know. That hurts me Charlie. Gets me where it hurts. Not long now boy, you know? Not long and I'll be lucky to see you again my little beauty. And you'll not be angry at your poor fuck father. I know. You with God and his boys and you seeing and knowing it all. That bitch and all. Your poor fuck of a da and all his drink and the evil ways and his bitch mother. It won't change your little smile, me and mine. Your face. My beautiful baby boy, lying in the dirt and broken. God Jesus, the drink, and that bitch, my poor broken boy and me that dropped you. I deserve it all. God. But me, fuck, I know, I know, a bad man but Christ, is that the way to punish me? Charlie, dead to fuck and slipping through my hands onto the dirt. And broken, Charlie, your poor little face. Smashed. God I know, I can see it, I can see it now. Broken. But not your smile, not your smile. And your mother. My Annie. God pity the poor, poor girl, who loved me and I killed her baby. God. I pushed you as much as I let you fall and she knew it all. Her arms waiting for you and you so still, like you never were and she could see it was wrong. And she held you up to her face and it was like I'd never seen, so sad, Charlie, so sad. And the tears running down her face and onto yours and she never looked me in the eyes from that day. So sad, she was, that poor, poor girl and she was cold in her heart. And I was the last that could warm it and she wouldn't look at me. Couldn't. And I could only look at her. I killed her only boy, you Charlie, my son, dead and me, full of drink. God fuck. And she was right to hate me like I hate myself and it's only you, Charlie, with a smile for your da as least should have. Me drunk to fuck and you with no sense for the world. A child, with no knowledge of the world and falling and there's no escape from that, not for anyone, not even for my beautiful boy. God Jesus there's no escape from that. Not for you or me, Charlie boy. And these lads are the boys and they're kicking me down but I can see you now in them. You, Charlie, my beautiful broken boy. It's not long. Not long for me. The concrete burns my cheek, just like yours son. God, just the same, the two of us, at last, lying on the concrete in the dirt and all but dead. Just like you boy and I picked you up and you breathed your last, looking your sick da dead in the eye and me too drunk to feel it. And me too drunk to ever want to feel it. Can you understand me Charlie? Who is only a fucking baby, no more than a baby for God's sake. God knows. You Charlie, you and the baby Lord Jesus himself know everything, don't you boy? Looking down on an old man on the edge of death and dying on the ground. Those laughing boys, Charlie, those laughing boys at their game as you never were. Never could be and me to blame, letting you fall down the stairs, the drink, as much as pushing you off and you to lie there broken, God, with one last breath to curse me and there was your smile. Standing at the bottom of the stair, of the long concrete stair with the sun on the back of my neck and the smell of whisky and even the bastard drunks deadly quiet. And you in my arms weighing nothing. And not a word of anger, not a word, just your beautiful smile. Running to me and me too drunk to come for you, running down the stair and falling. And there's no escape from the ways of world, not even for you and you had to fall and you had to die and a smile for your poor fuck of a father. Jesus, it's cruel. And me without the balls to end myself, me without the balls. Years of the drink and your face and your smile and nothing. Just the road and me lying there for as long as there is, God, and your little smile. You see me son and I see you and God knows if I don't deserve every second of it and worse. And all I see is you Charlie. Sweet Charlie. And me without the balls to end it for myself. A coward, a dirty coward in the road and here I am and fuck it if I'm not on my way out despite it all. And at last I lie, God, when I've done myself near to death for all these years and the children do my work for me, finish it. And in them I can see you Charlie. Is it you there? Charlie. Is it you there kicking and laughing. My poor broken child come back from the dirt? God Jesus, I could never blame you, my love. It's what I deserve, and you know and so does He. And so do I. Is it you my boy? Is this God's work, my little boy? Have you come to save me? My beautiful sweet boy. Is this the way? Saved by a kick from my own broken son? Then let it come. And let that be an end to it. God, fuck, I know now. More than even you Charlie, God, more than even Jesus himself, I know. All the years of pain. I see it all, your face and mine, broken in the dirt and God above us and that's it for you and me both, together. God fuck, it hurts. Charlie, my boy, it hurts and I'll soon be with you. Soon. Please, fuck, God, let it be soon. Let it be today. I won't ask but let it be today and end it all.

LOSING GROUND

One morning the newspaper doesn't appear
and the guy in the corner store forgets your name.
The street sweeper who jostles you with his broom makes no apology
and 46 Alderman's Square is nowhere to be found.
The banknotes in your wallet bear the faces of strangers,
they're the wrong texture, the wrong size,
and the cabbie is abusive. You leave your umbrella in his car.
The pay phone won't take your coins and reversing the charge
    brings no response.
You wait twenty-five minutes for a shepherd's pie that never arrives;
the waitresses are identical and all of them ignore you.
Your mistress isn't expecting you.
She serves pork braised in red wine and won't use your pet name.
(Normally you come with flowers.)
You arrive at the Head Office at three o'clock sharp;
the secretary has no record of an appointment and won't
    take your card.
You want your leather armchair, those slippers, that reading lamp,
but the dogs won't let you near the front door
so you loiter in the hedgerows,
fingering your keys.
You catch your reflection in a wing mirror.
You hardly recognize yourself.
You spot your wife leaving the house in heels and a red sequin dress.
You call her name.
The dress shimmers as she turns, looks right through you.

QUELQUES MOTS DE CONSEIL

You must, he says, be *trés maigre.*
You pad the midsection and insert
a sack of pigeon blood mixed with vinegar,
pour éviter la coagulation.
The costume you must embellish
with a certain quantity of sequins
to mark the place where *l'épée*
devait entrer et sortir le ventre.
It is preferable to request a sword
from any military man in attendance,
for then there will be no questions
regarding the quality of the blade.

BAD BLOOD

by Alex Mitchell

As a boy, Jinjo thought he knew all that there was to know about his father.

His father's name was Ichiro. Even to those who knew him well, he was a dull man, a good man but a dull man. When not working or sleeping, and such times were few and far apart, Ichiro had no real interests in life beyond watching the evening baseball on television with a glass of whisky in his hand. He was never cruel or angry, like some of Jinjo's friends' fathers, but it seemed as if there was nothing of any importance he had to say or to pass on to his son. If asked a question, he would take his time and do his best to answer, but there were just so many things he knew so little about.

By the age of thirteen, Jinjo had come to believe that his father had told him all he had to tell. As it turned out, this was not quite the case. The one thing he did not know about his father was the one thing his father did not want him to know.

Ichiro was Buraku, and, if you believe what they say about blood lines, so was Jinjo.

Jinjo would almost certainly have remained unaware of his family heritage had it not been for the sudden reappearance of his uncle, and Ichiro's brother, Bintaku-san.

Bintaku arrived at their apartment on the day of Jinjo's fourteenth birthday. On hearing the doorbell, Ichiro had guessed it to be one of his son's friends come for the party, and had not at first recognised the middle-aged man who stood on his doorstep. The two men had neither seen nor heard from each other for over twenty years. Only when he heard him speak in his thick Osaka accent, did Ichiro take his brother in his arms. Both men were soon in tears. Jinjo saw all this from the living room. He had never seen his father cry before.

After the two men had laughed, drunk beer together, and commented on each others' changed appearance, Ichiro discovered the real reason for his brother's visit. Their mother had died the week before. There was little more said after that and the two men left the same day for Osaka, in order to put her affairs in order and to take part in the passing away ceremony.

On his return, Ichiro appeared changed to both his wife and his son, older and even less attached to everyday life. Soon after, he took Jinjo for a walk by the Meiji river. As they watched a school baseball game on one of the diamonds that lay beside the riverbank, Ichiro told his son the real story of his life. Jinjo listened and remained quiet. It meant very little to him at the time. He had never heard of the Buraku before, but could tell that his father took the issue seriously.

Ichiro had been born into a large travelling community of Buraku people outside Osaka in the 1920s.

When he was a child, it was still believed that the blood of the Buraku was thicker than that of normal Japanese. The only time Ichiro would ever speak to an outsider would be at work with his own father in the family business of butchery. In charge of what was seen as society's 'unclean' activities, the other Buraku men also worked in leatherwork and the execution of criminals. They rarely mixed with outsiders.

The turmoil of Japan in the 1930s and then during the war changed all that. There were too many other things to worry about than keeping up the old barriers between neighbours. Ichiro joined the Imperial Army in 1940. He was sent to fight in Manchuria. At first it had felt good to be away in a foreign land. For a young man like Ichiro, it was an escape from the normal divisions that had so enclosed him, but the last two years of the war were hard and he was fortunate to come back alive.

When he did return to Japan in 1946, like many others he found himself drawn towards the rubble and ruins of Tokyo. It was during that difficult time that he first met Jinjo's mother in a food queue. They married soon afterwards. At that time, there were many things people did not want to speak of from their past, and it was not until their first and only child was born in 1950, that Ichiro decided to tell his wife of his Buraku origin. After living through the horrors of the past few years, she was not upset. As a girl, it was true that she had heard stories of the Buraku people's dirty way of life and of their position at the bottom of society, but now she didn't care. Having lost her younger brother and her parents in the American air raids, she was just happy to once again be part of a family. They spoke about it once and then agreed there was no need to discuss it again.

When Ichiro told Jinjo of all this, it was the first time he had spoken of it since.

When Jinjo reached the age of sixteen he left school and went to work in the clerical department of a large manufacturing corporation. It was the 1960s, a busy time for Japan as it entered a period of great growth, and a good job was easy to find. He moved out of his parents' home and into a company dormitory, where he shared a room with three other young men. Soon, he developed a taste for modern jazz, cold beer and Marlboro cigarettes. For the next two years he was moved from one section of the office to another, learning all of the different areas of the firm's work. In the evenings, he either stayed in his room, smoking and listening to records, or travelled into Shibuya to meet friends and walk the streets together, talking about music and girls.

He enjoyed his job, worked hard and was quickly promoted within the company. After five years, he was given a new position with more money, and told he must move office to a high-rise building in central Tokyo. There he met a new set of work colleagues. On his first day, he noticed a shy young woman from the north, whose desk was not far from his. She was very pretty, and Jinjo soon found out that her name was Mimiko. At first, they did not speak beyond polite pleasantries, but after a few weeks Jinjo plucked up the courage to ask her to accompany him for lunch in the work canteen. She had noticed him too and so happily agreed. Soon they started dating. They would go to see foreign films in Shibuya and afterwards visit cheap and smoky izakayas to eat and drink late into the evening before catching the last train home. Within a year, Jinjo had been introduced to Mimiko's parents. The couple were soon engaged to be married.

At first, the marriage was a success. With the help of their parents, they found the deposit for a small but neat apartment only a twenty-minute walk from the local train station, or five if you went by bicycle.

Life was good. In the summer they would go to the beach every weekend, and for the New Year they would visit her relatives in Hokkaido. Jinjo even learned how to ski and how not to smile at the strange accents up there. In Tokyo, they had a few close friends from work who they would often meet on Friday evenings for drinks and a meal. Sometimes, Jinjo would drink too much beer and Mimiko would have to pay for a taxi to drive them home. She would tease him when his head hurt in the morning but they would always end up laughing about it.

When Mimiko reached the age of twenty-five, it was time she gave up her job; they decided to start a family. All of their friends were doing the same thing, and, although Mimiko was sad to leave the work she had so enjoyed, she was excited about bringing a baby into the apartment, and immediately cleared out some space in their bedroom to make way for a cot.

Things did not work out the way they planned. The child did not come as expected. Neither of them were impatient people, but, after two years, she was still not pregnant and they began to argue and to worry. He would come home later and later from work and they gradually stopped seeing their friends who by now were all raising families. Where once had been laughter, a silence in the apartment now emerged and then grew. Mimiko retreated into herself, and their conversations died away.

When Mimiko did speak to her husband, all she would want to discuss was the child, or lack of one. Some days she blamed herself, on others she blamed Jinjo. She became superstitious and visited the local temple every day. She began to believe they were being punished for some unknown crime, and wanted to know what they could do to escape their fate. When she brought this up, Jinjo never knew what to say. He just wished that she could be happy again.

Eventually, Mimiko decided they should visit a clinic to find out if there was a medical problem. At first, Jinjo was unwilling. He was afraid of being found infertile, and of how his wife might react if such a thing happened. This did not stop Mimiko from asking however. Eventually he gave in and Mimiko booked a visit for the following Saturday.

Before speaking to the consultant, they both had to take a rigorous medical examination and blood test.

After all the tests, and with his mind deeply concerned for his wife's well being, Jinjo handed his medical card over to the nurse.

They returned a week later and held each other's hands as they stepped into the doctor's office. He told them he could find nothing wrong with either of their reproductive systems. Jinjo's sperm count was a little low, but this could easily be improved by an exercise regime and a change in diet. Apart from that, there was no reason why they could not conceive a perfectly healthy baby.

Delighted with this news, Jinjo left the hospital to pick up the car from the nearby car park while Mimiko remained behind to leaf through the various maternity leaflets. It was at this point, while separated from Jinjo, that an elderly nurse approached Mimiko and asked whether she could take a moment of her time. The nurse knew it was not for her to say, but she wondered whether the beautiful young lady was fully aware of her husband's Buraku background. Mimiko did not say a word in reply but took and read closely the medical card that proved the truth of the old woman's claims.

At first, she said nothing of this to Jinjo. Of course, she had heard of the Buraku and of their status. She knew that her parents would be upset if they were to find out, but also believed it to be an old person's way of seeing things. In this modern age, surely such things had no real importance anymore? She loved her husband deeply and could not see why the actions of his ancestors should have any relevance for the young couple.

But the months passed by, and their marriage remained childless. Jinjo stopped eating hamburgers, ate more sashimi and cut down on his smoking, but still Mimiko did not fall pregnant. Her mind began to drift back to the sharp words of the hospital nurse. Sitting alone in the empty apartment, the long summer afternoons would drag Mimiko to the thoughts of her husband's family's past, her barren womb and to the shame for which she was surely now being punished.

She finally broke down and unleashed her pain and anger at the end of a hot and heavy day in August.

A school friend had come to visit that afternoon, bringing her two young boys along with her. Mimiko had sat silently on the sofa watching the children play as her friend complained about the meanness of her husband. Jinjo was home late that night. He had told her that morning that he was going to be late as he had to attend a colleague's leaving party. The truth was that he did not know the man all that well and was only going as an excuse to delay his journey home.

When Jinjo finally arrived back at the apartment, it was after midnight and, even after the long train journey, he was still a little drunk. He went into the kitchen to make himself some instant coffee and a tuna sandwich and found his wife sitting in the darkness. He put his hand on her shoulder and asked how she was. She screamed and hit out at him. She called him scum and a butcher's bastard. His blood was thick with the dirt and filth of his family's past. She blamed him for everything. He had ruined her life with his lies. He would never come near her again. She wished she were able to find a real man who would give her the children she deserved.

He told her she was hysterical, and she was, but in the morning, when she woke, her views had not changed.

After that night, their relationship was characterised by long and painful periods of silence. Unable to keep it all within anymore, Mimiko eventually told her family that her husband was Buraku. For a while, Jinjo received a series of threatening phone calls. When he did not respond, her family stopped speaking to him entirely. If he picked up the phone when they rang, all he could hear was silence and he would pass it over to his wife.

He suggested divorce, but she would not agree. She believed her status as the divorced woman from a Buraku marriage would, if such a thing was possible, be even lower than her current position. She moved his clothes and possessions into the living room. He began to spend occasional nights at the office, sleeping curled up beneath his desk.

One morning, snapping the brittle silence of their breakfast together, she told him that she had started praying to the gods that she could be a widow. In reply, Jinjo said nothing, but watched as the seaweed in his soup slowly swirled around to the bottom of his bowl.

GALA DAY
by Irene Garrow

Johnny said that he could take them home but only if they left by midnight. He didn't like talking on the phone. Every year his sister and her husband relied on him for Gala Day, 'I won't stay late Jess, Helen's tired out from everything ... and she can't stand for long.'

'That'll suit me fine.' Jess's voice didn't sound the same. 'Robert has work on Sunday so he'll have to take it easy.' She hesitated, 'How's Helen doing?'

'Not too bad ... she's on the mend. It's tired her out ... and she can get very down ... I've told her it'll take time, the doctor said so.' His sister could tell how worried Johnny was by his voice. Most phone conversations were punctuated by laughs and jokes.

'It all takes time; she's been through a lot. She'll be looking forward to her holiday, I bet?' She spoke with force.

'Aye, aye – a week on Monday we're off. Listen hen, I'm at work so I'd better go. We'll collect you about ten on Saturday. OK?'

Johnny sat for a few moments trying to remember what he'd forgotten to ask her, before he hung up. Something about his Helen, it had gone from his head. Some friend of Jess's was into alternative stuff and she'd suggested some kind of tea was good for women who had Helen's problems. What was it called? He'd ask her on Saturday.

Gala Day was as wet as usual. He'd left Helen with Jess holding the umbrella, watching the parade, as the rain hammered down. The men folk had gone into the pub. Mary, Johnny's older sister had gone ahead to prepare the food. Children walked by splashing their feet in the puddles, their elaborate outfits covered in fluorescent rain jackets, their fancy hats standing upright in the wind. Helen and Jess waited for the final float to arrive: the Gala Princess and her handmaidens.

'Are you all right Helen, why not go and sit down outside the pub, you'll still see the float – and you can rest your legs.'

'No, I'm doing fine ... I'm fine ... Look! There she is just round the corner ... I can see her crown. The float's much bigger than last year!' They both stood on tiptoes to get a good look. Helen's face was wet; her eyes were heavy with thick black mascara and blue eyeliner. She took out her camera and began to take snaps of the Princess – one, two, three, four, five – she lost count.

Later on, back at Mary's house Johnny asked in a low voice about Helen, 'I'm sorry you had to wait like that … I thought Helen went back with Mary to the house. I wouldn't have stayed in the pub if I'd known … the pair of you must have got soaked.' There were lines of anxiety etched on his face. Johnny gnawed at a bitten-down finger circled by a loose gold band. He could see a worry on Jess's face. His voice picked up. 'You and Robert and Mary should come over for one of my famous curries. One Sunday soon eh … as soon as Helen's on the mend.'

He looked over at the table, 'I'll give Mrs Gordon Ramsay a run for her money!'

Mary had made a big lasagne and a chicken casserole and the oven was packed with baking potatoes. There had been a plan to barbecue as well but the rain looked set for the whole evening. Including a couple of neighbours, there were twelve of them sitting down for the meal. Everyone had a glass of sparkling wine, the seats were squeezed together and plates were piled high with food. Johnny sat beside Jess and Helen was on his other side. Helen was eating very little. Mary's neighbour was cracking jokes, and Robert was laughing; he wasn't a drinker and often avoided Gala Day. Johnny sipped his glass of wine; his mouth ached for a pint.

It was after eleven, the table had been cleared and more drinks poured for everyone. The rain had finally stopped but everyone sat in the main room ignoring the patio doors to the outside. Johnny looked around for Helen; she was talking to his niece. He hated to think it but from this distance, even with the make-up, she looked hellish; her skin was the colour of cement and her shoulders had shrunk. He looked around for Jess. He couldn't see her.

'Where's our Jess?' he asked Mary.

'She's gone to get a couple of chairs from next door. We're too old to sit on the floor now.'

Mary leaned over. 'How's Helen doing? She'll be back on her feet soon enough.' Her face was flushed from the heat and a couple of glasses of wine and she touched his arm as she spoke. 'You look ready for your holiday eh …

more than ready?' Johnny heard the catch in her voice. He turned away from her, his eyes faraway.

'I'll give Jess a hand – she should've asked me.'

Mary straightened up; she folded one arm over the other and stood watching Johnny walk away. He thought for a moment that he heard her say *don't forget your key,* like she used to when he was a boy.

He walked out Mary's side door along the path, which led to an identical house without a front gate. There were two windows in darkness. He called out for Jessie as he walked around into the back garden. There was no sound. He should've taken a right instead of a left. It was the wrong one. This house was all locked up, a small semi-detached with a square of garden at the back and a small shed. There was one rhododendron bush on the left and a pole with a *For Sale* sign lying against the shed door.

The estate was on a hill and the view from the back was dramatic; the tops and chimneys of all the other houses lay below. The roads with ants of cars in the distance and beyond them the hills; three hills, two identical soft green hills and one smaller one at the front. The clouds were moving to the west and he could see a rain cloud over the horizon. It was cold and he felt himself shiver. He had a crazy idea to get in his car and drive to the base of the hills and climb to the top of one of them. To look the other way, to face where he was standing full on, and to see how he would look from there.

'Johnny, Johnny … I thought you'd got lost.' It was Jess. She was standing behind him holding a folded chair. She walked towards him, she was smiling but her head tilted to one side, as if in doubt. 'You went the wrong way. All of these houses look exactly the same. I don't know how many times I've been here but I still get mixed up. You better go in. The singing is about to start.' Jessie was talking fast, as if there was a rush.

'If the singing is starting … then I'd better get in there … I don't want anyone to nick my song … do I?' Jessie and Johnny laughed at each other as they spoke, 'One singer, one song'. Johnny lifted the folding canvas under his arm. 'Here – I'll carry the chair … you go ahead and warm up the audience … that's the trouble with driving, I'll have to sing sober …'

Inside, the windows had steamed up and the drunken neighbour had just finished telling everyone a smutty joke. Mary saw them and pulled a face,

'Johnny, do me a favour, get him a whisky but top it up with water, he's had too much to drink. I don't want jokes all bloody night!' Johnny saw the whisky bottle and poured it out for those in need. He caught Helen's eye; she was talking to his niece. Not long to go, he should really leave now but Jessie and Robert were enjoying the party and Mary had put on quite a spread. He saw Robert pat Helen's shoulder and offer her a refill as he squeezed past her chair.

Helen needed him more. She wasn't getting better. Sometimes she would say, 'Oh I don't know when I'll get back to normal?' And he'd try to gee her on, point out she'd been through a lot, she'd be back to her old self, in her own time. The doctor had said so.

He went and stood behind her chair and placed his hands on her shoulders. He smiled at his niece, a tall, blonde girl who he no longer recognised, grown-up and unknowable.

'Hi Uncle Johnny – here sit down here,' she patted the seat beside her, 'I'm escaping before my dad asks me to sing. Helen, can I get you something, a sandwich, a soft drink?'

Helen shook her head. 'No thanks … we're leaving soon … aren't we Johnny?'

He nodded. 'Let me see if Jess and Robert want to come now … it's nearly twelve.'

Helen raised her hand, 'No, no Johnny, it's all right, we can wait a bit, they're enjoying themselves. Look! Over there.'

Jess was standing at the door of the kitchen bent over laughing at something Mary had said. Beside them, a guy was standing with a football scarf tied around his head, holding a pint glass. Robert had disappeared into the back room where there was the sound of a football game on television and a lot of cheering. There was a child crying in the distance from a house nearby. Five minutes passed. The room was quiet as if everyone stopped talking at the same time. The clock above the door ticked a minute past midnight.

Johnny sat down, put his arm along the back of Helen's chair and whispered into her ear, 'Two weeks today, we'll be sitting in the sunshine drinking our cocktails. No Glasgow rain for us.'

She nodded but kept looking ahead, not turning towards him. He thought she hadn't heard and was about to repeat it, but then he saw her eyes blink, and a tear run down her face. At the back of his throat he felt as if something was stuck. He followed her gaze; she was looking at a tall man sitting beside a shrunken-looking woman with sparse hair, pale skin and a half-eaten plate in front of her, in the glass patio doors facing them. Their reflection was crystal clear and framed only the two of them for what seemed a long time, until a passing hand pushed the door handle and closed it shut.

FOTHERGILL
by Ross Raisin

I

Ramblers. Daft sods in pink and green hats. It wasn't even cold. They went along the field bottom swing-swaying like a line of drunks, addled with the air and the land, and the smell of manure. From the top of the field I watched their bright heads down by the bottom wall, peeping through the fog.

Sat up on my rock there, I let the world play out below me. All manner of creatures going about their backwards-forwards same as ever, never mind that the fog had them half-sighted. But I could see above the fog. It bided beneath my feet in wispy puffs and spread out five miles over to the hills at Easington, settled in the valley like a drain-puddle. And all above was fierce blue and clear.

The ramblers hadn't marked me. They'd walked past the farm and down the field without taking notice, of me or of Father rounding up sheep from the Moor. I laughed on at them from under my cap. Oi there ramblers, I'd a mind for shouting, what the fuck are you at, talking to that cow? What the fuck you talking to a cow for? And they'd have bowed down royal for me then, I wasn't doubting. So sorry, Mr Farmer, we won't do it again, I hope we haven't upset her. For that was the way with these ramblers – so respect-minded they wouldn't dare even look on myself for fear of crapping up Nature's balance. The laws of the countryside. And me, I was real living, farting Nature to their brain of things – part of the scenery same as a tree or a tractor. I saw one of them, him that went last over the stile, fiddling a rock on top of the wall. Thought he'd knocked it out of place when he weighted himself over. Daft sods these ramblers. I went toward them.

I came down off the rock, and halfway down the field the fog got hold of me, feeling in round my face so as I had to stop a minute and tune my eyes, though I still had sight of the hats, no bother. There's nothing moves itself so slow as a rambler. They were only so far as the next field, moving on like a line of chickens, their heads twitching side to side. What a lovely molehill. Bob, look, a cuckoo behind the drystone wall. Only it wasn't a cuckoo, I knew, it was a bloody pigeon.

I hadn't the hearing of them just yet, mind, but I knew their talk.

I followed on, quick down to the field bottom and straight over the wall, not troubling with the stile. Tumbled a couple of headstones to the ground with heaving myself up, but no matter. Part of Nature, me, I was licensed for that. And them in front couldn't hear me anyroad, their ears were full of fog. I dropped down the other side into the field next theirs and sidled close up to the wall between, until they were near enough I could see them through the stone-cracks. They'd not heeded me. I could've had an eye out with a pebble if I'd wanted. I slunk along the wall, listening to them breathing, heavy, like Towns always breath, when they were on farmland. Weekend exercise for them this was, never mind that they moved slower than a sheep to dip. Weekend exercise, like sex, so of course they were going to buy a pink hat to mark the occasion. And what about it Bob, maybe we can use that hat tonight too, eh? Wink, wink.

A middle of the way down the field and they stopped. They plonked down in a circle like they were for making a campfire but instead whipped out foil parcels and a thermos and started blathering.

'I've got ham. Who wants ham?'

'I'll have ham.'

'Oh, wait a moment. We have a choice. Ham and tomato. Ham and Red Leicester.'

'Mmm, tomato.'

The ham was passed about, and they stuck into what was left besides, the thermos stood up in the middle of the circle.

'Nasty old day still. I wish it would perk up a little.'

'I know. Doesn't look too promising though.'

I teased a small stone out the wall and plastered it in cow shit.

'That is such nice ham.'

'Yes, isn't it. From Tesco, you know.'

Crack. I hit the thermos bang centre, tea and shit splashing up the fog.

They hadn't a clue. I had a job on to keep from laughing as they skittled about and scanned the sky as if they were being bombed. Or maybe they feared they'd pissed the cuckoo off – upset Nature's balance with a ham sodding sandwich. Didn't once look over to me crouching behind the wall. So down I went for the cow pat and I threw another, but it missed and hit one on the foot. I could've flung the whole wall at her and she mightn't have felt it through those walking boots but it wasn't going to stop her screaming her lungs out her windpipe. They were all on their feet, grabbing up the picnic and making a flee for the bottom of the field. And they'd got wind of me, for one of them

– Pink Hat – turned over his shoulder and blabbed something about a peaceful day out, and they meant no harm please leave them alone.

But I couldn't be bothered with them any more. I waited for them to scarper then I started back for the farm. The pups would be needing a feed, and I was rumbling for a bite myself. I upped speed. When I got near the top of the field I turned round and pierced my eyes into the fog. They'd come back. At first I couldn't make out what they were up to but then I saw Pink Hat pick something up from the ground and it glinted an instant before he put it in his rucksack. They'd left the tin foil behind.

I sat a minute and watched them from on top the trough outside the kitchen door. They must've levelled up some since I'd met them because they were in line again and they splish-splashed over the beck, water all over the shop. I lost them after that and went into the yard. In the old stable the pups were asleep, the four of them piled up snuffling against Evie's side. She had an eye awake, looking on while I pulled a plate of chopped liver off the shelf and lay it by for when they were ready.

Nobody was in the kitchen, but there was a smell through the air that got in my nostrils and reached for my stomach. Biscuits. I walked to the oven and opened the door but there was nothing inside so I closed it up again and put my hand flat on the glass. It was warmish, like a cow's underbelly. I left my hand pressed there a time, letting the heat slug up my arm before I stood straight and went for the cupboards. I looked in them all. No biscuits, so I sat down by the fire.

Mum was in the other room, and she was all I could hear but for the fire and the honeysuckle flapping against the window. She was on the phone to Janet. That, or she was talking with the budgies. Fat little fuckers them budgies, up to nothing all day but rubbing their heads together and gawping in the mirror. I got up and pushed the door to the other room, just a nudge, so as I could poke my eye in. She was on the phone, and she had the biscuits. She was loading them into her mouth whole while she gabbed on to Janet.

'Happy as a pig in trough he were, Janet, happy as a pig in …'

She might've made a second tin. Most times she did. I left the door a bit showing and searched over, checking if she'd put a batch in the freezer. Nothing. I gave it up and stood at the window, where just a chunter of talk came out the door-crack with the scratch of fingernails on the tin. The fog had cleared some and I could see the lump of Easington Top on the other side of the valley. I knew those ramblers were headed for the Top, filing downriver till the path jutted left up the hillside. Blimey, it's a fair old climb, but not to worry, there's a pint waiting for us on the other side. The pub round the Top would be heaving today, it being Saturday. Stuffed with Range Rover folk.

I humped up in a chair by the fire and felt my body go to peace, crackle crackle, it wasn't long before I dropped off to a kip, cosy with the warmth and the tap of honeysuckle on the window. Mum had quieted – Janet was on one – so I drowsed on, the biscuit smell sinking right through me and my eyes closing a moment until I came to, my head bare of thought. A wind was up, for the tap had sharpened but when I looked out the honeysuckle didn't move. Tap, tap. Then I jolted up, for it wasn't the wind, it was boots, Father's boots, on the path.

He came in, didn't speak. In his left hand he held a dead rabbit. I sat up straight but he didn't look on me, he came right past and went for the table. I saw in his face something was nettling him. He strew about the letters and papers on the tabletop, turning them over and knocking the salt so as it sprayed on the cloth. Next thing he was in the cupboards, as I'd been, but he left them open, then he turned back and the rabbit's head banged the sofa. He had it by the legs, ears drooping over eyes, and there were spots of red on the floor where he'd walked through the kitchen. He took the cushion out the armchair aside me and jammed his hand down the back of it. He wasn't after the biscuits then. I kept my quiet while he frisked the inside of the chair, dangling the rabbit by my feet. Mum came in, the tin in her hands.

'Ian. Have a biscuit, there's some left. What you looking for?'

'Whistle.'

'Here,' and she walked by him to the table, picking his whistle out the egg bowl before she righted the salt up. 'Near put it through washer, I did. You left it in your other trousers.'

He took the whistle from her and tucked it in his pocket before slumping into his chair. Then he took a biscuit. He bent toward the fire and set the rabbit on the hearth, laid out on its side so as it seemed to be stretching in the warmth with its eye fixed on me. Mighty fine spot for a snooze, this, it said. Father gave a stab to the fire and the room swelled with heat. Then he spoke to me.

'Them who've bought Turnbull's farm move in day after tomorrow, d'you know that, lad?'

'No. Who are they, Father?'

'Towns. And you'll let them be an'all. They've a daughter.' He took another biscuit. 'I won't have 'em up here banging my door five minutes after they're in, you hear me?'

II

I sat up top the field and I watched them all the afternoon while the pups scuffled about me and my arse proper boned into the rock. They were moving in. I'd been in the yard buggering about by the sheep-dip when I heard the cattle-grid rattling other side of our hill and I thought, hello, they're here, for I could tell between rattles and that wasn't one I had the knowing of. I was in my place before they even showed on the skyline. A blue van lurched along the track, heavy and wobbly, and as it got near I saw that something was wrote on its side, though I couldn't mark what it was until they pulled up to Turnbull's old place and my range fixed. I saw clear then, never mind Turnbull's was half a mile down the hillside among a snug of trees. PICKFORD REMOVAL SERVICES. I fetched the pups and sat them two each side of me, fooling myself they'd be mooded for staying put, and I settled in.

And look who was first out the van. The girl. Young. Sixteen maybe, a few years younger. Not much of a looker, mind, I shaped that from a half-mile. The rest of them got out – Mum, Dad, kid brother, two furniture lugs – and they went at clearing the van, Mum and Dad pointing to the house, the fridge, yes, that goes inside, like they feared the lugger-buggers might set it in the vegetable plot, and the boy skittering about, unsure, like a louse on the flat of your hand. The girl got stuck in, mind, bounding back to the van after each round, her ponytail flop, flop on her shoulders. I watched on, all the afternoon, with the whelps racing and tussling round me on top the rock, never losing sight of me, never jumping down. Big jump for them that, small souls as they were.

They were seven weeks. Not a bad lap of life, when fighting is all play and most the times you're not asleep you're chasing Twat the cat round the yard. And seven weeks was old enough that they'd live on. It's the first month which is dangerous, while they're still soft to the cold and the cat, and to each other, so that come morning you have to ready yourself for a warmish lump or two trod into the straw by the other little guzzlers. We lost three that first few weeks. None but the strongest survived. You had to be hard to be a sheepdog. Or a farmer. Or a furniture-lugger, come to that. Sod knows what I wanted to be myself mind, though no question furniture-lugging would come bottom of the list. I had too strong a brain on me for that. And while I sat mulling on the rock one of the lugs was searching about for his mug of tea. He'd left it on top the wardrobe aside him. He had a shufty all round the wardrobe, well bugger me I know I put it somewhere near here, I wonder where, before the girl came over and set him straight. His tea must've gone cold by then but he slurped it down anyroad, both hands, like a knobbly-arsed monkey.

Sal was biting on my finger. I let her do it, because it didn't smart much and she needed to train up her teeth. She was the bravest of the whelps, spite of being a female. The other three were happy to get mother-smothered but Sal had started to break from that, partial now to following me round the place. Sometimes I'd know she was there, with a tickle on my trouser leg, sometimes not, and I'd kick her five yards forward so she'd yap on back to me, what you do that for, you big old bastard?

She was the biggest of the litter too. The size of my head, pretty much exact, for when I put my cheek to the ground as I did now she fit snug against my face, a damp spot of nose on my forehead. And I had a big head. A long, thin head. A long, thin body. Lankenstein, they'd called me, in those days I still went to school. That was before I was sixteen and I fucked off from there, a fire brewing nicely in the sports storage room where nobody looked except Wednesdays. Cheerio, Lankenstein, we'll not be seeing you again, I hope. Too fucking right you won't.

I sat up and rubbed my cheek. The inside of the van had been gutted out and most of their belongings were lined up on the path to the front door. The pups had quit scuffling. Their heads were up, taking a gawp, same as I was. Five of us in a row, picture-house style, curious over these town folk. A person might have looked on us and guessed we were having the same thought, though they'd be wrong, probably, for I was eyeing up the furniture and figuring how much it would sell on for. A fair pocketful, that was certain.

The girl let her hair out. A blondie. The family were all indoors and she was leant up against the side of the van talking to a lugger-bugger. A nice chat they were having. He had his arms folded all attentive-like but I couldn't get a proper sight on him because he had his back-end to me so all I could see was the great stump of his back. Probably looked much the same both ways round, mind. Us five kept up our watch.

She touched him on the arm. Then the wind gave a gust and our ten ears pricked up as it wafted up the hillside toward us. Laughter. Her laughter. A bonny pearl of a noise it was, that danced about our heads a moment then spun off over the Moors behind. She must've laughed first, touched him after. Sound is light's clog-footed brother, always lagging behind. The touch on the arm had overtaken the laugh on the way up to us so we'd got them wrongways. What had a lug such as him said, that tickled her down to her bones? I'd never forced a laugh like that upon a person – not a girl, certain. What was that funny? Myself, I'd more likely rile folk up, cause them to shout – or bluther, than honey-talk them. That was my talent. Perhaps that was what he'd been telling her, perhaps they could see me up here with the whelps and he was having nine yards of fun out of me. There's a lad lives up there, do you see him? Sam Fothergill. He's mighty popular round these parts – you won't find a sheep that has a bad word to say on him. Ha, ha, that's a good one, you are funny Mr Lugger-bugger. Oh, I don't know about that. Not half so funny as Fothergill's face, I tell you. Ha, ha.

She was at it again. Laughing away, what a man you are, let me just steady myself against the van here. But she didn't touch him that time. Not so funny as before, then.

She'd know me before too long. Not me, course, but my history, painted up in all the muckiest colours by some tosspot just gagging to set her against me. A piece of gossip travels fast through a valley. The hills keep it in, so it goes from jaw to jaw all the way along till it's common news, true or not. Specially when the valley's full of tosspots, such as this one. And the worst of them lived just round the hill from us. Mrs Delton.

You'd see her each time you passed by their farm at the bottom of the track, before it joined the road down to town. A crick of the kitchen curtain, that was her, spying out and brewing up gossip in her head. The Deltons were sheep farmers, same as ourselves, but for we kept a small herd of cows on the best fields, and they hated us. Specially me. They always had, even when I was a bairn and I hadn't given them the littlest nub of bother. So I knew she'd be out for me now, old Delton, round the hillside, brooding, with her cats whipping round her ankles. Just ripe for an introduction to these Towns, and the second she sees her chance – that Sam Fothergill, let me tell you what he does to young girls like you.

Bugger that. I'd let them know I wasn't so foul-smelling as Delton had me for. I'd meet them flesh to flesh before they met with my shadow.

WHAT WOULD I DO WITHOUT YOU?

by Penny Hodgkinson

If he dies today here on the beach at Mundesley I have a plan.

On this bright afternoon in the hottest summer on record I will go up to the lifeguards' hut and speak in a calm, quiet voice to the two boys. They are sitting there on their foldout chairs, scanning the surf in an idle manner. I know my judgement is unfair. They are just local youths, spotty and gangly. Not quite men, but more than children. An apology for the cliché of Californian hunk life-guards but attractive nonetheless to the teenage girls who sashay up and down, between the flags, swaying their hips and tossing their hair back.

My plan is this. I will say, 'My father-in-law has died. Look, there he is.' And I will point down the beach to the small man folded like a dead moth. 'He's wearing the beige anorak.' In the beach chair his bony knees are covered by a woolly blanket. 'He was eighty-five, yes and in poor health.' The green-and-white striped chair seems pinned to the sand by a large pebble. A kite string runs from the pebble to a red and blue kite flying limply in the sunshine. He couldn't hold it, not even on this still day with no wind coming off the metalled waves.

'No he's not asleep,' I'll say. I had thought so, too, standing down by the sea edge with small waves breaking and frilling over my toes and sucking me back towards my daughter, paddling and shrieking. I kept looking back to where he was. The angle of his neck, I wondered was it a clue – was he? Had he? And then I checked, slipping through the sand in my bare feet, going up to him, bending my head and putting one hand on his shoulder, listening and feeling for his breath on my cheek. The sea air thick and unmoving. I held his wrist to feel for a pulse. Blood bruises from falls bloomed across the back of his hand under the papery skin.

And so I will ask the lifeguards to make the call, to summon an ambulance (I wonder briefly if any other types of vehicle are ever summoned?) And we will walk over to him, the lifeguards and I and we will lift him gently in his chair. An ambulance will arrive and park at the cliff-top. This is my plan. It will be like a scene from a film.

He didn't die that day, of course, and later we sat side by side and ate rolls with ham and lettuce and gritty sand in the butter and supping water from a Tupperware container. 'Like the one Nancy used to make salad cream in,' he said. 'Yes, made from evaporated milk, I always wondered how she did that.' I invited the wartime reminiscence, but he looked out far away to the horizon of the North Sea and the soaring sky. And then we walked back to the car parked at the cliff-top – me using the excuse of the burden of picnic box and blanket and chairs to keep pace with his small steps and the rhythmic tap of his walking stick. In the bath that night my heels were smooth; the beauty treatment in the friction of sand walking. No longer the heels of a middle-aged woman.

I am nineteen years old, gauche and raw, in a green jumpsuit tucked into high boots. I am meeting my boyfriend's parents, Nancy and Hodge, for the first time. They are staying at the Randolph Hotel. They come here every year from their house abroad and stay for six or eight weeks, living in the hotel, using it like home. I have no sense of what that could be like – it seems an impossible, almost glamorous lifestyle. We meet in the bar – later I realise that this environment comes closest of all to their lifestyle. Alcohol, social chit-chat, the transience of bar regulars. I am worried about what I should drink in front of them. Sherry – too suburban, whisky – too sophisticated, fruit juice – too cowardly. I delay my decision; I will wait and see what they are drinking. We enter the smoke and hubbub of salesmen going over their days, of professionals putting off going home.

Over the other side of the room a man in a checked sports jacket and a cravat gets up from an armchair; the woman stays seated. She is smoking and as her hand moves from ashtray to mouth there is a flash and sparkle of rings. My boyfriend shakes hands with his father who has an RAF moustache. Then he leans over the sofa and shakes hands again. This time, with his mother. A fleeting black-and-white newsreel image comes to mind: Prince Charles, four years old in short trousers and awkward blazer, on a station platform greeting his mother on her return from some foreign trip. What kind of family is this? In my family we kiss and hug and hold hands. I step forwards; I smile and ask for a glass of ginger wine.

The nightly whisky or two. The drumming of fingers and thumb on a side table. Every seat had a side table allocated – ready for the glass and the ashtray. 'Has the sun gone over the yard arm?' Hodgie's nightly question to Nancy as the Grandmother clock struck six. We gave away a dozen bottles of whisky after his death and we still have some left on the high shelf in the cupboard under the stairs. I poured away the cherry brandy and the rum, and the last day in his house I dropped a bottle of brandy; it fell on the thin blue dining room carpet and smashed. The empty room swirled with the fumes. The nightly whisky was a ritual – a routine to hang onto, to mark the folding up of the day into evening, the relaxation of the working day into the comfort of home. The evening of Nancy's funeral, Hodgie sat in the armchair and drank his way through a bottle. Making up for the empty space and empty glass next to him. I carried him to bed at midnight. He wanted to sleep the sleep of the dead.

'Will you help me have a bath?' It is eight o'clock. I am nearly ready for work. Hodgie stands on the landing in his silk dressing gown – bought for him from the factory silk shop, the factory where they made Princess Diana's wedding dress silk. Even the most tenuous of threads to royalty made the gift special. Another excuse for snobbery, I thought. I run the bath and pour in Badedas – the only bath essence he will have. It was Nancy's favourite. Perhaps he thought he was the gallant officer on horseback coming to help the damsel wash her back. I help him in; naked he is peeled, skin an old pink, the pink of dried up Elastoplast, the wrinkles hang loose at his wrists and elbows. He lies back and the foam billows around him. I arrange the towels on the radiator and leave him. Downstairs I phone my colleagues; they understand. We all work with people, with vulnerable people – patients and families, we think we know the dependency models. They warn me: the line between family and carer is blurry. Be careful what you do, they say.

He cannot get out of our deep Victorian roll-top bath, his hands slip on the curve of the edge. I reach around his frame, remembering my back just too late; his hollowed out armpits rest on my fleshy upper arms. I lock my wrists behind his back and like some monstrous fairytale animal we lurch up from the bath and I swing him onto the mat. I fold him into the fluffiest towel; his hair is coiling in damp baby curls along the line of his neck. I make tea and toast while he dresses. I kiss him goodbye and his moustache leaves the faintest taste of pine on my cheek. I smell it on and off all day.

Nancy wore Estée Lauder mostly. Occasionally Elizabeth Arden's Blue Grass. But mostly Estée Lauder: Alliage, Knowing, Youth Dew. In later years it became Chanel – Coco and Yves St Laurent – Opium. Heavy, oily, cloying. Perfumes with a presence even when you had left the room. After her death I cleared the bedside cabinet to find gift boxes from ten maybe twenty years ago – Paris by Yves St Laurent, Givenchy's Amarige – still sealed in the cellophane wrappings – the scent decayed into the faintest of traces. The talcum powder dried into round slabs like cheese. Nancy was glamorous, a lady doctor from the 1950s, bright lacquered nails, a designer bag and jewellery. Solitaire rings, a pendant from Cartier, a diamond brooch like a swallow. The brooch that now belongs to my daughter, the brooch which is hidden in our freezer in a plastic box labelled 'Ratatouille September 2001'. Old lady or granny jewellery she calls it. Like the Queen Mother wore. When the tests came back and I knew I was having a girl, Nancy's first words: 'Oh good, now I have someone I can leave my jewellery to.'

I cleared the drawers; the suede roll held just a locket, her engagement and eternity rings and the brooch.

The receipt for the engagement ring was in another drawer with a little note from the jeweller in Southport: I hope the enclosed ring gives you *many years of pleasure.* Regards to you, J Prince. It was written in ink and the underlining had a tiny blot – as if the fountain pen had dripped a tear of ink. In 1952 it cost £110.

The small fissures a diamond can cause. We'd arrived in the villa; we had some news. Nancy and Hodge have guessed and have champagne on ice. I show off my ring – the tiniest of sapphires and a chip of a diamond – we are, after all, poor students. 'I think we can do better than that,' Robin's father huffs. Nancy tut-tuts and goes off to get some brandy for a champagne cocktail. Neither of them like champagne.

Later we talk about weddings, ceremonies, guests and lists; I have a copy of *Brides* magazine with a handy pull-out instant wedding list. I laugh about the contents – 'Who needs grapefruit spoons?' I giggle. Nancy puts down her glass of whisky and soda, 'I've always found them very sensible.' She has half a grape-fruit almost every morning and the tiny serrated blade slices through the pith breaking up the segments quickly. I retreat – I have made a faux pas. Used the wrong cutlery.

Landing in Malta at Luqa airport, I had stepped into an ex-pat world which had gone on too long. Malta was Mediterranean but poor, underdeveloped except for cheap tourism. The villa felt like a film set from the 1950s; middle England in a hotter climate.

I was a 'curate's egg' of a daughter-in-law; one of Hodgie's expressions. He said it came from a *Punch* cartoon. *Punch* was a magazine I knew only from dentists' waiting rooms. I was at least white and middle class, well-educated but not, thank God, as far as he knew, a champagne socialist. University inoculated you against voting Labour. I was not a rebel. Perhaps my only defiant act was to wear a purple silk dress at my wedding. 'I didn't like it,' said Hodgie, 'but you looked nice coming down that aisle.' He was never a man to embellish the truth.

In the bay on the ward, he is sitting in the armchair by the bed; he is gaunt wearing the Granny Smith apple green hospital pyjamas and his maroon Pringle sweater. His eyes are closed; I lean across the trolley table and kiss him.

'It's Penny, Robin's wife,' I murmur.

He stirs a little. 'I want you to go.'

'But I've only just got here.'

'Please go, you need to go back upstairs.'

'Upstairs?'

In the bed opposite Edwin, the patient with the bad leg, calls out. 'For God's sake, nurse, why can't you come and cut me in half?'. I throw a smile somewhere past Edwin's head and pull the curtain along a little.

'How are you, Hodgie?'

'Please go, you need to go back upstairs. I want you to organise a party for the children.'

'Which children?'

'For Robin and the others.' A nurse is passing. She collects the undrunk cups of tea; congealed rings overlap on their milky surface. We exchange glances. I sit on the bed.

'Who shall I invite?'

His shoulders relax a little: his eyes are still closed. He lifts one hand to his moustache, brushes his spotty handkerchief across his mouth. 'Gatto,' he says carefully, 'and the boys from school.'

It is 1962 or 3; he is living in Manchester, he has a six-year-old son and a housekeeper called Gatto who looks after the domestic side while he is at work running the family wholesale fish business and his wife is working as the local GP. I have seen the flickering cine films and the photos; the Tudorbethan house, the sweeping garden, the red E-type Jaguar in the drive, the gardener in the rose garden, the basset hound. I sigh and take his hand.

'What shall we eat?'

'Jelly', he says, 'jelly and cake and get a magician.' The nurse comes back with his tablets in a small plastic pot. I leave him to sleep upright in the armchair. Behind his closed eyes children are chasing each other around the garden; Gatto is setting out sandwiches and jelly in cut glass dishes. Somewhere a conjuror is pulling a rabbit out of a hat.

I stand in front of the cupboard. There are dozens of shirts in plastic wrappers; a legacy of Malta when all the laundry was sent. Sheets and towels had little tacky squares of laundry labels on their corners and the shirts were ironed and folded like new. I rattle the coat-hangers, half expecting something shocking to fall out. Why does it fall to women to sort the clothes of the dead?

In his wardrobe I find:

Red waistcoat

One dozen silk cravats

Sports jackets made from Harris tweed and smelling of a Scottish loch at dusk

An RAF uniform including some knitted striped stockings

Flannels – the trousers he preferred

Silk pyjamas and dressing gown

A monocle

Dozens of red and white spotty handkerchiefs

A set of tails – he had told me that they were made for the Stork Ball in Manchester; he had gone to a Jewish tailor who was thrilled. It was the early 1950s and the tailor hadn't made a set of tails since before the war. The button-holes were hand-stitched in silk. There are photos taken at the Stork ball and countless other cocktail parties. Black and white photos of men in tails and women in ball gowns – all big skirts. Dior's New Look. And Nancy in a froth of tulle with a fur wrap or a dress covered in pearly beads from neck to waist. Clearing out her drawers, I find one full of the free sachets of face cream that you find in magazines, and gloves in bags. Hanging in her wardrobe are five pairs of identical cream trousers and two suits – the skirts taken up by chopping off the waistband and making a new waist with a fold and big stabby running stitches. I smile; my own mother darns nylon tights invisibly. There is old make-up in the cupboard, and an ocelot coat, a mink and several fur stoles, her doctor's bag with letters about patients – long dead.

He wrote silly, affectionate letters to Nancy. From Bahar-ic-caghaq in 1975, their house in Malta where they have retired; they are both living there together but Hodgie sits down to peck out with two fingers a love letter on the old typewriter:

My darling Nancy,

As no one appears to want to write to you, I hope you will find this letter a small substitute for external mail.

The weather here is very mixed. Today it is very windy with very little sunshine.........too many verys............I will not be going out today as Tuesday is staying in day and also laundry day.

I hope your health improves. When you are not well, I worry tremendiously, bad spelling and feel sick myself. I love you more than anything in the world and wish I could do more for you, but I'm afraid I'm a bit of a dead loss. I love your dexterity in stamping on spiders. What would I do without you?

I will finish now as I have to write to the cesspit cleaner which is rather urgent.

I love you and offer all my love, darling.

Yours always,

Hodge

His prayer before each bombing mission: Bring me back alive and I'll sweep streets for the rest of my life – this was the pact he made with God. After his funeral service two Jaguar jets flew over the crematorium garden; they took the 'missing man formation'. A kindly friend had used a contact at RAF Coltishall; two young officers who had never met this wartime pilot, agreed to fly over. 'An honour,' they said, 'flying a Lancaster was like flying a bath-tub.' As they crossed the outer boundary of the Crematorium one soared high up into the clouds and the other sped onwards out across the winter fields and on over the unseen North Sea.

DE-COMMISSIONING [OCTOBER 25TH, 2001]

Glinting in dark sunshine
The guns are left in jagged piles
Silent, unrelenting.

In the pits dug for their burial
Damp, rich peat
Offers its skeletons as bedfellows.

FECKIN' FOCAIL: A DICTIONARY OF AN IRISH TEENAGER (PLOTS)

by Jennifer Winters

The trip to the town jeweller's, ear piercing, a female initiation rite, a mother and two daughters. Rings, necklaces (on chains), religious medals, charm bracelets and The Watch which was the biggest initiation of all, as it was, the un-surprise Christmas present of the first boyfriend. As a child my wrist seemed to have an anti-watch paint on it, leather, plastic and metal simply slid off. Down the backs of sofas or drains or in fields. Refusing to wear one I looked blankly at the (surprise!) watch my first boyfriend gave to me one Christmas Eve. I knew that it really represented a certain strapping in of expectation, of living the life already written in puddle splattered stone. Preparation for this life was known, somehow, a watch one year, a proposal the next and after the primary engagement of staying in either parent's house the final full stop of building your own home.

To ease us into the plot, subplots, which could have lead us astray, were provided. Not suggested in the margins (this life did not allow for marginality of any description) temptations were handed to us on plates. They were, of course, sex and drink. I have a photograph of my sister and me aged fifteen and thirteen, we are in a pub after a local football victory. Beer glasses raised in glee, we are caught mouthing a word, which I remember was *gubock*. This was the name we called the team who our village had defeated earlier. It is a derivative of *go back*, a demand shouted at anyone who wandered into our patch. My mother had taken the photo so half our heads are missing; her finger is in the lens and is pointing Monty Python fashion at my sister's boyfriend's head. A suitable guess, the caption entry could be 'The Rest of Your Life.'

Boyfriends, local, known, easily identified, were encouraged. Few questions were asked if I arrived home late, half-merry and school tightless. Which I did with increasing frequency. My excuse was 'The fan belt broke.' A coup, I thought, explaining both the absence of (expensive) school tights and a reason for being so late. There was also a possibility that any reference to a car would detract attention from my pitiful state to my father's. He had failed in his role of Provider by refusing to buy a family car. I was encouraged with the wild excesses early in life as young womanhood did not exist. If there was fun to be had, it was now, just before the next chapter of marriage and homemaking. Just as I had juggled *Anne of Green Gables* with porn with Milton, I could juggle boyfriends with school with drinking. And also, trying to formulate an imaginary future.

So, The Future consisted of a possible teenage pregnancy with Mr Local, who must be related to someone you know, or indeed to yourself. Inbreeding was sanctioned by the Pope when he gave special permission to two cousins of mine to marry. A hasty marriage followed by an inheritance of either father's house. Father's premature death from a heart attack caused by drinking, smoking and poorly paid ceaseless labour was An Expectation (one of the few). And so while secretly reading through the night I began the public showdown of My Future.

Peers praised me for my catch, an older boy with a car. I'd plead for him to collect me after school, *please please please, if you don't write poetry at least collect me in a car.* I'd run out the school gates to see Brian's green (for Ireland) Ford Fiesta parked between the red buses.

Had I stayed in this plot I could still be snug in Brian's mother's house, which was doubly horrific because it was on the outskirts of a provincial town, too small even to be considered suburbia. Not that the word suburbia meant anything to us. There was Town and Country. Next, the battle against babies. Babies were a constant presence in our house, like potted plants they sat around, gaining nurturing and attention from all females present. Having forty-five cousins on my mother's side alone provided us with a steady supply. So I took to denying Brian His Onions, which was the euphemism of the time for sexual concession.

'I don't mind,' he'd say as we wrestled about in cornfields and on beaches, my tights lost in the undergrowth. That particularly insidious term 'prick tease' shouted once in a row, was in fact, a cover up, a deliberate verbal blaming. A pointing towards a lack of libido, when in fact it should have been a screaming headline As if in a Million Years I'd Let Your Expectations and Future Within a Ten-Mile Radius of My Body. So I shouted this back. In my dreams. I was fifteen and living a myriad of lies and instead I lied again and said, 'I love you too.'

After a year of squirming on top of each other like fish I sensed my time was running out. In my diary I wrote *He has a gentle soul but is slow.* Slow at what? Certainly not at diving into our future. Once in a moment of vulnerability Brian confided to me that he had seen a porn film. This was Ireland, where such things were unspeakable, unobtainable (supposedly) and never ever mentioned to women who had, after all, the Virgin Mary as a role model. After a pretend shock I suggested we watch one together. Really it wasn't *that* thrill I was after but the thrill of seeing Brian dig his own grave. He saw it as an act of consolidation, a bonding ritual and a chance of finally getting His Onions. I had found his tragic flaw.

Ducking into the garage-come-video-shop-come-off-licence while I whistled outside, Brian emerged somewhat shamefaced. I watched the film for about twenty seconds, as I was truly horrified, not so much by the sex but by the display of female flesh. I had never seen a naked woman before and by association I too was capable of such things. My whole identity up to that point was based on what went on in my head.

'You're a pervert!' I exclaimed before running out the house, adding for effect, 'and a murderer.' Brian had recently expressed support for the IRA. As he stood at the doorway, baffled, hurt, I pointed at the car and hissed, 'And a capitalist.'

The ending, when it came was less obvious, less dramatic. A fizzle-out rather than the drama I craved. I had a red canvas schoolbag, bought by Brian's mother. In biro, I had taken to writing misquoted lines of poetry alongside names of pop bands. *The world will end with a bang* was scrawled on the front flap. We had the continual threat of nuclear war so *bang* was a much used word. I wanted to end it with Brian but not in his meaning of the word *bang*. I wanted a betrayal, an affair, an assassination even. Then at least we could play out the ritual of survival; he in his heartbreak, me in my confusion. Guilt edged its way around all possible outcomes. I could stay in a life out of duty so underneath the flap of my bag I wrote *there will be time to prepare a face to meet the faces that you meet.* By now I felt like a six-faced monster. Worse, I felt there was no one who could see all the faces and determine which one was the truth.

What was my truth? That I just wanted out and knew for sure that if it wasn't soon I'd get pregnant. Then someone who didn't posses an imagination would write the future I couldn't imagine for me. The day my Intercertificate examination results came out I called into Brian's to tell him the good news. His mother began a celebration tea. 'Sure now you're educated you can get engaged,' she said joyfully. I asked Brian outside where I told him I didn't fancy or love him. We met once more on a romantic strip called The Green. Brian was full of hocus pocus stories. He claimed to glimpse The Other Side. I listened, appalled at the lack of originality in his stories. Each predictable twist and mythological feature confirmed my worst fears. His tale, meant to induce sympathy or passion, left me cold and relieved.

Weeks later when I had bounced up into the arms of someone and was even beginning to see, on the horizon, a future, I received (after a delayed postal strike) a parcel with the instantly recognisable dyslexic spider of Brian's handwriting. Inside a brief note and a plot. Literally a plot, a map of a piece of land he had wanted to buy for *us when we got married.* And in the middle of his map, his plot, Brian had drawn a bungalow. In a fit of uncharacteristically dreamy creativity (that's what becomes of the broken-hearted) he had written in hybrid of Celtic and heavy metal calligraphy The House of Our Dreams.

Then I met Sean. We met where everyone met, at the boxing club, which transformed into a disco on Saturday nights. Within hours of meeting he told me that he was in a band and that he wrote the lyrics, which even I knew was the only way a boy could admit to writing poetry. He also told me in a serious hushed voice that he was an existentialist. I asked my father what this word meant and he gave me books on the philosophical exploration of the question of suicide. Sean, however, provided ample explanation. 'Life is essentially futile,' he'd say while walking me to the bus stop.

'Maybe it is, but I like it,' I'd reply.

Sean had already decided that the body too was futile and we spent many a chaste night sleeping in our day clothes, talking, arguing and reading. I smuggled books from my father's attic to Sean who devoured them and passed them back to me. I'd lie and say I had read them but secretly I was tired of reading plotless books about the uselessness of everything. Some days I'd leave him stoking the iron in his soul and walk the five miles home on one of the old overgrown roads. One such morning I passed my mother in the kitchen. She gave me a smile that suggested approval of my nocturnal adventures. I glared back and said, 'Have you ever considered the futility of housework?'

TIME AWAY
by Tom Levine

She had been leaving a trail of clues since Valentines. Somewhere sunny, some water, some culture. Nowhere too biddy.

'And nowhere too French,' she said.

'Is that only France out then?' I asked.

'Not only,' she said, as if it was obvious.

It couldn't be somewhere childish, and not somewhere 'done to death'. Not Venice or Copenhagen. Nowhere she had been before, and preferably nowhere I had been either.

'It would be nice to discover it together,' she said.

Definitely nowhere I had been with Veronica.

Still, it was fun looking. I had ended up on the Zimbabwe Tours website. They have more gibbons in Zimbabwe than anywhere else in the world.

'Found anything?' she said walking into the lounge. I shrugged and quickly hit the little x to close the page. The computer jammed showing the bottom half of a bikini clad girl, half a white sandy beach, the lopped trunks of palm trees and a volleyball cut in two. I had to reboot.

'Honestly, I don't mind too much,' she said, 'Just somewhere nice.'

I tried a few capital cities, planning to surprise her. Ljublijana. St Petersburg. Are those sort of places relaxing though? Communist customer care. She fetched me a cup of tea without asking if I wanted one. Sometimes that annoyed me.

'It doesn't really matter where we go,' she said.

Doesn't really matter, I thought, and that from someone who always claims to want to do her best. Think what had to happen for us to be sitting here. I mean evolutionarily speaking. From amino acids to fish to monkeys to grandparents to Executive Officer to Ted Baker, and here we are in a flat in London, given this fortnight to try and get everything right. We have no second chances. Life is not a dress rehearsal. And she says it doesn't matter.

'What about Luxor?' I said, pointing to the pyramids.

'Michael says Egypt is too hot in July. It's horrible if you haven't got air-conditioning.' I imagined Michael in Egypt. Or worse, in the pub afterwards, telling us all about his night in a Bedouin tent, about the elders inviting him to smoke a hookah, and riding a camel across the desert. I don't need Michael's advice, I thought.

'Do you want a biscuit?' she said.

I pushed on with the web-search. Two weeks, long enough to get somewhere great, somewhere by a beach, perhaps. Greece. Or is that too clichéd? To judge by the adverts it was either dwarfy little grandmothers and their donkeys, or tower blocks full of ravers. Young, successful professionals – we deserved more. Maybe Turkey, that had culture, sun, mountains. Would she think it odd? They had just had the earthquake and I didn't want to be a disaster tourist. I started looking at America. Then South America. I'd love Peru. She'd say the weather was wrong. Iceland, but look at the cost and what do you actually do there?

I tapped more firmly on the keyboard. Two weeks, two weeks, with jet travel and night flights, two weeks is almost infinite. In New Guinea you can stay with tribal families, or there's a five-rhythms dance retreat in Goa. They still have a nudist camp in Lesbos.

'Is it stressful?' she said, rubbing my shoulders.

'No. Fine,' I said.

It was 1am when I got to bed. She was sleeping with her book on her face. Switching the light off woke her up.

'Any joy?' she said.

'You know what, I think we should just stay here,' I said, 'Enjoy London for a change. Two weeks isn't really long enough to go anywhere good.'

'Oh,' she said, and rolled over. I put one arm over her shoulder and held her breast. She moved my hand to her belly and slept.

That summer she went away, away with Michael, to Cornwall.

FREIGHT TRAIN BLUES

by Yinka Sunmonu

Chicago called me like manna and I drew my fingers over the black and white keys singing with my life, phrasing the stories of this world for the man they threw out of the window. Chicago called me like manna and I drew my fingers over the black and white keys knowing I'd take whatever they gave me. Window man said they owed him. Said they didn't pay what they agreed, so he paid himself. There was no noise in that hazy club when it happened. Just another dead nigger with his wailing monkey woman. But her sounds cut through the pretence harmonising my midnight blues as they danced on, on and on.

Black and white notes can sound way off-key sometimes. You've got to listen to them. You've got to know when to pound and when to stroke. When to stroke and when to pound. But the keys were beginning to feel heavy under my fingers. I could no longer jingle jangle them together. Hell sat on my shoulder.

I boarded this freight train to take me home. Home where mama begged me to stay when the Cannonball started flashing through my mind. Home where Leonora waits down by the sleeping water. Leonora. Just the sound of her name makes me break sweat. She's so fine she could pass and make the masked ones reveal themselves.

I pick up my shoes and blow off the dust. They sure have kept my company these few months. We've been sidestepping and slip-sliding for miles through Chicago, Frisco, Memphis, Tennessee . . .

I count my dollars thin from the exchange of hands and steeped in the smell of tobacco and music of sin. This life's been about economising, sacrificing, learning to survive in this skin. I pray for the day when I can quit this Cannonball mojo and settle down. The freight wheels keep turning, churning to carry me home, humming the dusky town blues.

The power of the sun, drifting through the chipped wooden planks, is enough to turn me into a balloon head and the pain accompanying this buttock-pinching plank is no help.

I'm having trouble breathing. My body feels weak, my throat dry. Why, I wouldn't be able to rise to defend a curse against my mama. I sit and listen motionless to the sound of the chortling train, spluttering to its destination.

Suddenly I gasp for air, raising my head to the unwelcoming ceiling. I can't breathe. My life moves in slow rhythmic motion. I see it moving away, going astray, rolling, a rolling on this gravy-less train.

I stare at the gaps in the roof and see the blue sky weaving its way into the Bayou as the clouds merge into the steaming heat rising from those cruel calm waters. I glimpse at my alligator skin remembering when we accidentally-on-purpose saw Satchmo into the river. He with the prissy lips and running mouth we curbed that day when we watched him rise and fall, fall and rise and apologise. Billy, my ace, and me laughed so hard running off that we fell on sun-ripened cow dung. We picked up those patties and threw them at the raggedy di rak, raggedy tak tak kids who lived in the shacks on the dirt roads.

You've got to move on freight train. Air sure is getting tight in here. My chest is so strung up I'm heaving. I try to moisten my throat, think some more memories but, as my head hits the floor, I know this is a bad bang. The slits in the ceiling close in, close out, move in, move out and I'm drifting. Up, down, sideways, lengthways, every which way and I'm just babbling on about mama's salt pork and hominy, brother Savion and congalene.

My body jerks.

'Keep still, keep still.'

'Yes Sir,' I say, fixing the smile. I look up. Nobody's there except me and the walls closing in, setting in.

The train stops. I hear tick ticking and despite myself I start singing *I'm a rollin', rollin'...*

The train chugs off.

... transporting the blues.

Leonora sure likes the blues. And does she like to Ball de Jack? Oh baby … I smell the pomade from her red hair, the hair that matches her dress and I want to strip that fire hazard from her body, stoke her heat with mine. I feel my manhood swell.

Saliva drips from the corner of my mouth. My chest is still heaving. It's tight, tighter. I pray for the train to cross the line and take me home quickly.

Chicago called me like manna and I dragged my two-tone fingers over the chipped plank, tracing the stories of this world for the men they throw out of the window.

Angela Cleland

APPLE

I
was by far the
most perfect apple in the fruit
world, I could have been eaten
by a handsome prince;
I was red one side,
green the other,
like an acutely
romantic still life,
until a naughty boy
took a bite right out of me
and then put me back
in the bowl.

CARDIGANS

It must be years since we lost him,
but every now and then I still see him.
I catch a glimpse out of the corner of my eye,
a black shape curled on a chair, on the floor,
most often in the hall.

And in my mind something fires
and before I can stop it I am overjoyed
to see him. Of course as this happens,
sometimes before it happens,
buttons catch – I see – it's
a cardigan. It's a malfunction in that
fond bit of my brain.

I was given thin lenses
in a thin frame,
so I would see cardigans right,
as bundles of wool and air posed
by chance like cats.

And though there was a gap at either side
between the lenses and corners of my eyes
I never took them back.

READING SAPPHO

I heave the window open
to hear the flautist's music.
Still it comes in fragments,
each far sweeter than any voice,
notes like blossom blown past
on the wind. She must be close.
My fingers sweat, darken paper,
smudge poems, relics, notes
that begin and end in the fantasies
of scholars. They vanish
into lines of dots, lines of stars;
are pressed petals, echoes
of some beautiful whole.
One long disembodied passage
reaches me and then
is gone; what comes before,
what comes after, is lost
somewhere between us, swallowed
by heavy summer air. I sigh
into the wind. The wind, the heat,
blank spaces and lines of stars
keep her music from me.

THE RAIN GAUGE

Your words
trickled in my ears, filling me,
inching like a rain gauge
from the feet up,

- Legs

- Loins

- Guts

- Heart

- Head, till I was so

- Full

that they started leaking
from my eyes.

ZENO'S PHILOSOPHY

'Before the clock bell can strike the hour,
the little hand must make the journey
half way to the hour marker, that is,
to the mid-point of now and the hour,
but first, it must move half this distance,
which, in turn, it must first travel half of,
and so on, ad infinitum,' I tell
my lover's eyelids as the sky lightens.
'Infinitely small, and infinitely
numerous. No thing, no clock hand can move
fast enough to outrun these divisions.'
She wakes, has dreamt a tortoise was racing
Achilles. I kiss her sleep-limp neck and
say nothing. If I do not let her know
that this minute is ours forever, she
will love me as if the dawn approaches.

FRIDAY NIGHT

by B Theo Mazumdar

It was no night to be out, but there was Wayne Tomlinson walking with Mike Jalcott and Curtis Leahy along the old dirt road on the northwestern side of Polk Junior High. The road was marred by overgrown weeds but definitively marked: faded red ribbon-tape hung taut between sycamores lining the sides, and made the lane clear enough for the Pepsi truck to make its monthly deliveries to the eighteen-table cafeteria. There was a peeling iron gate leading to the detached cafeteria building and the boys passed it and stepped onto the long grass that began just past the school at the western end. It was late November and a lone wreath had been placed on the back side of the gate, clusters of the plastic green stripped off to reveal a wire frame where the fake holly used to be.

Wayne hurried to keep pace with the others. Little Mike scampered along, had to struggle to stay beside Curtis. Wayne felt he was negotiating new territory, even though he'd grown up playing in the area, in every dried creek and every trail and yard the town had to offer. But he never took this route; his dad warned him off the path behind school. Wayne didn't take much stock in what his dad said anymore, but he always tried to stay well away from Polk after dark. He might have gone to the high school game at Ropers Coliseum if his parents hadn't already made plans to go, decked out in their favorite matching orange sweats to support the team. He'd wanted to stay home – alone – but Curtis had laid on his sweet voice, threatened to take back best friend status. And there was always Delilah.

Wayne swatted a resilient mosquito and shivered. He wanted to stop, let the other two rush ahead – it would serve Curtis right for not looking to see if he followed. Wayne supposed he could find the others if he got separated; you always could find anything in Sulphur Springs. But it was cold, and tonight the idea of walking by himself seemed a good bit less attractive than teaching his friend a much-needed lesson.

Curtis forged ahead. He was Delilah's brother, blonde hair, on Thursdays he lined up as defensive end *and* tailback. Curtis was also a schemer. Last fall he'd organized a betting club on pro football. The idea was simple: everyone in the group bet against the spread in all sixteen games and the one with the greatest win tally collected that week's pot. Curtis held the money; his real bet was the other sixth graders wouldn't take time away from their video games to find out how the others fared. Curtis won three out of every four weeks, and it wasn't until the first week of last December that the boys asked him if they couldn't just quit with the whole damn thing. Curtis had ringlets of wild hair that he wore intentionally unkempt. He was tall and well built like his sister, and just like her his eyes shone like a moonlit stream.

Mike Jalcott was nervous. As the boys neared the end of the long grass and Curtis led them on to the parking lots, he kept lifting his left hand and pushing his glasses up on his nose, even though he'd just had them tightened by the Polish optician down by the Dairy Queen. Mike slipped a skinny hand to his breast pocket and mouthed the words for a full five seconds before he allowed his voice to sound out into the night.

'Hey, you guys . . . you, you guys have to take a look at this.'

'What the fuck you talking about now?' Curtis always swore when he didn't have to; he thought it kept him sounding in control, made him the one with guts.

'You gotta check this out.'

Curtis slowed but Wayne kept going, his mind on the way Delilah's ears stuck out at angles when she swept her golden hair back and bunched it between fingers, her even nails perfectly painted.

Mike and Curtis stood shivering. They'd just reached the edge of the TG&Y variety store, the cars long gone but the bright lights still illuminating the lot and casting pools of yellow on the hard cement, highlighting the white lines outlining the parking spaces. There was a blue dumpster near with an upturned chair poking out of the mouth. Wayne dug his hands in his pockets and walked back to the others.

'Look, I don't want to be out too late, wherever in hell you're leading us. I still can't believe most of our class is gonna be there. Who's fightin' anyway?'

'I already told you, moron, nobody's fightin'. And we got forty-five minutes. Relax, Wayne Bradford Tomlinson. You don't have to run off to mama yet, do you?' Curtis raised his voice at the end, and the shrillness echoed in the deserted parking lot.

Mike squirmed, balancing on the outsides of his feet. 'You have to . . . to . . . you have to check this out.'

'Yeah well it's cold and I wanna move on. It's creepy around here,' said Wayne.

'The only thing creepy round here is how you're all agitated and rushy. This got to do with my sister or something? I told you she's gonna be there.'

'Shut up Curtis.'

'You're not gonna make me are you? You and Mikey couldn't do it together! Now let's see what the fuck he's holdin' us up for.'

Wayne inched closer to his friends and sat down on a step just outside one of the store windows. Mike unzipped his corduroy jacket – slowly – one of the teeth near the bottom had chipped and he had to tug on the zip.

'Look Mike, we don't want to see your puny body,' Curtis grinned.

Wayne smiled for the first time that night. 'Damn right.'

Mike stuck his tongue to the side of his mouth and brought out a wad of folded glossy magazine pages. He cradled the pages like he was holding a bird's nest filled with eggs. He looked up at his two friends and lowered his voice for emphasis. 'I got a porno.'

'You got a what?' Curtis demanded.

'I got a porno.'

'You don't have a ... Let me see that.' Cutis ripped one of the sheets from Mike's unsteady hand.

The boys moved closer to one of the stark circles of light and near to a sports equipment window with Texas Rattler memorabilia stacked from floor to ceiling: baseball caps, T-shirts and plastic helmets not meant for real contact and painted boldly with the green Rattler logo.

Curtis unfolded the page roughly and Mike winced as he looked on. A young woman lay draped in three-quarter profile across a chair. Her red hair spilled across the back of the chair, almost touched the carpet, and she held one of her bullet-like nipples between two fingers, so delicately. Wayne leaned in close and saw that one of the creases from Mike's frantic folding aligned perfectly with the patch of dark hair just above her leg.

Curtis scrutinized the page, flipped it around for a better view.

Wayne fiddled with a single door key in his back pocket.

'Where the hell's the rest of the magazine?' Curtis growled.

Mike gave him the rest of the pictures and Curtis unfolded them one by one, surveyed each one thoroughly, then handed them to Wayne. A bed shot, a dark-skinned woman in white underwear, the last a legs-open pose that sent a burst of color into Wayne's face.

Curtis spat and turned back to Mike. 'I said, where the fuck is the rest of the magazine?'

'That's it.' Mike's voice was softer than before.

'That's it?'

'Yep.'

'Come on Mike, how'd you get these? You find them under the PE trailer? Your fat cousin give 'em to you?'

'No, I have a mag . . . azine.'

'Then where the hell is it?' Wayne's sharp voice made the other two turn; the new tone to the lifeless air made them glance out to the parking lot for signs of lurking adults.

'I thhh…rew it away.' Mike shivered, wrapped his arms around his body like a vice. He snatched the pictures back and tucked them inside his jacket, tight against his chest. 'I took it from Yin's store on Oakfront.'

'You took it?'

'Yeah, w-w-w . . . well, I bought it.'

'What?' Wayne felt a frustration swell that he couldn't pinpoint.

'I just said "and this for my daddy" and looked the other way.' Mike grinned. 'It was easy.'

Curtis placed a thick arm around Mike. 'So where the hell is the rest? The stories are the best part.'

'I t-t . . . told you. Maybe I forgot to. Sorry, Curtis. I threw them away. My mom would've killed me if she . . .'

'And these are all?'

'Yeah well . . . I think they're pretty hot. They are, right? I didn't have much room.'

'Where'd you keep them anyway?' Wayne asked.

'I just kept 'em in the binder behind my '86 Astros complete set.'

'So why these pictures?' Curtis laughed. He slapped Mike hard on the back.

'Because,' said Mike, his voice barely audible. 'Just because.'

'Pussy.' Curtis turned and started to walk again. 'P . . . P . . . P . . . Pussy.'

They finally made it to the break at the beginning of the junkyard. Smoke floated up from a fire blocked from view and swirled into patterns like signals as it rose and mixed with the atmosphere. There were little rings of rocks and leftover wood spread around the junkyard, with beer cans piled inside some of the rings and littered around the other areas that had been fires. Abandoned appliances and TVs with their electrical wires swirled out like worms dotted the yard, and at the far end away from the light and the noise was a mammoth junk heap surrounded by a jagged barbed wire fence.

As the boys drew close they heard a chorus of high-pitched laughter. An occasional deep voice broke in as if from the sky. The fire was from a metal barrel, bright light jutting out and giving off intense heat. It had been burning for a long while and the barrel had a slash of fluorescent paint on the outside, midway down.

To the left of the fire barrel was a submerged area sectioned off with hard, frayed rope. The uneven ground hid a mass of legs from the knees down. There were more than thirty kids in the little pit and a few milled around the surrounding area.

Wayne turned to Curtis. 'You wanna tell me what the hell this is all about?'

'You've got the money, right?'

'Yeah, but . . .'

'But what? My sister's already here.' He smirked.

Wayne saw at the far end of the pit a long row of wood boxes turned on their sides. Ragged wire mesh blocked the openings. Wayne's eyes grew used to the fiery light and when the flames leaped high the contents of the boxes looked like picture-book sketches. Bright, majestic feathers of red, white and brown stuck out from the holes between the mesh.

Wayne edged slowly to the row of boxes and bent down for a closer look. A dense line of cocks pecked nervously at each other through the mesh. Even at close range the boxes stood so near to each other it was hard to see which feathers belonged to which bird.

Just below in the pit most of the other kids Wayne knew in his grade were standing around drinking and smoking, waiting, their bodies close together to conserve heat.

There was a second, smaller fire barrel further away from the pit and flanked by a massive blue cooler. Delilah bent and took two beers from the cooler; the light from the fire danced jigs across the back of her tight jeans. She was in eighth grade, only one grade ahead of Wayne and Curtis, but a full year and a half older than Wayne. Wayne shared fifth period Earth Science with her; he was in all advanced classes. He didn't think Delilah was in any. But Delilah had already started dating the guys with the letter jackets, the guys who could drive. She had hair the color of sand, pouty lips; she had a body that made Wayne blush the few times he'd talked to her. Funny thing was she stared at him – not in a way that could ever cause a stir at Polk's gossip lunch tables – but it was the way she locked her blue eyes on his as she turned to look at the topography map when Wayne sat behind. Fifth period never arrived soon enough, flew by faster than gym.

In front of the main fire, Mike looked skittishly to the group of kids in the pit and Curtis stood with his hands in his pockets, taking in the whole scene, his lips turned up in a self-satisfied smile.

'Wayne, give me the money,' Curtis said.

'Why? I don't get this, I don't …'

'We're gonna bet, dumbass. I swear, sometimes you're worse than Mikey. Hand it over.'

Wayne passed a cluster of bills to Curtis and he snatched them and started counting. Even with the noise and the chatter in the background Wayne could hear the whoosh of the bills as Curtis counted them in exaggeration.

'Let's see here. I've got forty dollars. Here's a little bet, boys. I bet we walk out of here tonight with at least four times this much.'

Mike grinned.

Wayne stepped up close to Curtis. 'Did you organize this? How the hell did you get all these birds? This is what you've been planning? Why didn't you tell me?'

'Whoa, Wayne. The fun hasn't even started yet. You know that no-good father of mine that coach is always saying I take after? He loaned them to me. Said he had some extra this month. Got tired of me whining on the phone about the Spam burgers Mom cooks for dinner. Wants me to have money for my own goddamned food. Gave the birds to me last weekend, brought 'em over from Louisiana. Mom says the bastard's makin' a nice bundle over there. She says it's legal over there, not like this goody-goody bullshit here.'

Delilah sauntered up to her brother, her hips swaying back and forth like a runway model's. She sipped delicately at a beer, and held another in her other hand. 'Hey bro,' she called. She handed Curtis the beer. Wayne could see her hand outlined against the condensation on the can. 'Hi Wayne, hi Mikey. Sorry, you guys can get your own.'

Wayne stole a glance at the way her chest bulged, visible even under her padded hiking jacket. He lowered his eyes, but it was the first time she'd mentioned a beer to him. He tried to hide his smile.

Curtis put his arms around his two friends. 'Come over here boys. We got work to do.' Curtis swigged the beer and the smell on his breath made Wayne turn away and gulp for fresh air.

Mike followed and when Delilah went to talk to Brooke Bowson, Wayne followed too. From the wood cage farthest to the right, Curtis bundled out a struggling, pecking cock. Its head darted back and forth and its eyes were like weird little light-colored BBs.

'Wayne hold him down here by the neck. Watch your hand don't get too high . . . his beak's sharper'n hell. This one's supposed to be good. He's big too. One of Daddy's pride and joys.'

Wayne didn't want Delilah to see him near the cock, but she'd wandered off and there was no trace of her shiny hair. Wayne held the thing down by the neck. Its body felt lean, too lean, and the feathers were strangely soft in his hand.

From his shirt pocket, Curtis drew out a flat three-inch steel blade with a thick rubber band attached to a hole in the tail of the blade. He grabbed one of the cock's legs and twisted the rubber band around the claw four times, the pressure making marks in the claw of the bird like creases on a worn leather belt. The cock's natural spurs had been filed down so the knives could be tied on.

Wayne stared up at his friend, but Curtis didn't meet his gaze – he was so intent on his work. Wayne let go a powerful impulse to free himself of the thing.

Then Curtis produced from his front jeans pocket a shorter little blade. He held it up to the light from the fire, his arm straight and ridged with muscle, and only one end of the blade was sharpened. This time he looped a piece of string around a notch in the blade and tied the blade to the left heel of the cock. The bird scratched and hissed and squawked but Curtis held its legs down and his face twisted up in a ball of concentration like he was taking a shit. He knotted the shorter blade again and yanked his hands out of the way of the sharp edge.

Wayne tightened his hold on the cock's neck. The bird's squawking grew muffled and strained like when you have someone in a headlock and they try to talk.

'Whoa, Wayne,' Curtis chuckled, 'Don't kill it. I like your style though. Bring it down to the middle of the pit. We're first. Of course.'

Wayne followed Curtis and Mike down to the pit and the other kids parted and made space for the boys like they were celebrities or football players. The few kids wandering around the perimeter or fishing beers from the cooler made their way to the edge of the ring.

'Alright folks!' Curtis yelled. 'This is the first match. Mine's going up against DeAndre's.'

At the other end of the ring, bathed in shadows cast from the fire, DeAndre Jackson clutched a bird in his arms. He towered over the others and his dark skin blended into the night. He walked as on a tightrope, gingerly forward as he tried to stop from being scratched by his bird.

'Place your bets now over there!' Curtis screamed. He pointed for a quick second and when Wayne lowered his gaze, Curtis was shielding his cock's claws from view like a guilty little kid hiding a piece of candy.

Wayne moved over to the crowd and stood next to a group of girls huddled together. A cold front; it was never as cold as this in November. He moved in closer; the girls' faces were painted and they wore heavy black mascara like at the Davis Disco last March.

Curtis strode into the middle of the pit and DeAndre followed his lead and edged closer too. Rivulets of sweat flowed down DeAndre's face as he tried to control the bird.

'Now,' Curtis shouted, his voice tearing up and going hoarse at the end. 'Get out of the pit. Stand around the edge so you can see!'

The two boys met each other in the center of the pit. 'Just drop 'em on each other and get the hell out the way,' Curtis whispered.

'Drop 'em on each other?' DeAndre's deep voice resonated in the air. Wayne wondered how old he really was.

'Yeah.' Curtis moved his hands up higher on the bird.

DeAndre caught a glimpse of the blades flashing intermittently in the fire-light. His eyes grew wide and he looked up at the crowd. 'What the hell…?'

'Just drop him,' Curtis hissed.

'I ain't droppin' this thing in with that.'

Curtis leaned in close. 'Look, I'll split tonight's entire profits with you. Do it!'

DeAndre hesitated. 'Whatdya mean entire profits?'

'Half of all the money I make tonight.'

DeAndre glanced around, avoided looking straight in front of him.

'Come on D! Just drop him! I'm running the show. Half my money!'

DeAndre still didn't move.

'Do it, OK!' Curtis shrieked. 'OK?'

DeAndre took a tiny step back. He shrugged.

'Get ready! One ... two ... three!' They dropped the birds and ran out of the pit. Curtis caught his foot on the edge and his "Shit!" was lost in a haze of voices and cheers as a blur of feathers tangled for a minute and then stopped. The cocks fell apart and stayed away from each other. They squawked louder than before and moved their little heads back and forth in succession. Feathers floated in the air and the watchers grew silent. The birds screeched at each other but stayed apart.

After a minute Curtis ran into the pit and kicked at his bird. The animal jumped and skidded and pecked at air when Curtis moved his foot. DeAndre followed into the circle and chased his bird around for a few seconds. He jumped out of the pit, wind-milling his arms in a kind of dance. The crowd cheered and the noise drifted around the makeshift pit and remained.

Wayne closed his eyes and felt the alcohol rush to his head. He let himself go, then he started. He could feel the body heat from the girls behind, and when he inched back their bodies felt very different to his; they felt frail.

Curtis trapped his bird against the side of the pit and grabbed it around the neck. He lifted it up. The cock clawed frantically and its feet made little quick circles, the knives a whirl of silver and steel. DeAndre grabbed his bird and the boys threw them together. This time there was a greater swirl and a dense cloud of dust and gravel kicked up like a dust storm. More feathers floated up and fell down to the ground in groups. Then Curtis's daddy's bird moved back a few feet and launched itself at the other cock. A new roar came from the crowd and for a second no one could see what was happening.

Curtis's bird moved away from the other animal and ran wildly back and forth, its feet making loud scratching noises on the hardened and rain-starved earth. Bright blood marked its feathers and again the chatter died. The other cock lay twitching at the opposite end of the pit near DeAndre, its head severed and hanging by only a thin stretch of skin and feathers. Blood trickled and pooled and its beady eyes opened and shut madly a few times before the life went out.

Curtis looked on and opened his mouth to yell. A trail of steamy condensation was all that leaked from his mouth into the chill.

The bird stopped twitching and Wayne could scarcely tell who stood opposite in the little pit. He found himself totally forgetting the cold and the beer and the girls behind him with the bright cherry lipstick and the flowery shampoo.

'Well I guess I won. How much do I …?' The voice was even and strong, loud from behind Wayne's left shoulder. Janie Cohen – she had a locker below his last year.

An even louder cheer erupted and someone handed him a can and he popped the top and took a deep, long pull. The liquid frothed in his mouth and he felt it slide down his throat and burn as it settled into his stomach.

Wayne backed away from the crowd. He couldn't find Mike and he stumbled in the direction of the blue cooler. As he neared, from the corner of his eye he saw Delilah sitting in profile. He could see her jutting breasts, her long legs stretched out on the ground. Her yellow hair flowed back and almost brushed against the dirt. When he moved to the side he could see her counting, and in her lap was an open, square metal box. She looked up at him and smiled, blue eyes standing out against her smooth skin, the painted lines. She moved her lips silently, slid the bills one over the other like Curtis.

Wayne walked past and wondered if she followed him with those blue eyes. He looked up at the open sky. A shiver ran through his body and Wayne wished he'd remembered a sweater beneath his jacket; it was way colder than he could remember.

Wayne looped around again and walked back toward his class. He stayed behind Delilah and she was hunched over. Her spine was outlined against her clothes. She still counted. There was another burst of cheers and a single brown feather rose up, caught on a little gust of wind and landed on top of someone's head. Wayne neared the pit but didn't stop to watch with the others. Now there was a steady chorus of cheers, squawking and hissing as he moved past the group to the smaller fire barrel.

On the ground next to a makeshift pile of trash and discarded cigarette cartons there was a ragged mess of blood and feathers. It was the mangled body of the beheaded cock. Wayne stopped, and looking down there was a little patch of intact and unstained feathers on the belly. The little patch was still white and the feathers overlapped each other in perfect order, like a seashell. Wayne knelt, and near a silver candy wrapper its legs were twisted and spread unnaturally apart, and there was a great stain of crimson where the genitals should have been.

Wayne straightened and took a last look down, then snapped the top button on his daddy's jacket and walked away from the fire. He felt in his pocket for the key.

VIOLE REMEMBERS
by Julia Napier

They'd flown to Miami on a Friday night and the plane sat on the runway for an hour, so the stewardesses handed out peanuts but no drinks and that made everyone thirsty. It was after ten by the time they took off, but Viole wasn't tired. She liked flying, especially the round windows and plastic shade you could pull up and down, but not the smell. It was like blowing your nose in an old Kleenex. What she loved was the tucked-in feeling, the tray over her knees and the food held in separate compartments.

They landed in Miami and then drove to the island in a rental car that wasn't what the travel agent had promised. Something about the difference between 'family' and 'luxury', but there wasn't anything else available, so they kept it. The car was a metallic fly-wing green that didn't exist in Argentina, and looked cartoonishly bright in the airport parking lot. She liked it. Her mom drove a grey Renault station wagon that they all called 'The Tick.'

The vacuumed-felt of the seats smelled dry and stale, and even though it wasn't like the plane smell, the effect was the same. Gabriel discovered the electric lock and kept tripping it. Viole remembered the noise and the low jolt as the doors shuddered: locked, unlocked, locked, unlocked. After ten minutes at the wheel, her dad announced that the car handled well, and her mom answered that she was still going to complain to the agency; the same thing had happened the year before.

They always went to Florida in the winter. Her dad spent most of the vacation catching up on a year's worth of medical journals – which he could have ordered by mail but he loved travelling to get them. Sometimes people brought him a *New England Journal of Medicine* back from a trip and he read it, but never with the same pleasure as sitting beside a pool in Orlando. He also liked repeating that it was a great opportunity for them all 'to work on their English'. He read better than anyone in the family, and flexed his vocabulary at restaurants by asking the waiter detailed questions about the food's ingredients or how it was prepared. Her mother said that English was fine for staying abreast of medical developments but that she'd spent a lot of effort learning French and wasn't about to forget it so she could order a hamburger. She took classes at the Alliance Française in Martínez.

The drive to the island lasted forever because they missed an exit leaving Miami and had to turn back after an hour. Viole looked out the window at the flat green landscape, reading the billboards and sketching some of the pictures that whipped past. It was a game she played with herself: to see how much she could draw from a single glimpse. She wasn't allowed to make up anything she couldn't remember, but she cheated at the place where they stopped for lunch. The sign was a giant boy in checkered pants and suspenders, holding a hamburger in one hand and a piece of pie in the other. He had swollen pink cheeks and a black ringlet in the middle of his forehead. Viole drew him in pencil, shading in the checks, but without the restaurant's name on his belly.

They sat down to order from menus, but the food came as quickly as at McDonalds and shone under the light. Her father said that you could starve to death on the road in Argentina, and Gabriel said you could make a million dollars selling empanadas in the States. Across from their booth was a woman in a fuchsia shirt that gathered around her breasts. Her skin looked like dried orange peel and her hair was crimped into a peroxide fuzz. She barked at her kids, who were eating fish sticks with fries, but Viole couldn't understand her accent. All the words twanged together into one sound. After their fish sticks, the kids drank milkshakes through white straws with pale pink stripes. She caught Gabriel staring at the lady's boobs. Gross, she thought, but didn't say it.

When they got back in the car, her mom went on a rant about skin cancer. She'd just been to a conference in Brazil on recurrent melanoma and wanted to start a public service campaign in schools.

'I mean, good god, Roberto, these girls start lying out all day in the sun slathered up with baby oil at the age of twelve – eleven even! If you believe the statistics, a quarter of them will have skin cancer by the time they're forty. It's outrageous!'

'Without a doubt, Alicia, but a third of them will be dead from lung cancer by the time they're fifty, so maybe it's a kinder way to go.' He laughed at the wheel and changed lanes, floating past an eighteen-wheeler. This was the kind of thing he loved to say to rile her up. Gabriel smiled next to Viole in the back. He was reading *Mad* Magazine. She hated the drawings, especially the fact that everyone always had giant zits with puss oozing out.

'Roberto! We're talking about girls Viole's age and younger.'

'I know, but Alicia do you *really* think you can get Argentine women – even in their larval stage – to prioritize health over beauty? Don't be naïve.

Think about how many of your own colleagues, trained professionals, still smoke. Save your strength for your own patients. And anyway, we're doomed as a race. Between Peronism and tobacco we have no future. We'll die out and the Chileans will finally inherit the Patagonia.' He chuckled into his shirt collar.

'I just won't accept that complacent attitude of: "Well, it's always been a disaster, so let's just leave it at that." So Argentine. You operate all day – they're just bodies to you, but I see the girls at Viole's school and I want to stop them from ruining those beautiful faces and bodies. I'm going to talk to Clarissa about this. She has a friend at the Ministry of Education.'

'You should, Alicia.' Viole watched him wink at Gabriel through the rear-view mirror.

She slid forward and put her arms around her mother's neck. The landscape outside was unchanging and scrubby, green-grey in the afternoon light. Telephone poles threaded black wire in regular dips above the trees. Her mother's skin was moist and warm. She could feel the breastbone rise and fall.

'Thank you darling,' she patted Viole's forearm, 'I'm just a little annoyed at your father. These things matter very much. I don't want your friends turning out like that woman back at the restaurant.'

Viole thought about the orange lady and her frizzy hair. It seemed impossible that anyone else could be like her, no matter what they did.

'Don't worry, Violeta, that'll never happen to you and most certainly if you don't smoke. Which is her real problem.'

And then conversation began again, a ping-pong of mortality rates and prevention. Viole took the wrapper off the game she'd bought at a gas station. It was supposed to be a picture that appeared when you drew over it with a special marker, but it only left black smudges on the paper. She dozed, waking to find the same scene outside the window, her parents still talking, before dozing off again. Then something was different and she opened her eyes as they bounced onto a bridge and the road whirred underneath the tires, humming through her body. Gabriel told her it was a drawbridge and that they'd waited ten minutes for it to go back down. She wished he'd woken her. Her mom said they'd be sure to see it again, and then, finally they were there.

The resort was a self-contained 'plantation' with paths that cut through thick, low vegetation; guests, they were told, drove down them in golf carts, but their dad didn't want one. They would walk. That's why Americans are all so fat, he said under his breath at the reception desk. You could also rent bikes, and there were windsurf classes in the morning. Viole's mom asked about tennis courts. Though she didn't look the part standing there in linen pants and a knotted silk scarf, she could beat the pants off everyone in the family. But Gabriel's serve was catching up with her, and Viole knew it made her mad.

It was almost dark by the time they'd checked in and eaten at an open-air 'pavilion' surrounded by a tangle of trees. 'Live Oaks' the waiter had told her father. 'As opposed to dead ones?' he'd joked to their embarrassment. Gabriel wanted to go explore. This happened every time they went somewhere new, even at restaurants in Buenos Aires. Gabriel would finish his spaghetti and say, 'OK. I'm done. Can I go look around?' The first answer was always no, but their father got bored of the back and forth between mother and son. Viole would spend the rest of the meal doodling on the napkin while her parents talked shop. As Gabriel got older, his range increased and sometimes they had to wait by the car until he appeared. A 'plantation' on foreign soil was irresistible after so many hours in a seatbelt.

Viole could tell her mother willed herself not to worry – in the same way she studied irregular French verbs – but she never relaxed. Their dad would say something to distract her, usually a provocation: 'Why shouldn't we let him go, Alicia? He's a perfectly capable boy and if he gets lost, he'll learn something.' But Viole felt sorry for her mom, whose taut mouth gave her away.

Now, too tired to argue, she said, 'Fine, but take your sister with you – and watch out for those golf carts.'

'Whatever. Come on, snot-nose.'

'Snot-nose yourself.' But she was thrilled. He never took her along.

Back in the room, Gabriel inspected the mini-bar – just Coke and peanuts – while Viole changed her sneakers.

'Come on, scaredy-pants, or I'll leave you here with the killer bugs.' They'd seen a giant cockroach lumber across the porch in front of their door. It moved like a fat old lady. Gabriel poked his foot towards it and it flew away, which made Viole scream. She'd never seen a bug that big. That it could fly was doubly disgusting.

'OK. OK. I'm coming.'

The air was warm and heavy. After all that time in the plane and then the car, the humidity felt silken against her skin and fattened her lungs. Twenty-four hours ago they'd been in sweaters and coats; now they were walking down the resort's main road in T-shirts. It was summer. They passed a low white house lit up with floodlights. A wooden sign with soldered letters said it was the resort commissary. Mosquitoes and gnats clustered in the glare.

'We can check that place out on our way back.'

That was the way Gabriel talked, like he was on a mission, reconnaissance into the jungle and the white building was a target they had to secure. When they were younger she helped him plant walkie-talkies around the Christmas tree to spy on their parents, but they never managed to stay awake long enough to hear anything. To be part of his plan, even a tiny part, was the best thing she could imagine.

Then the path forked, one heading deeper into the green and the other closer to the road. Gabriel hesitated.

'Let's take this one.'

'Don't be boring, Viole. If you come with me, you have to follow my rules,' and he strode down the darker path. She hurried after him.

The sky was clear overhead and she walked with her chin up, looking for stars, but there weren't any. The moon hung alone in the darkness. It was yellowish, furry. Gabriel kept moving, and she ran after him, feet slapping against the asphalt. The ocean whooshed close by.

'Gabo, do you know why you can see Orion's belt in both hemispheres?'

'Something to do with the position of the earth at certain times of the year. But there are parts of Orion you can see here that you can't see there. It's the same with the Big Dipper.'

'Maybe if we get to the ocean, we can look.'

'It's gotta be up ahead somewhere. I bet all the paths lead there.'

But the sound was everywhere, and the trees shuffled into it as a breeze moved through them. Viole hadn't slept much on the plane, but now she felt dreamily awake. Out alone with Gabriel on a summer night in a strange place. He slowed down.

'Hey Viole?'

'Yeah?'

'You shouldn't worry when Mom and Dad talk like that.'

'Huh?'

'You know, that whole thing about cancer. He just likes to tease her, and they're doctors. That's what they talk about.'

'Yeah, I know,' but she felt like she'd been caught. She didn't like it. She was used to the cancer part by now, but she hated the way her dad never let anything slip by. It always had to be his version, his winning goal of information.

'He's just a hard-ass, but he doesn't mean to be mean.'

They were walking side by side now, and the white rubber on Gabriel's

Converse peeked out of the dark with each step. A hazy ring shone around the moon. He probably knew why. He'd gotten into El Colegio Nacional de Buenos Aires, but Viole was going to stay at St Andrew's because she was 'so comfortable there'. That's what her mom said. Her dad said that tests weren't her strong suit.

'Yeah. But it's easy for you to say. You're the math genius. Dad loves that.'

'Don't be stupid, Viole. They just want us to be happy and stay out of trouble, and you're going to be a great artist one day.'

She blushed in the dark and looked down.

'You really think so?'

'Óbvio.'

And then they heard the noise: a rat-a-tat growl from somewhere in the brush. Like a kid imitating a machine-gun. Gabriel stopped short and Viole jumped behind him. Her hands landed on his shoulders and she flattened her head against his back. The ocean filled in the silence and then it came again, this time a little deeper, longer.

'Gabo, what is that thing? Can you see it?'

'Shh, it's OK Viole, just stay there.' And she felt his right arm move. She looked down and saw him pull a Swiss army knife from his pocket.

'What do they have here that eats you?'

'Nothing, Viole, just be quiet.'

It growled again, and she imagined it was getting closer. Every bone had come alive inside her. But Gabriel didn't move a muscle, pointing the tiny blade against the dark, his body firm and solid. His shoulders felt knotty and warm under her fingers. The creature was silent and the ocean came back, but now it was just sound.

They stood there for what seemed like forever until he spoke, 'OK, now just walk backwards, with me. I don't think it's going to do anything, OK?'

She took one step back and he moved with her, still facing forwards with the knife. They did that until the path curved, and then he turned around and snapped the blade shut.

'That was some fucked-up noise, eh?'

And she hugged him like she hadn't for a long time, 'I was really scared, Gabo. Weren't you scared?'

'Nah. I had my trusty knife, here. You'll always be safe with me, snot-nose. Now get a move on or Mom will think we got run over by a golf cart.'

And they walked back in silence to the main road, passed the white house without looking in the windows and got in their beds to watch TV. Tucked under the stiff printed comforter, she remembered hearing him pop open a bag of peanuts and a Coke, wondering, as she ebbed into sleep, if their dad would mind.

ORPHEUS

'someone or other stood whose features were
unrecognisable … ' – Rilke

First he felt the snap of the taut hemp strings
sensed frayed edges, a phantom limb,

then he watched the carved frame
flex and soften like a cat's spine.

Tingling in the fingers of his left hand,
his plectrum nails cracking and underneath,

licking the tender nailbeds, green tendrils.
Tetany in his left arm, in the muscle

so purely sculpted to its purpose.
Lyre-buds shooting beneath the skin.

Before he understood the boundary.
His hand on his face. The smooth skin of the cheek

erupts, ridges of bark, whorls and wood knots.
His legs grow sluggish, exhaled breath turns cold.

In place of blood, pale fluid flows.
He is already root. Now the lyre invades.

Her body, coaxed at his command,
ransomed the Argonauts.

Now, reverting to a tree,
she moulds the man.

Loosened like a roll of linen or a sail
that shoulders the wind, the lyre exults.

In gentlest caress, she circles the strong neck
from which came songs of unsurpassed lament.

He tries to call out, gags.
Green fingers trace the memory of a cry.

She seals his lips and sings
of conquest and of subjugation,

II

of Troy, where scent of olive wood and pine can't suppress the stench from
putrid
flesh that smoulders on a funeral pyre at dawn,

of Babylon, where brilliant flowers once coursed down staggered tiers and
now
a human carcass hangs,

of a boy's corpse in a field outside Belfast; his blood waters the wild thyme,
his knees
are shattered bone,

of Belsan where Chechyna's war is marked by plastic water bottles in a
blackened
school hall,

of the white iris on the banks of the Euphrates that flares crimson as
Falluja burns.

III

The stars shift in their constellations
the winds still, as the furious music swells,

Earth, through the song of the lyre
mourns her disfigurements.

IV

His face sets. Wood rings encase his ears
but leave them clear.

In the deep rock pool of his eyes
something gleams, plant sap or dew.

He stands before the shining exit gates,
unable ever not to hear

the footsteps walking away,
the long dress trailing, unable ever not to see.

SANTA FE

The guy who came to empty the septic tank
– your shit is my bread and butter –
remember the sludge-coloured Coke he drank,
the faith he had in the company agenda?

The launch of Krispee Chicken with Garlic Fries:
your dad, his face caved in, hunting his dentures.
We ate to camera, smiled, evangelised
the gourmet pleasures of his latest venture.

Beneath blue grass, red earth spawned termite towers.
We tracked the antique railroad south to Lamy,
believed snow blooms on arid desert flowers,
saw yucca, chilli, guacamole, adobe.

My body trusting yours in a cable car suspended
above sunset on the Sangre de Cristo mountains.

WHAT WILL HAPPEN TO THE DOG AFTER WE ARE DEAD?

by Evie Wyld

A dog should smell something like old coats, but Boris smells of gunpowder. He looks at me in the eye twice a day to tell me it's time to feed. There's no 'brekky' or 'tea-time' light-heartedness about him. He wants me to know he needs nourishment and any more than that is a waste of energy for both of us.

The Notes I received before his arrival say 'Moderate dislike of other dogs, never bitten a human'.

Boris's hackles rising make me think of the warmth of a familiar body. The tired skin of knuckles, the waxy sole of another person's foot and the smell of two people's breath in one room.

The night-time yell of a fox makes my bed bigger and colder than it was this morning.

I have lived with the comfort of old dogs for seven years.

Since I retired the thing I do is I foster orphaned dogs. Dogs whose owners have died stay with me, until I can find a new person for them to live with. Often, a dog's traumatised after losing its owner and so with each new animal, I am sent notes, to help me understand their back-ground – past aggressions and illnesses, fears; that kind of thing. I take one animal at a time, or two if they're companions. More than two becomes tricky for me, so I leave it up to someone younger, or someone with a partner to share the work.

The rule for looking after dogs is to have a routine. I get up at 6.45, (7.30 on a Sunday) and we eat in the kitchen, both of us together. My guests have biscuits and mince meat for breakfast and I have taken to having a bowl of soup in the winter, apples and cheese in the summer. I don't believe in 'breakfasting foods'. I don't feel the need to 'inject a dose of fibre into my diet' the way they talk about on the television.

After breakfast, I pull on my dog-walking wellies (I have three pairs – dog walking, gardening and fancy) and pocket my silver whistle, (a gift from my late husband) two plastic bags for the poo, and a handful of brazil nuts.

A dog likes to watch your routine. They mark time by the putting on of wellies and the sounds of keys and leads and such. A dog likes to know where he is. When a dog's routine is upset, he has no way of telling time. You can't say to him, 'I feel a bit peaky today so I'm not taking you to the park,' and so the dog gets trapped in morning time all day, waiting for you to put on your boots and tie him to a lead. For dogs, a change in routine means that something is wrong. For the most part they are right.

We get to the park before most of the other people. Personally, I can't be bothered with the piddling conversation of other dog owners – the ones who keep them on a lead and get upset when they roll in fox. We, all of us, have to have our fun.

Back at home there's generally some kind of housework or gardening to be done. If it's gardening, the dog will usually follow me about, chewing the beetles and grubs I turn out, and sometimes digging his own holes, which is fine. A gardener needs holes to be dug. I grow my own apples and robust squashes – nothing that an enthusiastic animal could ruin or would want to eat. This means that flowers are not an option.

Dinner is at five: boiled chicken or lamb hearts. I will generally eat what the dog eats. Or, that is, the dog eats what I eat. Your average dog can't have a stroke, because they're too healthy, so it makes sense to lead a dog's life, as much as possible. I make the food carefully. I don't over-cook; I skim the scum and fat off the top and keep the juice to pour over their morning biscuits. It's a pleasure for me, to see a dog's eyes wet and bright at the smell of their tea. To see them hopping from one side to the other, arse up in the air, whole body wagging. The inability to not get in my way. Nothing makes me prouder than to see the licked dish of a happy dog.

Recently I re-homed two miniature dachshunds, known as The Boys. Their old lady (according to The Notes) had died at home alone, except for her dogs. When The Boys arrived they huddled in their fag-smelling basket, twitching like mice. They wouldn't go outside to the toilet, so for the first week I had to clear up every morning. However, after two weeks of carefully measured treat-administering and coaxing, they forgot about being locked in a room with death. No doubt it had crossed their minds that sooner or later they would have to start on the corpse. Luckily the nurse arrived before there was need to, and they were brought to me, two small black sacks of sand.

The Boys liked to chase bitches in the park, bitches of any size. They squawked at children and cars and big dogs. For dachshunds they had enormous energy and even bigger balls. They were a happy pair by the end of their stay.

A young family in Wandsworth adopted them. Nice long garden, azaleas just starting, which, even before I left, The Boys had begun to eat.

The couple had a small girl with a permanent ring of marmite around her mouth, which the dogs appreciated. The house was tidy, but their child was the type who would relish sitting bare-bottomed in the mud. I unpacked The Boys' beds then and there, and called the office to tell them 'mission accomplished'.

When I find a new family for a dog, I get the feeling I have delivered an important gift. To celebrate a good re-homing I always bake a cake. That day I baked banana bread with walnuts. That day The Notes on Boris arrived. Boris, said The Notes, was not to be re-housed for at least six weeks. According to The Notes, there was a 'high possibility of active trauma'. Boris required a 'low noise level rest period.' The Notes were very different to any I had received in the past. I had no (still have no) idea as to the meaning of 'active trauma.'

Under the heading 'Other Comments:' the author of the form had left a deep mark, like they'd been considering writing something else. Like they'd put the nib on the paper and sat, twisting the pen, before deciding not to write. It was a thoughtful dot.

According to The Notes, Boris's owners hadn't been old or infirm. Some kind of accident perhaps?

I had just enough time to get rid of The Boys' smell before Boris arrived.

Often, after a person's death it turns out they had a son or daughter or partner who's desperate for the last living contact with the deceased. Something of theirs that's alive, and that touched them and soaked up some of their personality. Something that lives, and still smells of the person they loved; that still has the echoes of their voice stored in its memory. But The Notes, where they would ordinarily say, 'No next of kin,' say, cryptically, 'No one was left.'

Boris was delivered to me by the Police Canine Department. Normally they come in an RSPCA van but Boris was unconventional from the start. I was surprised that the officer didn't use a lead, or even take his collar. He just stepped back from the van, and let Boris descend onto the pavement, where he stood, square and brown, without a glance around him.

'He's a quiet one,' said the officer. 'Normally, you'd expect a bit of problem behaviour after something like that. But this one, he's a good dog.' He gave Boris a respectful stroke between the ears, to which he glanced up with reserved politeness. I refused to be drawn in to the policeman's chatter. What I needed to know about Boris was written in The Notes.

Afterwards, I let him into the garden, and he peed without sniffing the ground. I gave him a drink and a bit of food, which was accepted in the manner of someone who must eat if only to please others; if only to keep up strength. There was no licking the bowl. Shortly after he went to his basket (which was specially bought, me having never housed such a big dog before), faced the wall and slept.

Around Boris's neck is a heavy chain with his name tag on it. Impossibly small writing on the tag, (I had to find my bi-focals) it reads:

'my name is boris I belong to moira and steve and the kids please call them im lost!'

It was printed in a wiggly font, without a jot of punctuation. The phone number was on the other side and had a suburban area code. Usually on a dog tag you just have a phone number. You shouldn't really have the dog's name, especially if they're a pedigree breed, like Boris. People are sneaks, and sometimes dogs (especially pedigrees) can be less clever than you'd hope. In our local park there was a man going round stealing greyhounds. If you've a nice looking dog don't let just anyone know its name, because it doesn't take much for a dog to be convinced they know you. If you know their name and have a nice piece of cheese for them in the back of your van – that'll more often than not do the trick. It sends chills.

It's strange to want to put your whole family on a dog tag. It makes me wonder what kind of people they were. They must have named him together. The name Boris, means something close to 'wolf', Turkish in origin, though I doubt that figured in their choice of name; either way, it suits him. I imagine the children taking turns to feed him, walk him, wash him. I have a picture in my head of a little boy pointing a hose at Boris in a dirty back yard; laughing and hooting when Boris shakes himself and sprays the kid with water. In the background I picture Mummy Moira watching out the window, making lunch or pouring a beer. She wears sunglasses, and she is young. She laughs at her child through the glass, and her laugh is far away and high like a cuckoo call.

Staring at the back of Boris's head, I think about hair. It's something that I have learnt to live with. Hair everywhere. It turns up when I wear anything that hasn't made abundant use of pattern. Hair from dogs of years ago still stubbornly refuses the vacuum cleaner. Sometimes on my pillow I'll find a long yellow hair, even though mine is short and dark, and even though the last retriever I housed left over four years ago.

It makes you think about what goes into the coffins. Boris's whole family underground dusted with light brown hairs. No amount of undertaker sticky-taping or dry-cleaning will rid even their best clothes of the love-hair of a dog.

It's times like these, when the hackles rise about Boris's shoulders and that line of dark hair along his spine stands up, that I think about the bird-voiced wife – imagine her in the back yard watching the children in the paddling pool – long-limbed and messy-haired. Orange bikini and stretch marks. I see the kids like yellow-haired shrubs, naked or wrapped in a towel, piping noise into the white clear air, the hot air that stands about waiting to be moved by breath. And then at her feet, by the base of the sunlounger, head on paws, eyes black and pushing up against his heavy brow, I see Boris. Boris watching. Boris guarding. And Daddy Steven calls out from the shed, 'Moira! Moira . . .'

It's been three months, but I haven't looked for someone to re-home Boris with. He makes me wonder the way he ignores me, the way I just get those two looks everyday. He does everything exactly right, he walks in the park at the correct pace; he is not scared by traffic, nor is he greedy or noisy. He is too busy thinking. He is thinking about something, and for this he needs my respect, he needs me to not pat him, not say soothing words when he wakes up from a dream which gives away his whimper. I feel uneasy having him sleep out in the kitchen the way I usually do with my guests; this one has his basket in my bedroom. At bed-time I pat the empty side of my bed, and occasionally Boris takes up the offer, and we sleep with the warmth of our backs just touching. But when I wake the next morning, he's back in his basket, and the only way I can tell he was ever there is the dog-shaped dent on the other side of the bed.

And when his hackles rise at night and he stands staring into the corner of the room, I don't point at his basket and say, 'here' or 'lie down'. I sit up in bed and watch his weary guard, wondering about the memories that make his hair stand on end, that draw the saliva at the corner of his flues so that it strings to the floor in silence.

HOW IT ENDS

by Sara Langham

EIGHT

It has rained now for three days. No break in the clouds. No glimpses of sunshine. Just the wind pushing against the window and the rain sliding down to the earth. Streams of water run down the roads and everything leaks moisture. But it's light when we wake up, dusk when we come home, and spring doesn't seem so far away now, not totally out of reach.

Tonight I get back early. There's a message from Paul on the answer phone. He's going to be working late again. He won't be back for a while. I think of all the things I could do, the boxes that need unpacking, then I look at the rain falling outside and get into bed instead. I stay there for some time curled under the covers, trying to read then just lying still, enjoying the feel of my legs stretched out warm and the calmness that comes to cocoon me.

But I can't make it last. It's too quiet here. I'm not used to there not being people around, with the phone always ringing, the TV on, and sounds coming from the kitchen. I get out of bed and start to pace round. I open one of my boxes. There on the top are my folders from college and underneath them my Russian books. I pick one up and flick through the pages, stopping at places I once underlined, at the quotes I knew by heart.

I open the fridge then quietly close it. I boil the kettle but don't make a drink. I pick up the phone to call Ellie or Claire then put it back down before it rings. I know what it is I want to do but it seems really bad, much worse from here. I'm in Paul's home now, not mine anymore, although I'm meant to think that it is.

The piece of paper is still balled up in the front pocket of those jeans I wore. I put them in the back of the cupboard after our lunch that day. I unfold it slowly, lay it out on my lap and stare at the digits, how they are written. I follow the lines with my thumb. Then just before I lose my nerve, when I think Paul might be back quite soon, and I realise I can't wait till tomorrow, it might not be possible, I won't be alone, I finally dial your number.

A pulse beats at the side of my neck. I can feel my heart beneath my jumper. My hands are trembling. My fingers feel cold. But as I'm about to put the phone down, just when I think that you're not there, and I'm staring at the rain still rushing, sideways now, in thick blunt lines, you answer my call at last.

I wonder if you're surprised I've done this. If you are, you don't make it known. You act as if it is normal, natural, as though we speak every night, or regularly. I, on the other hand, stutter and stumble. I'm not quite sure what to say, to suggest. But you take control of the conversation. You say, 'Will you meet me again?'

My head is saying, *No, don't do this. Think where you are now. Don't mess it up. Once was OK but this will be different. You don't need to see him again.* Every reason out there is dancing before me, each excuse I can make is here on my tongue. I shouldn't have called. You shouldn't be asking. Paul will be home soon. I want him to be.

But then you ask the question again, quieter now, in a way that makes me feel I have to, I can't say no, I'm not going to.

'Not tonight,' I say at last. 'I can't now. It's getting late. Could we maybe do another time?'

You suggest Saturday.

I say yes.

It's only when I'm trying to sleep as the rain continues to pound down outside and all I can think is, I called, I called, that I realise how rarely I did that before. All those times we used to meet, walking home or in the park, all by chance or not by chance, by knowing where each other was, which parties we were going to, the schedules we had, our library times. So much easier then. Less complicated by time and space and where we are now and the plans that we have.

Then I had no plans. Life after university stretched lazily out in a series of possibilities and no one thought to tell us – to tell me – that the choices you made, whatever they were, would affect what your future would be. They should have written it in the prospectuses. It should have been the motto.

I hear Paul come in much later. The twist of the lock and a quiet click. The scrape of his shoes as he takes them off. The stream of the tap. The snap of a cupboard. The push of the door as he opens it. He tiptoes quietly to the bed. I can feel his hand on my shoulder. Then, when he's sure that I am asleep, when I don't move at all, when I don't hardly breathe, he gently kisses the top of my head. He moves away and gets undressed. He climbs into bed beside me.

NINE

I tell Paul I'm going home for the night. That my dad's away and my mum's on her own and I said I'd keep her company. I haven't seen her for a while so it sounds quite plausible. I say, 'I'll be back tonight or tomorrow.' I say, 'I hope that's OK?'

Paul, in jeans, a light grey T-shirt, is sitting cross-legged on the bedroom floor. He's drawing some plans with a compass and pen for the changes we're going to make to the kitchen when we manage to save some money. He looks at me, pen in his mouth. I am hovering close to the doorway. 'Come here,' he says, 'before you go. I want to show you this.' I walk over and sit beside him and absently he strokes my arm as we look at the pictures he's made. There's an ache growing slowly inside my chest that I've tried to contain in the last few days but it's getting stronger now. I lean my head on his shoulder. 'Paul,' I say, in a quiet voice, 'I don't have to go if you don't want me to. I can stay, it doesn't matter.'

'No,' he says, he hardly looks up, 'it's fine, honestly. I said I'd meet up with David and Ben, and Ellie, I guess, if she's around. We can do something tomorrow.'

'Are you sure?' I ask. Then I suddenly realise I'm angry with him. Why can't he see what I'm about to do? How can he not say anything? I want him to say, *I want you here.* That it's me he wants to see tonight. If he only says it I won't go, I'll stay and I promise I'll never call you again. I promise that will be it.

'I'm sure,' he says. 'I'll see you tomorrow.' He kisses me quickly on the lips. I hold onto him for a second.

I turn round once before I go. His head is bent away from me. I can see the tendons on the back of his neck, the curl of his hair that needs a cut, and all I want is to sit behind him, stay, and rest a while. Instead I pick up my bag and my coat. I shut the door and leave.

I am lulled by the train. I almost forget what it is I am doing until, as we move across the river and I see the bridges lit up to my left in parallel lines like fairy lights, I suddenly realise I'll be there soon. It isn't just something I've hoped for or dreamt. I'm actually going and nobody knows. Not one of my friends knows where I am. There is only me travelling towards you, and only you, waiting for me.

You are facing the other way. You're on the platform alone. Your back is towards me, your hands in your pockets, your hat is pulled over your head. Everything is damp around you: signboards dripping, puddles in the concrete, pieces of newspaper stuck to seats. You turn as you hear the tracks swelling behind you and as you move I bend my head, hiding myself from you. I'm suddenly gripped by this thought that I have to stay on the train and not get off, to carry on down to Brighton. Instead I take my hairbrush out and run it through my hair. I stand up and walk down the aisle.

'I feel like I'm on holiday,' I say too loudly, as I step down, trying not to think how strange this is, or if we'll have anything to say. I move towards you hesitantly, aware there could be boundaries here, that three weeks have passed since I saw you last, that I was the one who made this call and who has a boyfriend at home.

You walk towards me. 'Hey,' you say. I bunch my fists inside my pockets. I try not to stare at your mouth. 'Come on,' you say. 'Let's go.'

The sun slides behind the tower blocks, melting against the concrete. The street lamps, already lit, blink faded orange overhead. The corner shops, the only signs of life, where groups of old men stand inside, shadowed by the grills. You point out landmarks, places, the names of streets, as if you are leaving breadcrumbs on the path for me, as if I will follow them again.

I thought we were going to go for a drink but we don't do that. We walk past the rows of cafés and pubs then turn into a quieter street and stop in front of a building. An old mansion house divided, it seems, into innumerable flats. 'This is where I live now,' you say, as you start to climb the steps. I follow behind you. My cheeks are burning. Is this how it's really going to be? Am I just going to let it happen? I swallow my questions. I want to stop. But there isn't time for anything, your key is out, the door is open, you smile as we walk inside.

Your flat, your room, your pictures on the walls, your records, CDs, your clothes in rails by the side of your bed, your table, your lampshade, your tablecloth, ashtray, your books piled up on the floor and me, standing in the middle, sliding my shoes off, placing my bag at my feet, and you, by the stereo, putting on music, moving towards me, pushing the hair away from my face, pulling me closer towards you and us, not even kissing, not even kissed yet, and me wondering how we left it so long, and how it is possible that one other person can make you feel like this again, can make you suddenly feel whole.

Before you begin to touch me, before your hand reaches out and brushes my cheek, before you move closer and kiss me, there is one absolute moment of peace and it feels as if these are college days, and this is the first time once more.

When the room is dark in shadows and the traffic beats down outside and we are lying together still touching, as entangled in each other as our clothes on the floor, you remind me of that first first time and I see myself that day again, after Ellie left and you were there, when I just went home with you. And afterwards, sunk down in the middle of my bedroom floor, I remember thinking my wish had come true, that once was enough and it didn't matter if it never happened again. Until the next time and the time after that and the time after that, at least.

THE ABYSS

by Max Mueller

Schmitt turned on the light. Along the factory hall, long rows of neon tubes rattled. Flashes of metallic light cut the darkness from the machines until their steel skeletons stood brightly exposed, submitting into dull reflection. Schmitt stepped into the hall. He caught the smell of musty wet cardboard. Passing the main conveyor belt, he reached the steel door of the compressor room. He entered, jamming the door open with his left foot to admit some light. Condensation glistened on the black walls. A dark round object stood before him. Schmitt reached down its right side and pulled a lever. With a light backwards step he skipped out of the room and the door slammed shut, just in time to confine the infernal noise of the starting compressor motor.

It's no use howling. I'm still too quick for you, he thought.

He walked down the middle aisle, along a row of riveting machines. His steps echoed faintly on the yellowed concrete floor. Beside the third machine he stopped. A thin plastic tube slithered with escaping air, hissing defiantly. Dust rose from a circle around the tube, drying the back of Schmitt's throat. He picked up the tube and forced its end back onto the valve on the machine. The hissing stopped and he felt the machine revive, vibrating gently under the compressed air. He inserted a steel hexagon into the machine and hit the trigger. The pneumatic tubes pulsed and rose under the mounting strain. Reluctantly obeying Schmitt's command, a piston emerged inside the machine cage and smoothly pushed two copper rivets into the hexagon. Schmitt smiled. He pulled a crumpled cigarette packet from his breast pocket. The first one this morning. He had promised himself only to smoke during the hours of daylight.

He looked at the cigarette and then at the skylight above, with the morning darkness beyond. Dawn would come soon. A distant, single click reached his ear from the far end of the hall.

He lit the cigarette and looked at the third riveting machine where the new girl worked during the week. A couple of photographs were attached to the frame. They showed a middle-aged couple in close-up, in front of a blue wavy curtain. Schmitt saw the family resemblance and decided that the couple were her parents. The picture had been taken in an automatic photo booth. Her parents were fooling around in the booth like newly-weds. No wonder their daughter liked to look at that picture often. She would look at the picture every couple of hours, when her left hand grew tired from pushing the trigger of the riveting machine. Schmitt looked at the trigger switch, worn smooth around its edges over the years. He would like to laugh with the new girl in a photo booth one day. They would be old but she would still be beautiful. They would have four children, and give them one passport-sized picture each. One each, out of the set of four, to pin onto their machines at work. Schmitt stamped out his cigarette. He liked dreaming about a future with the new girl. He would have to pluck up some courage. He would ask her to see a film with him. Tomorrow. Tomorrow he would ask her. Again there was the distant click. They're impatient today, he thought.

Schmitt walked on. He crossed the hall towards the mechanics' department and entered the office of his supervisor. A smell of soap and unwashed coffee cups hung in the sound-proofed room. He opened the fuse box and flicked several switches. Lights flared up to the rear of the factory. The hydraulic presses in the small hall at the back began to hum. There, there, have patience, he thought. Two minutes' peace. With a sigh, he let himself fall into the supervisor's office chair. The gas cartridge built into the seat compressed under his weight. Orderly stacks of catalogues were set out on the supervisor's desk. Catalogues of machine parts. Catalogues of cutting tools. Catalogues of pneumatic valves. The supervisor always read catalogues. He did not want to be near the machines any more. His respect had turned to fear. If you have fear, you should work with your head, not with your hands. One pair of hands can control many machines. But one good head can control many pairs of hands.

The supervisor was smart. His brain ruled over all the machines. When Schmitt tended to them, the supervisor could read catalogues. It's quiet in here, thought Schmitt, and the chair is comfortable. He got up and left the office. His blue service trolley stood in the workshop. One by one he checked the tools. The keys were polished to a shine. He felt the files, rasping his hardened fingers across their sharpness.

Schmitt made for the small hall, pulling the trolley along. The high factory walls echoed as he whistled. He repeated the last three notes of the tune, shrilly. A distant crackle came from the furnace room. Its door stood ajar, glowing with the flickering red of molten aluminium. The liquid fumes threatened to sear the back of his throat. He pushed the service trolley through transparent plastic flaps into the small hall. It was cooler here, with a calming smell of cold, yellow oil. Mineral oil, stemming from the centre of the earth.

A dark row of hydraulic presses hummed in indignation. Schmitt knew the sound each machine made. There, there. It's me. I'm here now.

At the end of the hall stood the two fly-wheel presses, coated in chipped green enamel. Schmitt slowly circled the larger press. In his mind he set out the sequence of the repair. First, he had to expose the flywheel. With a little luck, it was nothing. He unhooked the metal guard of the wheel and leant it against the wall. He took hold of one of the huge spokes, and pulled. The wheel silently yielded a quarter turn. The plates of the cutting tool moved upwards into a gaping yawn. The polished metal of the lower plate reflected the neon light. Schmitt switched on the mains and the fly wheel started to turn. From behind the press he saw its spokes whistle past, steadily gaining speed. The pitch of the motor increased until it held a high note. Soon the huge wheel spun at twenty revolutions per second and Schmitt could no longer distinguish the spokes. He inserted a piece of tin and hit the trigger. The clutch gripped, and two thousand pounds of rotating steel spun into seventy tons of downward force. Tearing metal shrieked between the cutting plates as the small hall shuddered under the thundering blow. The machine spat the cut tin into a metal cage beside the press. It tingled, steel on steel. It had the shape of a kidney. Its measurements were precise.

Schmitt shook his head. The clutch needed replacing. He hit the trigger again, and as the drive engaged he moved his hand inside the press where the plastic guard had been. An invisible beam from a photoelectric cell halted the advancing cutting plate. The safety device had interrupted the movement. It was very reliable. With the device he could control the might of the machine simply by waving his hand. Thus the human race ruled over these creatures. Schmitt smiled. He moved his fingers, observing the agile movements of the knuckles and joints. A few grams of flesh, capable of holding back seventy tons of force. Men and women had forged steel into this creature and harnessed its terrible strength. With time, flesh and bones would wither like dry leaves, but what did it matter? We have harnessed this unbelievable force. We have enslaved the beast that will bite its own kind into precise shapes. He felt the warm draft from the spinning wheel. He smelt the oily breath of the creature. He laughed, silently, at his reflection on the polished surface. Then he made sure his left arm covered the light beam of the safety device and reached inside with his right. He noticed some iron filings on the lower plate.

The abyss opened before him and took his breath, his breath was gone and everything was wrong, everything so wrong, just when you fall asleep at night wondering what death will be like, and will it be just like this, drifting off into black?

Had he heard the crash of the plates, the impact of steel on steel? Had he heard it? No. But he must not move, not move, not breathe. There was pain, some pain, but no blood. Should there not be blood? There was pain, but not enough. Should there not be more pain? But they say that shock is a powerful pain killer, and that the pain comes later, later it engulfs you with all its might. His arm was there. His arm was there but he could not see his hand. He had seen his hand, but now he could not see it. The view onto his hand was blocked.

A large plate of metal blocked the view. He had to slow his breathing and he must not move. What was it? Christ, what was it? He had brushed away the iron filings with his right hand. Yes.

And now he could not see his hand. His hand was under the cutting plate. He felt pain in his hand. Logic was needed. Much logic. If his hand hurt, his hand had to be there. For the pain to register as the hand's pain, it had to travel along the nerves of the fingers, the hand, the wrist, the arm and then the spine. Nerves that were cut could not transmit pain signals. Hence his hand was not cut. But if it was not cut why did it hurt? He could not see the hand. He could not pull the hand from under the plate because he could not move. He could not move because whatever had caught him, whatever had put him on this terrible brink, was still there. It was still there, and if he moved, it would throw him into the chasm.

A convulsion rose in his throat. He summoned all his body's strength, and suppressed it. It took much strength to remain still. He had to remain perfectly still.

A thought formed in his mind. It came together, mistily, assumed a shape, and waned. Schmitt forced himself, and the thought returned. This is what had happened. It was clear now.

The clarity of the thought swept over Schmitt with the force of a towering wave. He fought the force of the thought while its terrible draught threatened to sweep him off his feet. This is what had happened. It was clear. Crystal clear. He had bent down to brush the filings off the lower plate. Somehow, his left arm had moved. It had moved out of the light beam that protected him. How? It did not matter. The light had let loose the beast, and it had closed its jaw. It had sunk its enormous shining tooth into Schmitt's flesh.

And then it had stopped. In mid-motion, the mighty jaw had stopped. Somehow, his hand must have moved back into the light beam, disengaging the drive. A reflex, he thought. The fly-wheel made a ticking noise.

The thought sharpened. Schmitt could not move. He noticed the smell of oil close by, yellow and sweet. The slightest movement of his left arm, and the creature would bite. Schmitt concentrated on his left. He was still bent double over the cutting tool, and his left arm was up somewhere, behind him. But he could feel something by his left arm. It was a cold, even smoothness. The smoothness must be the frame of the cage, where his arm interrupted the light beam.

The thought grew thin and narrow and drove itself into his stomach, hot and tearing. He felt a slow strain in the muscles of his back. The position of his body would soon grow too tiring. He could stand in this position for twenty minutes. Half an hour at best. Then his back muscles would get tired and his body would begin to shake. It was the Sunday shift. He was the only worker on Sunday shift. The others would not find him for twenty-four hours. He tried his right hand. He pulled very gently. With all the care he possessed, he pulled. He took care, such care. Seventy tons were suspended half an inch into his flesh, a terrible sharpness, the beast two inches from grinding its teeth. The fly-wheel made a regular ticking noise. It was impossible. Schmitt felt the edge of the metal deep against the bones of his hand. The hand was still there, but it was caught, tight. Tighter than the tightest handcuffs. Seventy-ton handcuffs.

Schmitt stifled a sob. Tears dripped onto the metal surface before him. No hope. He would grow tired, and the beast would bite. He would lose blood. Much blood. He would faint before he could call help. They said this sort of thing did not hurt. When Bolenz had lost the tip of his finger, it had not hurt. But the other thing? People said we could not know what it was like. But he knew what it was like. It was like 1959. Or 1859. It was like time that happened without you, before you, and after you. He could not remember 1959 because he had not existed then. And he would never remember tomorrow because tomorrow he would exist no more. You could not remember sleep. Dreamless sleep.

Schmitt screamed, he screamed a motionless scream, shrill and hollow, at the noise of the car outside. It was the cleaner, twice monthly, Sundays. Today.

He stepped back from the chasm and sunk onto an iron crate. He looked at his right hand. It was bandaged in white gauze. Little red dots showed on the gauze. Next to him sat the cleaner.

'Imagine,' repeated the cleaner. 'Just imagine.'

The cigarette shook in Schmitt's hand.

DIPLODOCUS
by Jennifer Barker

I

I, Diplodocus. The sun running into the sea,
waves turning in tubes and then
breaking on the shore.
The tide washes in a lifetime of human experience:
nappies
needles
condoms
dentures.
The occasional whole human corpse, eventually followed by tents and police and pathologists and no lack of bad smells.

On nights where the rain never let up for a second, my father would take me down to the holiday camp swimming pool, and I'd flap amid rain drops as big as my hand, unsure whether I was doing the breast stroke, or merely rising from the waters for the third time. My parents were obsessed with the idea that it was necessary for me to swim
swim
swim.
I am, in fact, a
poor swimmer even now – overweight, ungainly – and the sea on a bad day could eat me whole: but I'll never drown in a swimming pool.

Above is only the sky. There's nothing to choose
the sea
between them, the sea and the sky; two patches of blue/grey/black that segue into each other. Two flat barren expanses only waiting for the next bolt of lightning. The gamut of human emotions is not comprised in the reflection of a thunder storm.

Suicide is the most common form of death in my family,
and
VOICE OVER: The sun, the sea, the storm
was all I ever heard as a child: my life as a storm on which I rode, throughout

trips to chapels of rest and crematoria. One of my earliest memories, it may even be my first, is of getting ready for my grandfather's funeral:

MOTHER: Come here, let me do it.
(straightens child's tie)
CHILD: It's too tight.
(Mother reties knot)
MOTHER: There.
(Child stares into mirror.
There is a red mark around his throat.)

So I went to the graveside with a bright blue scarf wrapped around my neck like gaudy bunting.

Some are out in the sea even now, though the sky is practically black. I regard them as predestined to drown, extinct already like the prehistoric creatures that turn up as stones all the way along the cliff.

At school, I'd sit in the headmaster's office for hours at a time, staring at the fossils that lined his walls: *Trilobite, Rizosceras,* the spine of a *Dimetrodon,* small shards of other creatures, even a replica of the claw called *Baryonyx Walkeri.* But the biggest, most complete fossil, donated to the school by a former pupil, was reserved for the reception area. It was huge; neck bones larger than my legs, head small and square and full of

teeth.

Diplodocus.

If the news was especially bad, the Head would meet me in that hall, touch my shoulder with his hand, two small and feeble humans in the shadow of a beast made of stone.

1991, my twelfth year, was a bumper year. I sat in the hall twelve times, and my mother alone clocked up seven serious attempts, so serious that I would be farmed out to other unhappy relatives while she recovered in hospital.

Sometimes, as I stared at the Diplodocus, waiting for the Head to come and meet me, I knew it would be her. Before, days before, she would grab me by the shoulders, and talk about the sea being so loud for the time of year. Everybody knew it was no louder; but on occasion she carried me away with her, and I could feel the waters surging in my ears, as though I was drowning in the noise, asphyxiated in a tar-pit of sound. At these times, she would try to kill herself, attempt to escape the encroaching sea. Ironic, then, that in the end she would drown herself, and I would stand in a cold atrium with a human skeleton for decoration, waiting to identify her. Remembering every time I had kept vigilance with the Diplodocus. In those moments, cold and solitary, surrounded by bone, waiting for the news of tragedy with a silent giant, I knew that my family's trait had not passed me by.

II

At night, the sound of the sea kept me awake. I choked down hot milk, I ran for miles, I lay in bed with my eyes shut – all of these on my father's instructions – but in the end I sloped downstairs to join my mother on the sofa: a mutual warming of hands on mugs of coffee, easy-listening TV and Penguin novels.

At six, my father would rise, dawn come or not. He had little sympathy with our reddened eyes, our relief at the arrival of work, and school.

'YOU NEED MORE EXERCISE.' He'd tell me, out of my mother's hearing. 'YOU'D SLEEP BETTER. WE'LL GO DOWN TO THE POOL TONIGHT.'

He'd never say anything to her, just pass her tea, not really noticing whether half the cup was sloshed on the floor or not:

HERE.

While I was still at school, Diplodocus changed its name, to Brontosaurus. Wandering through the town's museum, I saw the little curators with sticky labels, carefully positioning the new name over the old, tearing off the plastic backing, stepping back to examine the work.

At the same time, my mother's illness also changed its name, though not as efficiently as Diplo/saurus: rather more like a criminal – an alias

also known as

but shame and bigotry don't recognise any changes, and children ran after my mother, mainly shouting names, but once pelting her with plastic cola bottles. My father, hit a couple of times, said that it really stung. My mother, as ever, said nothing. I never heard it mentioned again.

I never mentioned, either, my own troubles at school. By the time I was in the final year of primary school, everyone knew. Knew that my mother was
a psycho
a nutter
a freak. Barmy, Basket-case. Schizo. Mad. Crazy. But mainly it was just 'psycho'.

Shouted out in the street, or whispered, as I was bumped into, in the classroom. I think even the teachers thought something similar; didn't openly call out, but slighted my mother on parents' evenings, barely saying 'He's doing fine' before moving on to the next child. They never accepted an excuse note if it came from her, and didn't speak to her in the street, though they greeted the other parents and children,

in their Sunday best, as good people.

They even refused her offers to 'help' during school hours, though help was needed. And they never stopped the children from openly mocking her.

There was no need to encourage them to mock me. The world is full of bookish children who successfully build normal lives, hardly ever bursting into tears on the train for no reason. I never fought back, my father said, that was my problem. If I'd just laugh it off, or respond in kind, they'd never do it again. Utter bullshit, of course. I was too tired; too well read; even at that stage too weird, ever to be acceptable to them.

My father couldn't deal with any of it. He was of Yorkshire stock, sprung from a tradition where, if a woman was fed up with her husband, she knocked him down the stairs, and the GP would come around and write the cause of death down as 'miner's lung'. He didn't understand a woman who could low-level bitch for hours, go to bed, and then resume the next day as though there had been no pause. She stormed out to the car frequently. He only left the once; and I've not had a word from him since.

III

Fire.

If anyone embodied that force, then my mother was it; the alcohol she drank that burned my throat every time she pressed a sip upon me, the sudden bursts of enthusiasm that caught up everyone in the room, like a chair burning up from an unattended cigarette. Dashing around the supermarket, coloured scarf flapping behind her, as unable to keep up as myself. Fire, fiery, firefly.

My mother always said she was Earth, that was her element; the rows of vegetables in the back garden. A bed or two for flowers, mostly thorny plants, mostly nettles and bindweed, but the loves of her life were the fruit bushes – gooseberries, blackcurrants – that needed careful pruning in the autumn. She pruned our poor fruit trees with the same vigour. I was there, never allowed to hold the saw, too dangerous. Instead I stood below, watching her red face as she balanced, one foot on the stepladder, leaning into the centre of the tree, chopping at great swathes of branch, cutting further back than it had grown in a year. I think, in the end, she killed one of them: certainly it never produced any more apples.

It was all fuel, you see. Fuel for the great bonfires we would hold on chilly, often rainy, afternoons. Wrapped in coats, the cold weather making our fingers shake, we would pile a mammoth sacrifice in one of the barren vegetable beds: branches from the trees, the prunings from the bushes, thorny sticks, and any number of weeds, all from the great vegetation massacre. The rest of the garden seemed shrunk back, as though fearful of sending forth a single bud.

I would stand on the grass path surrounding the bed while my mother started the fire. After a futile period holding a spluttering match to the damp wood, she would curse and look up at me, dyed black hair falling wet around her face, which was smeared with earth.

'Pass me that lighter. Watch out. BE CAREFUL. Thanks. Can
you get another one out of the box, in case I need it.'

I would shuffle back to the path, wind driving the rain into my face, envying my father for being inside. He never came out when my mother did the garden, he preferred to make tea.

'Sit about and fall asleep in front of the TV. Watch the football instead of helping me.'

I wanted to watch the football too, instead of being in the cold.

'I wonder if Dad needs me. I could go in and see.'

'He doesn't need any help being a lazy sod. Have you got another match? I think I'll need some more newspaper in a minute, you could do that. Like that, don't you?'

NO. But I did anyway. There was something magical about my mother's fire. When the matches had done their work, and there was a blaze, only a few inches across, in the middle of the sticks, my mother would take her metal stick, and fold the rest of the branches into the flames, so that eventually the fire was suffocated. Then she would shove paper randomly into spaces between the branches, and lift the wood about an inch into the air, shake it, and let it back down. For a minute, there was nothing, then she'd say, it's going, and the wood burst into flames as though she had willed it.

The fires my mother set never really went out. That was the secret to them. Even at their coolest, there was still a red glow in the middle. Eventually, the whole thing caught again. She had a Petoniasta bush in the garden, and we always included handfuls of the leaves. They contain oil, and once caught on fire, burn bright and fast, sometimes with pops and squeals.

It took a couple of hours to burn all the wood, and then we went back to the house. Once, as my father helped me take off my coat, I whispered

Do we always have to burn so much?

TELL YOU WHAT, SON, I'D PREFER SHE SET FIRE TO RUBBISH IN THE GARDEN, RATHER THAN ANYTHING IN THE HOUSE. SOME OF THE THINGS IN HERE ARE VALUABLE.

I wonder, sometimes, if my father feared my mother's moods, the sudden changes. I wonder, too, if his being there would have saved her, not just the last time, but from some of the attempts. Anything, any effort to stop the flames. Anything but the nothing that was done.

IV

School holidays, my mother and I alone in a tiny house that felt too big. During the day, the town was full of tourists, all squashed into B & B's, emerging in swarms like flying ants as the summer faded. I hid in my bedroom, reading a book, my only companions a cup of tea and a cheese sandwich, fair-weather friends.

In the evening, though, the beach was mine. I walked along it, up the path towards the cliff. For an hour or two, I picked up bits of stone, sometimes breaking them apart, trying to find fossils. The ground was damp, the paths slippery, and I had only a torch to see by, but I dreamt of finding some pieces of ancient rock. If a stranger had come across me, lying in a heap of battered stones, staring at the distant, yet visible, stars, and asked me what I wanted to be when I was older, I would have said 'paleologist'. The bones of the past were my future.

I left home for University when I was twenty-five. I'd done less well at college than I'd hoped. Not badly enough to be turned down for a place on the course, but badly enough that I felt ashamed, almost as though I'd cheated my way in.

That's where I was the night that my mother came ashore. Manic all that summer, she'd come down hard. Antidepressants that would normally have bounced her back to contentment were ineffective – 'like trying to kill an elephant with a butter knife' – and she'd refused psychotherapy, just like she'd refused it throughout my childhood. Sometime at the beginning of September, she'd thrown herself into the water. Living alone, friendless, neighbours indifferent if not hostile, she'd not been missed. The sea had taken her, as she'd always said it would.

Could I come home asap?

V

The taxi left me standing on the last inch of pavement, my former home a short walk through the dark. I stepped down from the kerb, and put my foot in a puddle. Yes, it was raining. Not storming, just the weary drizzle of early autumn. I was afraid. The dark didn't seem to draw back as I approached it, and I was returning to a haunted place.

At least in the
she wasn't house, I thought.

I would have bitten it back if I could have done so. I walked the rest of the way, thinking about making the journey as a child; the school bus roaring away from the pavement, sea reflecting the last line of sunset straight into my eyes so that I had to squint and trust to luck, mother shouting from the front door for me to hurry up, it was freezing.

It was cold now in the house, ice formed in stalactites under the window frames. It was early October, the heating hadn't been on for several days, but it still seemed, well, supernaturally cold. All imagination, but I hurried up the stairs to turn on the boiler.

The first thing they showed me at the mortuary was a bracelet, still smelling of the sea.

Is this your mother's?
Yes.
(pause)
It was popular in this area a few years ago.
It says 'to Mum, from Henry'. I had that specially engraved.

It was a bracelet I had given to her one Christmas. She had worn it for a couple of days, but it turned her skin 'green', as they call it.

She must have put it on
before.....
deliberately.

She lay on a common hospital trolley, as though she had died a few minutes ago and been wheeled straight in. Her face was swollen, or maybe fatter than I remembered; hair fanned around her face, as it never had in life. Her eyes were half-shut, like a naughty child pretending to be asleep, as I sometimes had, waiting for her to lean over and say, 'I know you're awake.'

I know you're awake.

Sorry, sir?
Oh, nothing.
Is it your mother?
Oh, yes. Yes, it is.

Wake up, c'mon. I'll
take you home, it'll
be all right. I forgive
you. Don't be dead.
Don't be dead.

VI

The house is in darkness, and the sound of the rain against the window just makes me think about the flimsiness of the modern tomb; the cardboard-thin coffin, the tiny grave, barely more than could be dug with a trowel, the speed of the memorial, the cross: two sticks for a headstone. All soon gone, only a little slower than memories.

If I go out, soon, to walk along the beach, out to the cliff face, will I come across my mother, her last steps into the waves? Reach across, save at least a little part of her, to keep in a box beneath my bed, along with the stones I collected as a child, all of them barren of fossils. Lose her, fail to catch her, as I never saved her in life, watching her slow drowning and not moving an inch. Fear of the sea, a fear she taught me?

Or not to go, stay here. Climb the steps I crouched on listening to them argue about HER drinking, HER flirting, until she ran into the kitchen, slamming the door behind her, and crying? Perhaps I shall find her there? Perhaps upstairs, hunting for a decade-old bracelet? The garden; I think the garden, hacking the trees more viciously than before, dancing like a jack-o'lantern around the bonfire. I'll find her there, hair fanned out behind her, skin still smelling of salt. My grief, my grief.

My notes are finished now, the pad lies beside the bed, and I'm staring up at the night sky. There are few stars; it's the wrong time of year and too cloudy, but that's all right. If I died tonight, I'd be on that cliff-face like a shot, still trying to dig a Diplodocus out of English soil, wanting to unearth a past that told the truth, or maybe just hoping that bones could be resurrected, and any bones would do. Watch myself wandering along the beach, still fearing the sea. Stare at the other strangers come down to the water's edge, the hundreds of others with a one-way ticket and an abandoned car, slowly rusting in a car park, eventually towed away.

I'll be scared silly in a minute, I shouldn't have stayed. I should have gone back to my halls. It's ridiculous: there's no electricity, she didn't pay the bill. But I know, don't I, that I'm not going back. I'm going to live in this house until it falls into the sand. I'll scrape so much earth off the cliff that it'll end up in Cambridge.

Perhaps I will leave. Not much point in just sitting here, waiting for the sea to knock on the door. My mother would have hated that. I could go back to university. I have people who'll miss me, not in any big way, but it's a start, isn't it? I might sell the house, move somewhere away from the sea; have a second chance. Get married, settle down. I might want to find my father.

NIGHT YARN
by Catherine Casale

I try and concentrate on what trick Jeanie is playing on Major Nelson this time in *I Dream of Jeanie*, but Mom and Dad's screaming down in the kitchen is really loud. It's flying all the way up the playroom stairs even though the door's shut. David is a blob on the floor in front of me. Is he alive in there? The pugs are conked out next to him.

I hold my knitting out, letting it hang down. I've never had such fun yarn. The purples blend into the blues, into the greens, turquoises, yellows, pinks, and oranges. It's a swirl of changing colour, like magic.

Dad is shouting, 'I've had enough. Do you hear me? Enough.' I can't understand what Mom is saying. Her voice is high and strange and the words are all running together. Wet, her voice sounds wet.

I jig the needle. I like the way the scarf springs up and down, boing, boing, boing.

I just wish they would stop. His shouting and her shrieking are like giant Pacific waves slamming into each other. David is completely still.

I could cast off now. It's long enough. We don't need scarves in California, but with a scarf you don't have to worry about following a pattern. You can just enjoy the fuzzy rainbow colours tugging along between your fingers and the sweet clicking of the number 8 knitting needles. My favourite size.

Oh-oh, something's broken. A plate? That wasn't the sound of something just falling. Tigger's noticed. He's sat up and started sucking his thumb. He'll sit in that pretzel position for hours now, his short body twisted backwards and held in place by his teeth clamped into his rear leg. His large brown eyes are rolling this way and that with too much white showing.

Oh God, please stop.

Maybe a few more rows. Then I'll decide. I slip the right needle into the stitch on the left, both hands working together, cross-click, loop-twist, pull-slide, hook-and-push. Repeat. Repeat. Repeat.

It's quiet now. No sound at all except for the rain hitting the windows.

Okay. Jeanie is batting her eyelashes and tipping her head to the side. I wish I had hair like her, shining and bouncing and twirling in the air. She has just convinced Major Nelson that she's not going to hold a party in his house, but really she is. I like Jeanie, but she's always fooling Major Nelson and I feel sorry for him. Not like with Samantha and Darrin in *Bewitched.* Darrin's just boring and stupid and won't let Samantha and Tabitha have any fun. I love it when Samantha ignores Darrin's strict instructions and goes ahead and does what she wants. Why'd she marry such a fussbudget anyway?

The playroom door jerks open. It's Dad, stomping up the stairs. He reaches the top and looks us both over.

'Cathy! Downstairs.'

Oh God, what have I done now?

Dad turns and pounds back down. I jump out of the rocking chair and drop my knitting in the basket. David doesn't move. I run down the narrow wooden steps, holding the rail so I won't slip.

I climb onto a kitchen stool. Dad is on the other side of the counter, leaning into it with his arms out straight.

'How much did she have?'

'What do you mean?'

'How much did she have and when did she start?' He pronounces each word very clearly even though he's shouting.

'I don't know what you're talking about.' My voice is going gurgly.

'Tell me where she's got her stash hidden.' He smashes his fists onto the counter.

'I don't know what you're talking about.' I start to cry.

'Don't lie to me.'

'I'm not lying!'

'Why are you protecting your mother?'

I don't know what to say. I just shake my head and cry.

'Don't pretend you don't know! She gets drunk every day of the week. Don't tell me you haven't noticed. Even David knows what's going on and he's three years younger than you. What d'you think she's drinking out of those coffee mugs? Beer, that's what. She's a goddamn alcoholic.'

'I didn't know!' I gasp. But I did, only I didn't. She's been drinking beer out of coffee mugs since we were little in Minneapolis, but I didn't know there was anything unusual about that. Or wrong.

'Where's she hidden it?'

I shake my head. I have no idea.

'Think! You're here all afternoon.'

It's my fault, I realize. I haven't noticed.

Some afternoons we drive to the shopping centre and I buy yarn and

Nancy Drew books. If we run errands, sometimes she gets me a treat. Lots of days I play outside at the Zelins. I don't know what she's doing then. But inside.

She stands over me while I'm vacuuming, screaming down at me. About David, about Dad. I can't do anything right. She says I do the vacuuming wrong on purpose so she won't ask me again. I look hard at the family-room floor, blonde wooden boards with dark round pegs, a fancy, beautiful detail, with the orangey-red carpet from Germany in the middle, two different surfaces, two different attachments, trying not to miss a single spot, but it's all blurry because I'm crying so hard, and it's so loud, over and over again, 'You stole your father away from me! You destroyed your brother. He was such a happy smiley baby. We had to take your door off its hinges.' Over and over again. 'We brought you home from the hospital and you rejected me. You preferred your father and he prefers you! You ruined my marriage. Your brother wouldn't have any fingers left today, if we hadn't taken your door off.' The things she says are so terrible. It doesn't matter what I say, she doesn't believe me.

Dad is staring hard at me.

Does David really know? How?

Suddenly I remember green coffee mugs tucked away in little nooks all over the house.

'Where's Mom?'

'She drove off in a huff. I've notified the police. She's in no shape to be driving.'

The police! He called the police! What will they do to her if they catch her? Arrest her and put her in jail? What if she crashes the car? I see our station wagon with its bright flower-power decals crumpled up like a mashed Sprite can.

'Look. Dad, up there in the plates.' I point to the glass-fronted cabinet above my head.

He walks around the counter, yanks open the cabinet door, and thumps the mug down on the counter. Beer sloshes up the sides. He snorts, lips pressed together, nodding. He's pleased.

'Now that I think about it, a good place to hide something might be the ironing board cupboard,' I say in a bright little voice, looking up at him. I had grown a jar of furry blue mould in there from a piece of damp bread for a school experiment. I needed a dark place and Mom had suggested the spot.

I'm right. We find a plastic-webbed six-pack. Three of the cans are missing. A fourth one is sitting there open. But why does she drink it from here, warm, when the whole bottom of the fridge is full of six-packs?

I seek Dad's eyes, looking for his approval. I might have been unforgivably dense up until now, but I can learn. We decide to make a systematic search of the laundry room and kitchen. Every time we find a new piece of evidence we exchange satisfied looks.

But where's Mom gone? How did I miss the sound of her driving away? Even though it's only got tiny windows on that side, the playroom looks over the driveway. Was I in the bathroom or just paying too much attention to the TV?

I imagine her hunched forward gripping the steering wheel, a crazed look on her face, blazing down unknown roads just behind the white of the headlights. If she drives any faster she's going to get ahead of them and be in the dark. Come back soon please.

What if she doesn't come back? What if she runs away or gets lost or, or worse? It's one of those California downpours out there. Why didn't he stop her?

We keep searching and find more half-drunk cans and mugs in the dining room, living room, and family room. I don't understand how she forgets about them part way through.

Dad and I wear ourselves out. He says I can go. I climb back up the stairs to the playroom. David is still sitting spaced out in front of the TV. Tigger is sucking his thumb and Snoopy is sound asleep. He's just a puppy and really tired by bedtime.

I go stand next to the television. Right next to it so that I can try and get David to look at me.

'David.' I say in a grown-up voice. David keeps his eyes on the tube. It's a laundry detergent commercial. Since we moved to California, he watches five or six hours a day. Mom lets him. He must come straight home from morning kindergarten and go upstairs.

What's a mother to do! the woman on the commercial wails. It's the husband's ring-around-the-collar and the kids' ground-in dirt again. I'm sick of listening to that woman fuss night after night when it's her who lets them play in the mud and roll in the grass dressed head-to-toe in white clothing.

'David. Mom's an alcoholic. That means she drinks too much beer.'

'I know.' He says it in a bored way.

I'm mortified. How could he know and I didn't? What's wrong with me that I missed something so obvious a six-year-old could figure it out?

I don't know what to do. I can't just keep standing here with David refusing to look at me or talk to me and knowing everything anyway. I go back to the rocking chair and fall into it. I pick up my knitting. I throw it back down. I hate knitting. It's stupid. And it's really dumb to knit in California. It's too hot in the summer and the wool gets scratchy and sticky and why would you make something you can't use? I'm never going to knit again.

MALARIA

When at last he came home on leave
to Spottiswoode, the Heights (our semi-d)
our family circle had grown too tight.
We wouldn't let him in,
this haggard absentee
with his Officers' Mess, his tiffin,
his 'best parties in South East Asia Command'.
Couldn't he have written?
And those sugar parcels, shipped
from Capetown, couldn't he have
addressed them himself, by hand?
I remember how pale he was
and my dad went outside to throw up.
Malaria, he said, *can't shake it off.*
But still the parasite persists – like love.

My father washes his hands

My father always turned away,
and washed his hands.
Must be cold water, he said.
A doctor's habit, no doubt, ingrained.
But it troubles me still,
as if he were absolving himself from love
over and over again.

BRIDGET'S WELL

The locals say *Come back in August,*
come for the craic on the Saint's big day
and not wishing to disappoint, I reply *I will,*
and mark the date, knowing I won't go.
Instead, on a quiet afternoon, I pull off
the cliff road, park outside the pub,
step down into the sunken garden,
with its privet hedge and rosary path,
and stoop to enter Bridget's Well.
It's nothing much – a moss-covered
overhang from whose lip a tiny waterfall
tips into a trembling pool.
It fills and refills, never overflowing.

On the cave wall – votive litter, coins,
wax hearts, crutches, letters biro-stained:
Blessed Bridget, thank you for the grace
to give up smoking, for mending my womb
so that I can bear more children,
for getting my husband off the booze.

When miracles happen, if they do,
they happen close to water,
there's refreshment to the spirit
in that constant tireless flow.
I cup my hands to trap some water, swallow,
it's cool and tasteless like the soul.

AT KIRSTENBOSCH

For Stephanie requesting tree oil.

The giant redwood stiffens from within –
the inner cells start dying first, but its highest,
furthest leaves still seethe with life.
Though some say greenness is a kind of grief,
the old sequoia doesn't just give up,
he keeps on growing like a buttercup
heaving his great hulk towards the light,
not ready, not by a long chalk, to become
a monument to himself.

This may be our autumn, dearest wife,
but in this garden of the Cape,
another spring has only just begun.
Look at that deluded sun-bird swinging
on yellow protea spikes. How fervently
he retracts his nape, puffs up his throat
and lets rip a love-song to his mate.
No matter that a twitcher armed with mike
records his song, and plays it back to him,
the little sun-bird, swaying on the flower,
keeps on singing, hour after hour.

THE LIBRARY

The National Library of Sarajevo, Vjecnica,
was destroyed by shelling on August 18, 1992.

The architect went to great lengths
to capture the gracious Ottoman style.
Everybody loved Vjecnica, the City Hall
that held the memory of a people.
The gunners on the hilltop were lucid, logical,
had it in their sights, took aim.
Their incendiary shells were meant
to erase by fire those signs
by which people recognise themselves.

These are not careless crimes.
Only conviction can breed the truly crass.
When Amr-al-Asr brought his army to the gates
of Alexandria, he said: *God the Merciful*
and the Compassionate. There is but one God
and Mohammed is His Prophet. You tell me
of the great library that contains all the learning
in the world, that it should be saved from the fire.
There is but one Truth.
What need have we of books?

THE MONASTERY OF PROHOR PCINSKI

The monastery of Prohor was founded by Czar Milutin in the l3th Century.

Even now, in time of war, pilgrims still come
to the monastery seeking absolution or chrism.
In the porch of the abbey church, we pause
to labour at some moral, blowing plumes
of frozen breath and gazing out at the valley
now oppressed by a snow-laden sky.

Casually we begin to argue,
sipping raki against the cold.
This so-called holy monastery, I angrily assert,
was Milutin's war temple.
It seems our sacred places only breed war.
We are born with cleft palates,
our most passionate prayers are flawed.

There may be another gentler form of speech,
I venture, *whose vocabulary is silence.*
But then I falter, losing the thread,
my thought pluming out of reach.

We go in. Above us looms the Pancrator –
harsh father. Some zealot from the nearby town
has cross-hatched the transept with crude new paint,
as if to restate some truth.

Beyond the iconostasis, some early frescoes
bloom faintly like girls.

AFTER THE *POSTUMUS ODE* BY HORACE

It seems only yesterday, Isobel,
that we sat on a beach
in north-east Brazil
washed by warm green waves
and I wrote your name
with a stick in the burning sand.

Your childhood has flown,
and I'm getting short of breath.
Yet our combined night prayers
can't rid me of the wrinkles
round my eyes, or put off by a single hour
my coming fatal bout with death.

Light candles? Yes, why not?
We should pray to Jude or Genevieve.
None of it will do us any good.
Sooner or later we all have to leave,
and creep down the darkened stair
past the room that's always locked,

Nobody's spared. You, too, darling,
you'll have to leave your mum,
your cosy flat with the river view,
your gentle lover when he comes along,
you'll have to leave it all behind:
your one-day one-entry diary

with its secrets and its scribbled notes
for stories you are never going to write,
each page ripped out except the last
in which some other girl will come,
sweeter and cleverer than you,

and write your requiem.

EVENSONG
by Jane Harris

This happened late on a November afternoon as she walked home from school, when the light faded and darkness fell like an indigo veil. At the age of thirty-nine after much deliberation, Miss Norman, who taught mathematics well, decided to take up the violin.

It happened at approximately the nineteenth of the forty-three paces she knew it took her to walk from one street lamp to the next. That is, almost halfway through the swath of cold darkness which connected one pool of light to the other. She slipped in and out of the wan sodium glow in five steps, a figure she considered disproportionately small even though she was aware that her stride was perhaps more vigorous than most. She had, after all, scaled Care Caradoc in Wales, Cross Fell in the Pennines and, just this past summer, the challenging Scarfell Pike in Cumbria; it was to be expected.

Her height was also a factor to be counted in the correlation between the figures. A lithe five foot seven. The simple mathematical constancy, the brevity and precision of the fact that a shorter person would naturally take a greater number of paces to cover the distance, a taller person less, was always a source of wonder to her. Just as Venus would always glide faster than Jupiter across the night sky. Numbers could be relied upon to fix the world in place. They made her feel there was a certain correctness in the world, that it had reasons for existing as it did, even if these reasons sometimes eluded her.

By the time she fitted the key into the door of her flat she had quashed any feelings of foolishness which welled up in her heart. She had never before attempted to play a musical instrument, but lately she felt a need, now growing more insistent, to unearth a little piece of good news inside herself, a snippet of potential to work at something new.

Although the ceilings were low and the walls plain, the flat where she lived alone was not unpleasant. It had a south-westerly aspect. From her windows she could see the street which was lined with chestnut and plane trees. In October she watched flocks of housemartins wing south and now, in November, seagulls wheeling away from the heaving sea settled nonchalantly on the frozen ground.

Miss Norman had had one big romance in her life. When she was thirty years old she fell in love with a man. In her mind she likened the effect of this love on her life, the enormity and completeness of it, the transforming quality of it, to Isaac Newton's formulation of his extraordinary equation of universal gravitation $F = \frac{GM_1 M_2}{d^2}$ which had led to landing a man on the moon. Love led her to see deep within and far beyond herself. It led her to the brink of the visible world. The instant she became cognisant of this love she recognised the uniqueness of its equation and thought the probability of such an event occurring twice in one lifetime was remote if not impossible. So she had loved him with all her heart, her body and her soul. The man, reading her mind in her face, could also not help noting in the same instant, as if catching his sleeve on a snare, how her contact lens bulged over her iris like a second membrane reminding him of a fish's eye. He blushed even as he fell upon her. Miss Norman read the blush as passion.

A short period of exquisite happiness ensued for Miss Norman until the troubles of love not returned in equal measure began to brew. The imbalance overwhelmed her lover with guilt and self-loathing and he declared himself unworthy of her. One night after a supper *à deux* in Miss Norman's favourite Italian restaurant *I'm sorry* was what he said, as they walked past a gaily lit bedding shop. *I'm sorry* was all he said stopping in front of the windows. Only three months before he had told her he knew by heart every part of her, the slightly off-centre peak of her hairline, the way she combed her hair more slowly after they made love than at other times, the birthmark on her left thigh; he said if someone were to show him a photograph of, say, only the small of her back or the arch of her instep he would know it was her. But standing in front of those windows, which were filled with a promotional display of mattresses made by a company called Comfilux, he looked at her as if she were a stranger. A life-size cardboard cut-out of a square-jawed man in striped pyjamas gazing hopefully at a smiling woman in a less demure négligé and robe was propped on the biggest bed in the middle of the window. Insisting that Miss Norman deserved better, her lover disappeared from her life.

It took Miss Norman some time to regain her composure.

For a time she came home from the supermarket without half the things she intended to buy. Twice in the first year she forgot to set the children homework. When she stood on playground duty her eye wandered to an isolated spot high above their heads where their shouts and laughter thinned and once ten-year-old Emily Bridgewater stepped boldly forward watched by two hundred pairs of eyes: 'Excuse me Miss Norman, I'm sorry Miss Norman, but aren't you going to blow the whistle, Miss?'

She felt temporarily unsound of mind. It was not what she expected of herself.

That was when she took to walking. She wanted to walk herself out of her predicament which was this: she felt completely baffled. Where that fecund fire had burned within her, somewhere within the left ventricle of her heart where the blood looks reddest, she sensed a futility which frightened her.

She immersed herself in the patterns and minutiae of Ordinance Survey Maps. She followed the clusters of undulating lines into the plunge of valleys and in summer sought a meandering thread of blue where a stream rushed through a crease in the dells. Soon she learned the intimation of a storm in the lift of the wind. The maps led her to days distant from anywhere. Like the dots and dashes, the exs and brackets, the numbers, the pluses and minuses of equations, she took comfort and pleasure in how the maps transcribed the intricate world onto a small bare page. On the ancient public byways she heard a thousand footsteps walk behind her, tramping on and on in time, and in time the patterns and soundness of nature dulled her anguish. She walked until she came to the sea where she stopped and stared. An understanding, stark in its brevity, struck her with such force that she leaned against the cliff face. Walking is a revocable process. Unlike a terrible insult whose harm cannot be repaired, it can be undone. After the time it took for the rising tide to begin to ebb Miss Norman turned and walked back inland.

She stood in her living room and looked around. She would not practice next to the wide window. She would stand unobserved beside the standard lamp whose light would benefit her music sheet. From here she would still be able to see the sky but not her reflection in the small over mantel mirror. Practice would have to be completed before eight o'clock in the evening. Any time later she deemed unsociable.

With every second Miss Norman grew more confident of her choice. One could tuck a violin under one's arm or hold it beside one's handbag without attracting undue attention, the paired harmonies of curves concealed in the zipped lozenge of its case. She would walk to the Conservatoire of Music and the Arts for her lessons with the violin taut and light in her grasp. She estimated a twelve-minute walk.

Having settled these matters she hurriedly put her briefcase down next to the table where she marked the children's exercise books and removed her woollen coat draping it temporarily over the back of the upright chair. Then she phoned the Conservatoire to explain her desire. In her enthusiasm she had failed to consider the time of year. The middle of term. It was incredible that she could have done such a thing!

The sensible course of action, the one Miss Norman knew would have most accurately reflected her usual frame of mind and sense of order, was to say she could wait until January. If nothing else this would have reassured the secretary who sounded young and whose voice had clouded with hesitancy. Miss Norman considered doing so for a split second. She could feel embarrassment rising from her chest right up to her throat. She considered how she would pass the coming night, Christmas too was coming, without having taken steps towards realising her intention, and discarded waiting as an impossibility.

Instead she swallowed hard and arranged to meet Rosemary Stevenson, Principal, the very next day at five thirty in the afternoon, which could not come too soon.

It had been a winter day thick with mists, when distant objects were not clearly visible. At five twenty Miss Norman sat in the corridor of the Conservatoire with her knees together and her hands folded in her lap listening intently. Behind the double doors of each rehearsal room every musical note was being played in a different order on different instruments. Piano, flute, saxophone, violin, cello, and from behind the last door, the human voice. The same set of notes, only the arrangement varied, but in that variety Miss Norman wondered how many possibilities there were. What further transformation was achieved when one introduced the modulations of rests and stops, sharps and flats, bars and beats, softness and amplitude and finally, interpretation? Yet always the notes remained constant like the square root of the real and imaginary parts of a complex number. Perhaps this was what kept the whole from chaos.

Miss Norman's mind bobbed like a gull on the overlapping waves of melodies, mysterious, elusive, no sooner heard than gone forever. When Rosemary Stevenson came and stood near her, so quiet and intense was Miss Norman's posture, Rosemary thought her stricken with sadness or some unearthly distraction. She almost regretted having to disturb her.

Reputation, age and character had all contributed to Rosemary Stevenson, Principal, ever being called or referred to as anything other than that within the Conservatoire walls. So accustomed had she become to her name being unfettered by any other title, now she believed it was her own express wish it remain so. It seemed appropriate to the singularity of widowhood and her age, sixty-one. A tireless crusader, she enjoyed bringing the benefits of a musical education to the community. She had been 'at the helm' as she described it, for twelve years. She thought herself fortunate to have found an employment which gave some meaning, however small, to her life. A keen defender of her personal freedom, she could summon forces of resistance against any who attempted to impinge on it. In her turn she respected this quality in others. She also considered scuffed shoes to be the end of civilisation. She and Miss Norman were destined to get on.

Alerted to Miss Norman's untimely request, Rosemary had consulted the schedule of violin lessons. There was not a violin teacher on the roster of instructors with a slot free in the middle of term. She was undaunted by this news. Not in the habit of turning people away, she carefully examined the entire schedule of music lessons. Miss Norman had told the secretary she was herself a teacher and required an evening lesson. There was one opening in Robert Morelli's schedule on a Thursday evening at six. He taught Classical guitar.

Rosemary's quick eye appraised the woman in the chair. Would she be open to suggestion? The navy blue skirt and green polo-neck jumper Miss Norman had been wearing since morning were serviceable, not stylish. The red coat suggested some exuberance of spirit. Her hands were unadorned, the fingernails neatly filed in short practical curves and there was about her person a faint scent of lemons. She was in her prime, past the inexperience of youth, yet Rosemary wondered how aware she was of this advantage. With a little coaxing, attention could be drawn to her startling blue eyes and long slender neck. The lively intelligence lighting the face would do the rest.

Miss Norman was listening even more intently now, waiting. She had just heard the moment when, by chance, the same note was sounded simultaneously by two people somewhere in their separate songs, as if two worlds had become indivisible for an instant, before they split apart once more. It seemed extraordinary even though she knew, because she was well acquainted with the laws of probability, that perhaps it was not. She wanted to hear it again.

For an instant Miss Norman wondered why the tiny, buxom woman standing in front of her was looking at her so quizzically. She had a beaked nose and very dark, bright eyes.

'Miss Margaret Norman?' The woman continued to study her, but it was with a frank and open look as if she intended to find a way of putting Miss Norman at her ease. She realised this was Rosemary Stevenson.

'Yes. You must be Rosemary Stevenson.'

'How lovely to see you, Miss Norman. Won't you come in,' she said, opening wider a door through which she had probably just come. Light footed, her movements were quick as darts. A bird, that was what she reminded Miss Norman of, a robin or a warbler.

Rosemary's office was more like a large storeroom than an executive chamber. There was an upright piano against one wall, two cellos, one in its case and one out lying on its side on the floor, a flute, a guitar and an assortment of several large curvilinear black cases which suggested the arabesque of a French horn or saxophone. Cardboard boxes of programmes and blank certificates waiting to be awarded were piled in corners. Shelves of sheet music and books lined the walls. Her desk and the two easy chairs to which she escorted Miss Norman formed a small oasis in what otherwise suggested a hive of activity.

Rosemary had already decided not to beat around the bush with Miss Norman and came straight to the point.

'So although I cannot offer you the violin at the moment, Miss Norman, Mr Morelli would be delighted to have a new pupil. He is very well liked by his students. Many stay with him for years. He is particularly good with adults, very patient. I have always thought the guitar such a gentle instrument. Why not have a go, if you are unhappy with it you can always switch to the violin later. To make a start on something new, that's the important thing don't you think?'

Miss Norman could still hear strands of music faintly in the background. Each note was an infinitely simple event which held a moment in place, each song moving through a particular sequence of those events. How pleasing the music was; how comforting to be able to divine the result of the entire process! But the guitar, it was not what she had intended. She had seen people walking with the instrument strapped to their backs almost as if it were a person, bearing the cumbersome weight of it. She thought again of the coming weeks of ever-increasing darkness, the very evening ahead. She imagined her wrist half pivoted around the neck of a guitar, her fingers stretching over the frets. The pleasure of being able to give herself to, and any who heard it, even one limpid note.

'Yes, to make a start. That's exactly it. But the guitar, I'd not thought of the guitar. You are of course right, it does make a lovely soft sound.'

She had not wanted love for the power it could bring her. She had never wished for all to adore her. For what then?

Suddenly Miss Norman doubted that she had any excuse whatsoever for being there.

'But my hands.' she said stretching her fingers taut and looking uncertainly at them. It was late in the day. Her knowledge of music was scant.

'What about them?' Rosemary said calmly.

'I have never played. I wonder if they're strong enough.' A worse fear was overshadowing her resolve, as when a flash flood suddenly takes hold and strips the riverbank of life; what if she stayed, had lessons, and was still unable to exhibit sufficient excuse for being there? This was not a detail she would herself be able to overlook, no matter how kindly the teacher.

'Ah, but they will be, with practice,' Rosemary said, placing her own hands flat on her lap and giving her thighs a little press, a gesture which always prefigured some new determination on her part. 'They become like the yin and yang to each other my dear, one with beautifully manicured long nails for plucking the strings and the other with equally beautiful short ones for pressing them to the fret. You will soon learn who the cognoscenti are as they will be the ones who will guess why.'

Rosemary was near certain that in Miss Norman she may well have found a walking advertisement for the Conservatoire. Here was a mature woman with no experience of music, who possibly had the perseverance and intelligence to some day reach recital standard and be an inspiration to all.

'Miss Norman, as, by a happy coincidence, it is Thursday, Mr Morelli is here now. It will soon be six o'clock,' she said, looking at her watch, 'Why not have a chat with him and a look at a guitar? He will be able to answer any questions you have far better than I can. Let's see if he has finished his last lesson yet.'

Before Miss Norman could say yes or no Rosemary was on her feet and out the door without a backward glance. Miss Norman followed her down the corridor and up a flight of stairs and found herself being shown into a small room where a man stood by the window. He was not at all like the stout-bodied, dark-haired personage with thick, closely-knit eyebrows over intense eyes whom she had imagined. Instead he brought to Miss Norman's mind a slightly dilapidated windmill on a breezy day. He was tall and his baggy clothes flapped when he moved. He wore a tie but the knot was inexpertly fastened and swerved dangerously off-centre revealing the buttons of his shirt. What wisps of hair he had gusted about his head in a tangle of sand and grey. His eyes were soft, green and kind.

Miss Norman looked at him with surprise and apprehension.

Rosemary announced that Miss Norman was considering studying the guitar. On hearing this news Mr Morelli returned Miss Norman's expression with one of such celebratory delight that she blushed to the roots of her hair. He bowed, shutting his eyes as he did so.

'Robert Morelli,' he said solemnly, his shoulders still inclined towards the floor. While he was thus bent toward her Miss Norman happened to glance past his shoulders and saw a music composition book open on a small table. The page was covered with pencilled notes dangling singularly, or joined in groups of twos, threes and fours stepping jauntily up and down the staves. Miss Norman gazed at the top of Mr Morelli's head with a sudden curiosity for which she did not attempt to account.

ME, MY MUG

Look at this mug I made at school,
more like a tall bowl, glossy, bold,
a solo, now as old as I was then.

Make this mug you. With three colours?
But here I am, sunshine with a burnt rim.
These black pictures are my parts:

Kylie Minogue and her microphone,
Villa Laila, the pool, the pine trees,
that's Popa Ted, they're his wings,

Becky, my rabbit; *Jane Eyre,* open;
that's a Cadbury's Crème Egg, frozen.
Joy, Mervyn, Nina, Nanny Nell and Rina.

This mug was me before I knew your name
now I'll make it a vase for your flowers.
First, let's have a toast: to us. Take a sip of me.

LONDON ROUTEMASTER

by Amy Prior

'Sick as I am
confused in the head
I mean I have
endured this April so far
visiting friends'

William Carlos Williams

An ambulance travels high speed down Commercial Street, making a cab driver pull in so sharply to make way he almost swerves into the front of an Indian restaurant. It is 7.18pm, a rainy Thursday night in April, and her breath makes strange patterns on the glass of the windowpane as she views this scene from inside the cosy domestic warmth of her flat. She pauses briefly for a second before hitting the send key. Sadie is emailing Richard Hell, a musician from New York whose CDs were first played to her by a boy she used to like, a boy from school who was chess champion, who was so cool he hardly spoke, the one who was the first she knew to be online. (Later she heard he moved to Tokyo, did sites for Pepsi.) She is asking Richard for an interview for her zine, one she photocopies for free when no one is looking at the offices of the corporate trade magazine publishers where she is temporarily answering telephones. She wants to meet him for a drink, maybe more, now that she sees on his website he is visiting London on tour. She thinks he might be up for it. She hears another siren, goes to the window, sees two fire engines and another two ambulances racing down the street. There's some kind of accident, she thinks, some kind of drama.

Richard Hell is staring at the keys of his laptop in Room 176 of the Great Eastern Hotel. He is wondering what to write next. Maybe he should use emoticons or is that too flirty? Her picture was good, sweet eyes like his first girlfriend Julie in high school, and she knew stuff about his films the others didn't. Once he met one of his online girls in a bar in Virginia who said she wanted to interview him for her dissertation on 'The Female Gaze and Rock 'n Roll'. He thought otherwise, but she really did just talk about her college courses, then asked him about the seventies, about the Blank Generation and what it was like living through all that and he paused and thought, then said, well it never really disappeared. He stares at his screen. It stares back. He lies on the bed, looks up. The ceiling is white, like the whole room; cream towels sit alongside lily walls, white-with-a-hint-of-pink bedspread and beige-white coffee maker and cups.

At that moment his girlfriend Ramona, who has already been away from the Great Eastern far too long just to be picking up some coffee, is emailing in a web café. Her fingers dance across the keys with lightness, but also with speed, like the way her voice became when she spoke to a guy she met at a record company party last week, the one she is emailing now, a music video-maker ten years younger than her, who is still at that brief and almost imperceptible early twenties stage when pretty boy is on the cusp of chiselled man, who sat out with her on the roof of 93 Feet East and rolled cigarettes while her husband was interviewed downstairs by a feature writer from *Rock Classic* magazine. She remembers him touching her hair, brushing it behind her ear when the wind picked up, had revisited this thought several times.

The electric pulse of physical attraction she is experiencing now as she formulates this thought again, moves from her fingertip to the keyboard and then – as she hits the send key – it is translated into more regulated electric impulses that are transported along a route miles and miles from her – first to the service provider in Holborn, then branching out along tightly entwined cables of tiny diameter. At that moment the web café is playing host to numerous other electric connections between lovers substitute, future and potential, networks of intimacy-at-a-distance communications from this tiny corner of East London; connecting up people right across the city so they are almost touching.

Though the place is in the main still, quiet, there is an oppressive background hum of keyboard movements, occasionally punctuated by short beeps of electronic affirmation, detraction or confirmation. A hundred, maybe more, bodies together in this strip-lit space, a flickering host for flickering screens and eyes (some tight and sleepless but coffee-sustained for hours through the night); some darting from screen to webcam and back again as if they were frightened animals caught up somewhere against their will, occasionally some furtive communication between them – signalling a hot photo of some body, a flirtatious email.

Jane, aka gothteen66, whose long-sleeved top hides a criss-cross history, posts intense messages to reno99 in an unspecified city location on the

Suicide.net noticeboard. Later they will meet, and it will transpire that reno99 is, in fact, in-between tenancy agreements so that the next day she will move in with gothteen66 who lives alone even though she is only seventeen years old, on account of being recently re-housed in a council flat to escape a step-father who used to black her eyes. Reno99 takes the sofa bed in the living room, and gothteen66 loves to have her around; most nights they sit close on the sofa watching soaps and quiz shows until after one, but after a few months gothteen66 starts to get annoyed at the way reno99 leaves her clothes lying around the kitchen, rarely buys bread or Coke or other foods, spurns contributions to the gas bill, the end coming soon after the time when gothteen66 comes back home early from her retail job in a supermarket to find reno99 on the Internet when she is supposed to be at work (the nature of which is unclear), specifically in chatrooms, and it becomes clear that reno99's attentions are now focused onto other suicidegirls and boys, and she moves out soon afterwards having acquired a copy of raya101's housekeys. Later, gothteen66 will end up in casualty suffering from hypothermia, having trailed the streets of London in bitter winter sleet trying to find her love that never happened, and this will continue to be the pattern for a number of years until someone kind and wise and much older than her intervenes. But this is before all that, before all these difficult things, when gothteen66 is just a pale, etched sliver of an unknowing girl, who is calmly sitting here typing in a strip-lit room with strangers.

And in a corner directly opposite her, though unhampered by the close attentions of other users and close to the gentlemen's toilet facilities, is Jesus Magdelanio, part-time English language student and waiter who has purchased the attention of Sabrina on SEXYCHICKS.com (off-line Shirley of Hackney) and is in lengthy and urgent discussion (where spelling and grammar have become quite irrelevant) regarding his current pleasure requirements. Shirley is glancing up at the clock as she is typing, calculating when she should wake her baby for a feed. Her job is a secret from her boyfriend, though unfortunately for her, it is not one that will be kept much longer.

In the other corner of the web café sits Melissa, currently studying communications at graduate level, who is mailing Charlie about flyer design for an arts project, but it is not actually about flyer design, though neither of them is aware of the fact at this moment; it is only something that will become clear in retrospect, after months of emailing and dates that are not classed as dates but meetings, ones that start with lingering glances at inappropriate moments over lemon and ginger tea, end being meetings of souls, so the flyers never get done but they do end up living in a studio just off Hackney Road, quite happily for a short while.

Outside now, Ramona rushes back to the Great Eastern Hotel, her passage across the highway blocked by lanes of traffic slowing to a stop and now an ambulance turning into the junction, then another waits behind, some kind of talk of a situation eastwards she hears but it is fleeting because she speeds by, making up time, her coffee under her arm, her eyes on The Great Eastern Hotel sign up ahead, her mind on her boyfriend's face, the way he will look when she walks through the door and smiles brightly. I had to walk three blocks for this, she will say breathlessly (though not suspiciously so) handing him the package, waiting for a reaction, and it's not Columbian.

The pretty boy, the recipient of all Ramona's mis-spent attention, whose online name is teenstar, whose real name is Lloyd, is at that moment, looking with his pretty eyes at the blog of someone he's never met. He feels like an intimate friend of this girl, though it's a relationship without the commitments of the real. He likes this, what's good is that he can check her out at a distance. He already knows Amber likes the same films as him, so that is a start, but he is worried about her obsession with Cindy Sherman, the way she snacks on pork scratchings for breakfast. He will have to take that one further, but not now. He is tired still from the club last night. He sits, a slight figure, clothes hanging off his thin frame, a loose arrangement of fleece materials, longish hair dangling down shapelessly like when he was a kid. The kind of androgynous look that's so fashionable at the moment he gets attention from style-magazine photographers when he goes out, which he simultaneously courts and spurns. He sucks on a cigarette slowly, flicks the ash on a textbook beside the monitor. He has just finished art school, is working part-time in a video shop, and looking back on these years later, he will view them as the slow ones, the ones where most of his key career choices were made without much deliberate thought or action.

At this moment, from her houseshare in Henage Street, Amber is updating her blog. Someone is calling her to watch *EastEnders* on TV in the other room, and there is dinner waiting. OK, OK. Amber has been typing her entries and emails for so many hours the joints in her fingers ache and her eyes are glazed over, straining to see the words on the screen. When she goes to eat finally, one part of her is in the real world, one part is still in the virtual. She will watch *EastEnders*, forking some tuna salad into her mouth every so often, but her mind will be on her In-Box, imagining electronic replies. She has an addictive personality. This is something a therapist will tell her later – and there are no boundaries to its nature. The TV will hum like constant background chatter, but over the top there'll be something else, the whir of helicopter blades circling up above the roof. She will hear them, and for a moment be distracted from the screen, then look outside. There is a kind of glow in the sky, a kind of dazzling, like there are searchlights or something.

Online at this moment and reading the blog a few streets away from Amber is Sadie who, through lack of an immediate response from Richard Hell, has begun to check up on people she has never met to see how they are doing. On an entry that interests her, she stops reading, briefly touches the glass of the screen, lacing her fingertips around its rounded corners, tracing a circular path that loops text and image and coloured advertisement. Then they move to a stuffed toy animal, a sloth, on top of her monitor, a present from her first boyfriend, who is helping the less fortunate make local communities in India, has been for two years now. You could have worked here, she always said. She'd just moved to London from the south coast, didn't know too many people. For a while they mailed, him snatching turns on an old Mac in an iron-roofed back-street – but long-distance never works. She picks up the animal, smells it. She can still sense his scent, like a mixture of smoke and joss sticks and cheap cider. She used to dream about him traipsing dusty tracks, on his face that intense frown he always had starting to etch lines on his forehead. Now she has begun to have a recurring nightmare. Always the same scenario: the whole world had been blown up two years ago, right to smithereens, and everyone was just floating around on parts like they hadn't even realised what had happened yet.

There's been some kind of accident, some kind of problem, that much is clear. In the next street traffic has almost slowed to a stop, and helicopters fly overhead to record the situation for the radio news. Things are not good: an aerial photo shows problems on routes within much of the London Orbital. A light map of traffic flow shows some continuous currents westwards, allowing for roadworks, but eastwards there is disruption in the charge of cars, interruptions in the chains of vehicle lights at certain points, and one black insulated spot where their conduction has completely malfunctioned. And it is here Sadie stands now, finally aroused from her virtual world into the real one by the sirens nearby. The fire engines got there too late, too much traffic with people coming home from work, and the flames are touching everything. Some kind of problem with the electrics, they said, some kind of short circuit, two wires meeting when they weren't supposed to.

On-lookers gather at the fringes: a teenager walking home past curfew hour; a man in a wig and stilettos going to a club where he would speak to no one, where he would sit sipping rum and coke in the corner all night on a high stool, legs crossed awkwardly to hide re-growth; a Bengali kid, fifteen, weaving his way in and out of the cars to get closer to the spectacle, his pupils dilated so the vision appears lighter and more dazzling than the real thing, like it is a kind of apparition or something.

An elderly couple next to Sadie are so shaken up they hold on to each other tightly, and after a while she takes them home to their flat, part of a block similar to the one that's been ruined. Standing in the kitchen, searching for glasses, Sadie hears the couple's voices, calm again in the other room, something about blackjack and poker, and remembers briefly her grandparents, the way they played patience for hours – outdoors in summer. There was nothing they liked more. She sees them on the patio with sunhats and iced tea, the way one's eyes would take quick glances at the other's hand, then read their face to second-guess the next move. She pours Bourbon into a tumbler, hears ice cubes fracture, little hairline cracks that grow then slowly melt away.

EAST MAIDENS
by Miranda Doyle

1938

EAST MAIDENS: Triple flash every 20 seconds. Visible only from S.23°E through S.17°W over Russell & Highland Rocks. White Tower. Black Band. Height: 95 feet.

At the foot of the lighthouse crouched the dwellings. The swell of the tower thickened at its foot, dwarfing Michael Doyle, the Assistant Keeper, in shadow as he passed between its curve and the line of the cottage where he slept. The buildings were penned from the sea and the crude jumble of rock by a white wall. Their light marked the Maidens, a hazardous group of islands and reefs, twenty miles north-east of Larne on the Northern Irish coast.

The East Maidens rock jutted out of the surf no more than eight metres, and grew slick and black as the tide rose. Beneath the breaking water lurked a chaos of whirlpool and swell, churning the limit of this tiny island white. There was no seaweed, no mark of high tide, for the water scoured the rock till it was clean. Even with their marker, the black scars of the Maidens' rocks had holed a fleet of ships: amongst them the Maria and Sumatra, square riggers lost in 1882; the Housatonic, the Dalriada, and the Albia, all wrecked after 1908; finally the Norseman, a steamer, which ran aground in December 1916. She lay a few yards from Michael's feet in six to ten metres of water, badly broken against the rock.

As Michael slipped beyond the wall's boundary, it was low tide, September 6th 1938. Europe argued over Germany's annexation of the Sudetenland, whilst in the Atlantic a weather system that had developed off the coast of the Western Sahara was travelling at speeds of up to sixty miles an hour. It was on its third day, and would continue its journey across the ocean, reaching America's eastern seaboard on the twenty-first. There it would drench Rhode Island in ten feet of water and kill over five hundred people as it hurtled past.

But on this particular morning dawn was crisp in the Irish Sea, a ripple of red weakening in the east. The lantern was quiet, the clatter of its clockwork silenced. Michael saw the shadow of Fiddler Boyle, the Principal Keeper, in the lantern as he prepared the light for the next night.

Michael walked down the steps to the water, and clambered round the rock.

He was a tall man, over six feet, with a thick thatch of red hair, bleached to the colour of sand. His hands were coarsened by years of sea work, each long finger marked with nicks and lines. The skin, parched by salt and sun, appeared decades older than his forty-one years.

Michael paused. A stonechat, its bulbous belly in soft ochre, sat agitated on the wall above him, stretching and pulling its squat wings like an accordion. And some feet away there was a chaffinch, the length of its tail brushing the stone. He must remember to enter them in the bird book. They were the first he had seen on the rock in days. Both rested, gazing towards the distant land.

It was relief day. His six-week sentence on the Maidens would end late morning when the inky speck of the relief boat was spotted against the horizon. Then, Michael promised himself, he would enjoy the last hour that it took for the boat to darken and swell till it was near enough for him to hear the splash of its oars against the sea.

Michael sat down. In his hands was a ledger, its pages filled with pale blue squares. He sat two feet from the rising sea, sheltered by the wind, which strengthened from the north. His pencil meticulously sharpened, he began to write. Where once the words were sparse so that the whiteness of the page eased his writing with light and space, now the boxed paper darkened beneath his hand. He liked the confinement of those vertical and horizontal lines and with his fingers tight to the raw wood of the pencil's end scratched ferociously between borders of blue.

His poetry no longer had form. Over the months he had lost the ability to shape it. Poetry allowed words to dangle into the empty space of the page, like a limb slung out of bed. He wanted his words to be fettered by one another, their tails and strokes overlapped. In this blank landscape of the Irish Sea, Michael felt like one comma on a clear page. To stay even another day, he thought, would be to leak into the vastness of sky and sea. Already he felt their whiteness upon him, skin pickled by a salty scum.

Behind him a rock pattered on stone. Then a second. Michael scrambled to his feet.

A third. His eyes skating back and forth, he turned to see a fourth bounce against the tower. A figure stood on the wall. Nelson, a slingshot tucked beneath his arm, balanced along its ledge. The other light keeper bounded up onto the roof of the dwelling where he stooped to retrieve his target: a pigeon, its breast feathers tousled by the wind.

'Doyle?' Nelson shouted.

Michael ducked down, crouched against the rock.

'Is that you? Come out, man,' said the younger keeper as he swung off the building with a thud onto the compound floor. 'Perhaps there'll be relief for you today. The sea is not moving round the way it was.'

Nelson, not able to see the older man hunched in against the wall, snapped the gun together and took the bird inside.

Michael slumped down. Forty-eight days on the rock. In the past he had sent up prayers to God that his relief would not to be overdue. But after fifteen years in the service he no longer prayed. He was at the mercy of that other god, the sea. He looked up. The morning did not taste the way it should. High overhead birds flew landward. Clouds were ragged. Perhaps there would be more wind, but he must not think on it. He opened his ledger, a third of the double page filled with microscopic words and, picking up his pencil, attempted to write on.

Yet words no longer worked. He had tried speaking, but his wife, Rose, and the other keepers folded his words back for him in different tones, undigested. His despair ran off them like fresh water down a windowpane. No salted mark. Words were without meaning. The slim margin of white page glared. Perhaps it had more sense than the letters filling it. He tried to erase white with black, each word stitched closer to the next. The ruled squares were choked with his striving for sense, but the page's emptiness glowered through.

He blinked. The sea, which crawled towards him over the rocks, was indistinct. Michael rubbed his eyes and got to his feet. Though he could not face it, he sensed by the gathering stillness that there might be no relief today. Tiredness overwhelmed him.

He must lie down.

The Principal Keeper had joined Nelson in the dwelling kitchen when Michael edged past his colleagues to bed.

'They'll be rowing towards us now, Doyle,' said the Principal. 'You're needing a bit of time ashore.'

Michael stopped in the doorway. This pair were fools, talking about relief. Michael sensed change like a distant song.

'Sit down man. Have yourself some tea.'

Michael hesitated. He was unsure how to excuse himself, and yet he was thirsty. He felt anguished. There was only one conversation he was able to have and he was sure they had no desire to hear it. Nelson patted the third chair. Michael sat down. He placed the ledger on the table and watched as the tea was poured. Principal Keeper Boyle added milk and slowly stirred before pushing it towards Michael.

The two men were talking. He could not follow what was said and, exhausted, watched the brown circle of tea wobble to stillness. Sensing their attention upon him he looked up. Their words seemed to swell and dim, like echoes. He would try again. Use words. Simple words to articulate despair.

'I cannot stay here.'

'As soon as the relief comes, Doyle, you'll be off,' said the Principal Keeper. He strained to look through the window. 'Though it looks now like the wind is picking up.'

'I cannot stay out on this godforsaken rock another day.'

Uncomfortable, Nelson leaned forward and touched the ledger.

'What are you writing, Michael?'

Michael looked down at the book. He opened it. Tearing a two-inch strip from the first page he stuffed it into his open mouth and began to chew. The bare dryness of the paper clumped on his tongue. He worked the pulp between his teeth, masticating words to a moist grey lump, and tore the sheet again. And again, eating as though he starved.

His life was a knot of mush. It thickened with each page, and each day till he choked.

'Nothing,' he said. 'It means nothing.'

'No. You must not feel that,' said Nelson, looking at Boyle for support. 'I am sure Mrs Doyle reads those long letters of yours over and over.'

Michael realized he should not have spoken. Words provoked more words. They believed they could fill the cavity with the sound of themselves. He stood up and leaving behind him the torn ledger walked the bare corridor to the foot of the light tower. There, he circled up the stone steps, fatigue causing him to lean against the curve of stone as he gazed up to the light. Out of a square window behind him, the stonechat and chaffinch flew west towards land.

In each of the lighthouses where he had been stationed Michael felt there was little privacy from the other keepers in the dwellings and no shelter beyond the tower. He was drawn up to the lantern, a window in the sky. There, crouched on the floor of the gallery, his back to the glass that encased it, he sat amongst the landscape of sea and clouds. In the hours between dawn and dusk there was a different quality of light from that which spun across the night sky. Sun reflected in window and prism, its rays iridescent, glancing through glass.

Up in the lantern Michael was bound like a sheet in light, oblivious to the poison which leaked from the lens's mercury pool.

Michael was woken where he lay on the floor of the gallery by a thud. Something had hit the glass. He climbed on all fours out onto the balcony, a platform ringing the exterior of the light tower.

He circled, the stillness broken by the livid cries of a bird. On the west side lay the broken body of a chaffinch. It had struck the lantern and fallen, still warm. Michael picked up the soft taupe form, no bigger than his palm. He pulled one wing out, admiring its concertina of brown and white and slipped the body into his pocket. The agitated calls of another bird bleated on. The stonechat, with its tiny upright body, wings twitching, hopped about the floor of the balcony.

Michael looked down at the rock beneath him. Boyle and Nelson, on the roof of the dwellings, watched the horizon to the southwest where a boat, its sails almost flat to the sea, tacked towards land. The blue of the day had been devoured and cloud, swirling like a sandstorm, towered over the sea, bilious and dark. Between it and them, the air had turned a sickly yellow. Thunder echoed from the shore, each clap nearing the rock. Then from beneath the rolling darkness a wild stick of white struck the sea. Nelson gestured to Boyle and they jumped down onto the wall and from there to the ground. The younger man looked up and saw Michael. He signalled with his arm beckoning. The wind was now strong, and nothing could be heard but the howl in Michael's ears, and the rattle of the glass above him. Exhilarated, he watched as Boyle pulled Nelson towards the door of the dwellings, the young man's mouth opening and closing like a fish in a jar. Michael's eyes slid back to the horizon where the cloud swelled to east and west, swallowing all light.

The sky had fallen upon the sea.

The waves were torn to white, their rhythm gone. They turned upon themselves, tangled, and bulged in messy knots. Uneven the swell crashed over the wall of the compound three times in quick succession and then not again for many minutes. In the distance, the boat, no longer able to beat a path to land, knocked to port and starboard, its mast lashing the sea on either side. Spray hissed against the stone of the tower and then rain fell.

Pushed back against the glass of the lantern, Michael closed his eyes. No longer able to hear the incessant calls of the stonechat, he let the rain scrub despair from him, and the wind sear his mind clear.

A crack of thunder exploded overhead. Lightning neared.

Oblivious, Michael, his clothes pasted to his body, let the weather pummel him, soothed like a child in a towel rubbed hard.

Down in the dwellings Nelson drew his gaze away from the window, and watched the echo of the heavy sea in the circle of his mug. The tea pulsed. Beside him the round face of the Principal Keeper was up close. He leant into the table as if he was trying to prevent the capsize of a boat.

'I tell you, Nelson, when lightning strikes, it leaves not a mark on the body, but blows a man's clothes right off.'

Seven miles away on the mainland, in the keeper's dwellings at Ferris Point, Michael's wife, Rose, swept her eight children beneath the kitchen table. She had covered the mirror with a blanket. All that glinted, the scissors and knives, were wrapped in socks and thrust into drawers. For those possessions that shined attracted the gleam of the devil, forking out of the sky. Then, with her foot, she pushed the door open. It let the lightning out easy.

On the stone floor of the kitchen, whilst the baby mewed and the wind stripped the hair from their faces, Rose's terror conducted through her children. A primal fear they shared till their deaths: the darkness that brings unruly light.

GREEN and PURPLE

by Gethan Dick

GREEN

I can tell you exactly when it was that my sister and I stopped making sense to each other. No, I can't, I can tell you exactly when it was that I realised that my sister and I had stopped making sense to each other. When we were little it was fine, like peas in a pod, that's what they said, before we sprouted up. Sometimes, when I look at photographs of us when we were small, sometimes, in the wooden-ness, you can't tell who's who. Unless you can see the eyes, hers clear and pale and mine with that weird leafy light behind them. People sometimes ask if they're tinted contacts. Pete, a guy I used to work with, said it was because of the chlorophyll. Chlorophyll is what I do, the biochemistry of greenness as a measure of plant health: vert, verdure, verdant, good, better, best. Designing sliding scales from verdigris to malachite, holding sample slips up to verlot's mugwort, sweet vervain, gooseberry and mint to measure their vigour. So Pete thought that looking at it all for so long meant my eyes soaked up the colour. His eyes were brown. Ha ha. Anyway, my eyes were the why of when I found out that my sister and I had stopped making sense to each other.

The restaurant she had decided on had things drizzled on the menu. Not actually, drizzled on the menu, you know, 'braised fennel with spinach drizzle'. Sometimes in French. Except there didn't seem to be a French word for drizzled. Drizzlé? Maybe.

It smelled nice though, of olive oil and apples.

I could tell she had arrived because people stared at the door, which I wasn't facing, so I had to tangle myself round to see. The Whiplash Kid, that's what they used to call her when we were in school. I used to hear them say it because nobody ever grafted her onto me. A waiter appeared, and she managed to make waving while taking off a coat look graceful.

The Whiplash Kid, I could see it in her walk towards the table. Because that's what makes her blonde and me fair, her slim and me skinny, it's movement. Something sap-like and willowy. She is to me as wind on a meadow is to mown hay.

She folded herself into the chair like something blooming in reverse motion.

'So, how are you, my God, it's been, oh. I'm so sorry I'm late. Have you been . . . ?'

'No, I, only,' pointing at the finger-width missing from my wine glass.

'Have you ordered?'

'No, no, I was waiting for you.'

'Ok, right, well.'

She glanced over the menu, sizing it up, 'I'm having the endive salad and the monkfish with asparagus. You?' She said it as if I wasn't me, peeked over the top of the menu as she said it, and I would almost swear she pouted. And said it, coyly is the word I suppose. I suppose she's just used to dining coyly. Of course, I'd been too busy watching her to know what I wanted.

She said 'blanc' to the waiter when she was ordering the wine.

"So, are you still working on . . . the same thing?" She has no clue what I'm working on. She knows I do something in a white coat with plants and possibly microscopes, that's all. I've never managed to explain it any better to her. 'Yes,' I said, 'yes still the same project, we got funding to continue, so we're going on to work with a bio-luminescent that combines with chlorophyll, for nocturnal crop monitoring.' I was boring her, I knew I was boring her. 'Cool.' She always says that when I'm boring her. So I asked her what she was doing. Though, of course, I know, because the guys at work keep me posted with information from papers that I don't bother reading. The food arrived. I think she was name-dropping, but I don't know any of the names. If a name drops in the forest, and nobody knows who it is, does it really make a sound?

Then, 'Did you get your hair cut? It looks lovely. I found this really good hairdresser, I'll give you his number if you like. He's just fantastic.' Popping a piece of asparagus into her mouth. I wonder if she practises that move in front of the mirror.

'Really? Well, I don't have much time at the moment. I'm going to be off to Scotland on Thursday. Maybe when I get back.' She'd die if she saw how I cut my hair, lopping it off, pruning it back from my face with the kitchen scissors.

'Holiday?' She grinned, slid her eyes sideways, 'Dirty Weekend?'

'Bio-conference.'

'Oh. Well, wouldn't you like to get it done before? Wow all those professors? Or don't they take you seriously if you don't look like you've been out in a field all night measuring lettuces? It's a shame really, that you don't get more of a chance to dress up.'

'I don't mind, I've got it easy, jeans, trainers, white coat.'

'Yes, I suppose. There's nobody looking at you really.'

Maybe I don't bother because I'd look like a callow copy. Maybe I look like a callow copy because I don't bother. She started fooling with her hollandaise.

'Are you going to have dessert? I was sort of thinking about the lime sorbet.'

'What? Oh. Uh, I don't remember what there was.'

I feel like I've escaped now, shortcutting home through the park. She probably does too, speeding away in her taxi.

As I said, I can tell you exactly when it was that I realised that my sister and I had stopped making sense to each other. I was fifteen and she was fourteen, and it was a summer Friday evening. I was sprawled under the open bedroom window, staring up through the leaves of the tree outside. She was at the mirror trying out different hairstyles. Every time she tried a new one she'd ask me what I thought. Then she called me over to hold a tendril of hair while she twined it in place. I was watching her in the mirror, the bud of bottom lip clamped between her teeth. When she got the sprig of hair pinned in, she looked at me in the mirror, but she wasn't looking at me. And she said, 'They gave you my eyes, you know.'

Sometimes I imagine that she hasn't looked me in the eye since. Sometimes I think I'm not imagining it.

PURPLE

What I've learned from last Monday is… Jesus, I don't know. No, I do. I've learned that if you lie in the bath and drink the best part of a bottle of wine and then pull the plug out you can feel your body getting heavier and heavier as the water drains away. It's not much, but it's something. Apart from that I feel like all I've done is unlearn. Unlearn self-defence for beginners and six sessions of Alexander Technique. Unlearn three years of feminist theory in art and The Female Gaze. Unlearn probably a lifetime of feeling, well, not exactly invincible but something not a million miles from it. I don't know how to explain it. I don't even know what happened. I mean, I know what happened, but I don't know what happened.

I work at home. I do wallpaper designs, not the blocking, the painting. The colouring in. I do it freelance so there's not a lot of money in it but it's nice work. Anyway, my studio is pretty much my flat, so I work at home and most days at lunchtime I walk down my street and along the road at the end of my street to a café and I have my lunch there. It's just an excuse to get out of the studio; it's nice, if you're in the same room all day every day, to get out for a bit. And they do stuff on tomato bread, which is a deep dusty orange, and almost matches the plaster-stripped walls.

So on Monday I was doing what I always do and walking along the road on the way to the café and this bloke pulled up beside me in a busted-up old bottle-green car and asked me for directions. I didn't recognise the name of the street he was looking for so I sort of shrugged and said sorry and I was about to walk off when he said, 'No, wait, there's something else.' I leaned down again and looked at him in what I hoped was an 'I-want-to-go-now-but-what-do-you-want' face and he said, 'please don't think it's weird, but, where did you get your tights?'

They were purple tights, a warm-toned purple, with maybe a touch of damson round the ankles where the fabric didn't stretch too much. I'd got them in Top Shop and I told him that.

'Top Shop,' he said, 'I've looked there. Did you get them recently?' I hadn't, I'd got them months ago. I think by now I was looking at him oddly and thinking why was this guy interested in my leg-wear. He must have noticed because he started to explain. 'You see, I'm a fashion design student and the project I'm working on is all tights, it's a big collage, made of tights, and they're all different colours, except I haven't been able to find purple ones anywhere. I've looked in lots of places and they don't have them. And, please don't think it's weird, but, can I buy your tights off you? I'll give you twenty-five quid for them.'

I was sure it was a set-up. That morning I had discovered that I was twenty-five pounds overdrawn at my bank. I'm not authorised for an overdraft and they were going to start fining me if I didn't pay up, and I couldn't pay up until they cleared the cheque for the last batch of designs I sent in. I only had enough small change for lunch. So I was sure it was a set-up. I looked carefully at the clutter in the front of the car and tried to look smart and said, 'OK, where's the hidden camera?' He said 'What?' I told him about the bank and the overdraft and the fine and all that and he said, 'No. No hidden camera. You need twenty-five quid and I need a pair of purple tights. Just blind luck.' He was smiling.

I still wasn't certain that it wasn't a set-up but I said 'OK.' I don't live far away, I'll go home, I'll change my tights and then I'll come back and you can give me the twenty-five pounds.' I turned round and headed back up the road towards my street. I figured I didn't have anything to lose, even if it was some sort of 'You've Been Framed' thing. I could just imagine some sort of weird publicity campaign that would involve stuff like that.

As I walked home I started to think it probably wasn't though. You remember that ad where a girl steals a pair of pale-pink granny-knickers off a clothesline and gets the man in the paint-shop to mix her up the exact same colour so she can paint her flat – I always knew exactly how she felt. Sometimes you see things that are just so the right colour that you have to have them. I bought a hideous print of horses from a pound-shop once, just because it had a beautiful violet sky in the background. And, even though I can't stand the taste of them, I'll buy aubergines because I have a cerise fruit-bowl and they just look perfect in it. So by the time I got home I was feeling all kind and virtuous inside that I was helping somebody who understood all these things about the right shade in the right place.

I took the tights off, put them in a plastic bag and pulled on a pair of jeans. I went back down the street and out onto the road where the car was waiting. I walked up to the car and looked in the passenger window and the man smiled at me. I handed him my tights and he handed me the twenty-five pounds. Then I was fiddling about for a bit; getting my purse out of my handbag and the money into the purse and then putting the purse away again.

When I got myself all organised I looked up to tell him thanks and that I hoped his collage went well. And he was, I think what they say is he was, you know, finishing. Into the tights; white onto purple.

I couldn't move. I just stared. He looked up at me and I think he might have been about to say something but I said, 'I have to go now!' I ran down the street and jumped on a bus that was stopped at the lights. I went and sat upstairs and tried not to think of anything. I stayed on the bus until I saw a branch of my bank from the window and then I got off. It seemed like the only thing I could do with that money. I couldn't have bought something to eat or wear with it. I just had to get rid of it. I don't remember much about waiting in the bank except not wanting to touch the notes as I handed them to the cashier.

I just feel so stupid about the whole thing. Stupid for having somehow consented to something without meaning to, stupid for thinking I consented to anything. Which I didn't, I mean, if he'd said, 'Can I buy your tights for twenty-five quid so that I can have a wank into them.' Would I have said yes? Not bloody likely. But it still makes me feel stupid. Stupid that I haven't gone down to the café since or worn purple or tights and can't even imagine replacing the ones I had. Stupid for avoiding amethyst and lavender and mauve and lilac and indigo and all of them in the design I'm meant to be working on. Stupid for having done it. Stupid for letting it make a difference. Stupid for feeling stupid.

All I've learned is how to lie in an empty bath and feel completely, completely stupid.

AFTERLIFE

Strange how my hair keeps growing,
spreads a shield of copper gauze

across my brow. My nails, too, lengthen
into brittle scimitars.

I try out new verbs, learn
to time-shift, swing jive, text. The pile

of bills, notes, pizza menus, parking notices
rises beside the stripped pine door,

even though you are gone.

HOLE

This earth's an icy bell.
The spade stutters. Chimes.
Opens a hole the length of you
when you were still full size,

and then some, six feet long,
six down. When I was six,
my heroes fell from rooftops,
bridges, aeroplanes,

through windows, leaving holes
their height, their shape, from which
there'd presently emerge a hand,
an elbow, then a grinning face,

not harmed, no damage, ready right away
to rise up, whizz off, trailing
fluffy puffs of smoke –
and words too. Vroom! Zoom! Wheeeee!

I slice down harder, further.
These cold earth walls are steep.
There's this hole in the world the shape of you.
It stays so empty. And it stays so deep.

MEMORY BANK

They're expensive, those shared moments.
They will be re-possessed. Your brief
has made this clear, and you are eager
to pursue my debts. A joke repaid
for every lie. Elephants, armpits, duchesses
shoved into tea chests, bundled into vans.
For each *wrong number* call, a page reclaimed:
that black tomcat we called Otis;
crescent moon ear-rings I won't wear again.
For each adulterous glance, a photo ripped
from the album: your ma and mine
in hats and heels, exchanging grins; my arm
slung loose around your father's waist.
A hotel night two miles away from home
costs three months' bedtime reading: *Steppenwolf;*
the first volume of *Gormenghast, White Fang.*
The lost weekend in Amsterdam? Oh God,
that one's priceless. The stages of my breath.
The tender stubble on his crown, minutes
out of the ambulance; that trough
between two waves, his headlong dive, the way
she placed him in your arms, his grip, his gaze,
my hand pressed close on yours, rough cotton gown,
stainless steel, sugared tea, his slippery limbs,
neon. The exact progress of your tears.

WHEN IS A DOOR?

Outside the window,
a strange hillside,
one these legs
will never climb.
The wood's dark verge –
a doe steps out.
I see her print the tip
of one front hoof
into the silver wet dawn grass.
She meets my gaze
and goes.

The trolley rolls.
Tea sloshes
into mugs.
I say *No thanks,*
but too late;
there it stands
all morning, cooling,
painting its white ring
onto the cover of the library book
I don't intend
to read.

The day lengthens
as slowly I unfold
a memory.
Hill-walking,
South Downs wasn't it,
with Arthur
sixty years ago.
I run three fingers over it,
find the rough edge of chalk. Enough.
Tuck it away
before the nurse appears.

Pills tinkle,
bells complain.
A Hoover mumbles
down the corridor,
and in the room next door
the TV drones.

Five in the evening.
At the window once again
armed with bifocals,
I recall my deer.
A holly tree
stands where I thought she stood.
The room darkens.
The walls come close.
At first it's just a tree
guarding a space;
sharp leaves
spiked with green oil.
But now it shines. It shines
and is a door.

A PERFECT DEATH
by Bridget Whelan

My father's last conscious act was to catch my eye and, with a small smile, raise an eyebrow. My mother was adjusting his pillows. Fussing again, he was saying, although by this time his paralysed lips couldn't say anything. It was a humdrum note on which to end a life, but it meant that on the very last day when he could still look about him, still make connections, Jimmy Malone was back. I was very glad he was dying and I was very glad I hadn't killed him.

His last years had been blighted by a savage paranoia. After retirement my parents left London, where they had spent most of their adult life, and returned to County Kerry. My father seemed to settle effortlessly into the village where my mother was born. They had honeymooned there in the early 1950s and returned for their fortnight's holiday every year after that. Together they enjoyed a comfortable life in their newly built bungalow until my father started to make phone calls.

'Do you know what your mother just said?' He rang me in London, as I was getting ready for work. 'Couldn't we put in another socket! Any fool knows that would blow the system.'

'Mum doesn't understand electrics as well as you.'

Silence. The phone had been slammed down.

He would ring again a few days later as if nothing had happened. His conversation became peppered with inappropriate pronouns as the words 'we' and 'our' disappeared from his vocabulary. The man who had never boiled an egg or driven a car now talked about 'my cooker' and 'my Escort'.

Soon the telephone – the only way my sister and I could maintain regular contact – became truly his. By setting up an elaborate wiring system, my father was able to move it from room to room. It meant that he could monitor all my mother's conversations while he was able to make calls as soon as she was out of earshot. His talk became heavier, darker; his anger more focussed. My mother was stealing his money.

'In the long years we've been married not a penny has she put on the table. I kept yous all.' Oh yes, she had always worked as a nurse, he would reluctantly concede that point. 'But in forty years every brass farthing went on driving lessons.'

Worse was to come. He became convinced that she was having an affair. He knew the man. Knew his name. Knew it all.

'She's out now.' His anger would blaze down the telephone wire.

'In town, Dad, in town!' Sitting on the edge of my chair hundreds of miles away, I tried to reason with him. 'She always shops in town on Friday mornings. It's the only time you're apart.'

'I'm not so easily fooled,' his voice was thick with contempt.

I wasn't the only one getting his calls. He was saying the same things to my sister, to our husbands, to nieces and nephews, to his in-laws, to the bank manager and doctor, to the chemist and the village publican. Even now we're not sure what he said and to whom; we conspired among ourselves to keep it quiet. We conspired too to keep the full extent of his malevolence from my mother, who had to cope with his frequent tantrums and serious health problems: prostate cancer, angina and chronic bronchitis all made worse by panic attacks and lifelong hypochondria. We presumed that Alzheimer's should be added to the list, although he always discharged himself from hospital before a firm diagnosis could be made.

His imagination was destroying the foundations of his life and his anger grew daily, encompassing his home, his marriage and his family. All was bitterness. All was betrayal. My sister and I began to fear that he would lash out at my mother; for such an ill man he still had remarkable energy. I wished him dead. To my sister he already was.

'Dad's gone.' She was brisk and practical. 'We have to deal with the man who's taken his place.' Together we contacted the local solicitor and bank manager on our mother's behalf as he talked of selling up and going on spending sprees to spite her.

'Are you scared of him?' young Dr Dooley asked my mother after yet another emergency home visit. My father insisted that all visits had to be treated as an emergency.

She refused to acknowledge the possibility.

'Well, I am,' the GP admitted. 'He's a bully.'

If I had been organised and single-minded, if I had taken charge and not waited for a final stroke, I could have killed him with the chaotic assortment of prescribed drugs he kept by his side. No one would have questioned an overdose, least of all Dr Dooley.

But I didn't. I talked about it and wished that I could. Death was preferable to the life he was living, and the life he was forcing on the people around him. But despite the painful things he said and did, he was still my father. More than that: he was Jimmy Malone and even close to the end he seemed too big a man to die.

My father had no special gifts: he was a Brendan Behan without the words, Count John McCormack without the voice, Jack Doyle without the punch. But all the same there was something about him, and he knew it. Perhaps it was no more than a deep-seated confidence. As a child he had been loved and cherished and petted; the only man in the household after his father, a soldier who served throughout the First World War, died from influenza when he was a baby.

Perhaps it wasn't just the doting women in his life who made him so sure of himself. Perhaps if he had been a few inches taller he might have looked at the world less steadily. At five foot five he made sure people did not mistake him for a small man, because there was nothing small about Jimmy Malone: not in his temper, or his laughter, not in his generosity, his self-centredness or his social grace.

Some boxers punch above their weight; my father had manners above his class. He knew when to say please and thank you, and say it with charm. He knew how to compliment a hostess, praise a host, buy a round and put his hand in his pocket without seeing what came out, and he also knew how to look the part. Never anything more than a poorly paid, semi-skilled worker, he always had at least two 'good' made-to-measure suits hanging in his wardrobe, each one costing more than a fortnight's wages. He never aspired to being more than he was; being Jimmy Malone was enough.

Brought up in a small town in the Irish midlands, he came to England in 1948 with a cardboard suitcase, a few pounds in a back pocket, and instructions to meet a cousin at a station called the Saint. It turned out to be the Angel, Islington. Glad to earn a wage, he coasted round the Irish areas of London, sleeping in comfortless lodgings, part of a drifting generation many of which discovered that, when they had no strength left for labouring, they hadn't paid enough stamps to claim a pension.

What spared him from Arlington House or some other hostel for the solitary Irish male no longer able to work because of age, or ill health? He would have said pride. And he was a proud man. But it wasn't pride that saved him.

It was the two-step.

The foxtrot.

The slow waltz.

Even in his corpulent sixties the magic was there. He could turn and glide, spin and twist and, like a true master, make it all seem effortless. And dancing – with his winning smile, Brylcreem bright hair and those good manners – made him popular with women.

What saved my father was marriage. My mother gave him a future worth planning for and the stability to achieve it. Perhaps he didn't immediately recognise those qualities when they met at a Holloway dance hall – they both told the story of how he turned up for their first date with another girl on his arm – but he must have done soon afterwards. The other girl was ditched; my father found the words to smooth things over and new arrangements were made. Then nothing. They lost contact and my mother, now a qualified nurse, transferred to another hospital. She hoped that she might bump into Jimmy at another dance but never did. He must have felt the same because, eighteen months after their first meeting, he began to loiter outside hospitals.

'Do you know Peggy O' Sullivan from Kerry?' He would ask nurses at the end of their shift. Finally someone did.

If my father's raised eyebrow on his deathbed suggested that his old self had returned to allow him to tease his Peggy one last time and die a gentle death, his last intelligible word had no special significance, although it did underpin the fact that he was dying an Irish death.

Propped up on pillows, my father struggled with a tongue too large for a mouth that would no longer obey him. Finally it came, just one word: 'Liam'. We nodded and he fell back satisfied. In the few hours we were away from the hospital he had had a visitor. Liam, a young man with a young family, was a relative only through marriage and they weren't even on each other's Christmas card list. However, hearing that my father was unlikely to last until the end of the week, Liam drove eighty miles after work to hold his hand for five minutes. And then he drove eighty miles home.

Other people made similar journeys in the days before my father's death. After he slipped into unconsciousness, more often than not Kathleen, my mother's eldest sister, would sit beside him, reciting the rosary. I joined in but, while I could give a convincing performance when following her example, I wasn't so confident about my ability to lead. And that was exactly what I was supposed to do at some stage. Whenever my aunt left the ward my mother scribbled prayers on the back of an envelope and passed them to me. The phrases were as familiar as breath itself: 'full of grace', 'forgive us our trespasses', 'fruit of thy womb', but when it came to what order they fell in I lost faith in myself. The more I thought about it the less certain I became. We weren't trying to pretend that I was a good Catholic – my aunt knew me better than that – but I ought at least give the impression that I had been well brought up.

We sat there, the three of us, around my father's bed as the light of a November afternoon faded to grey. My mother's decade of the rosary was coming to an end. She was trying to slow the pace but it had a rhythm and speed of its own. Soon it would be my turn. As I opened my mouth I wondered what I would say.

My father made a gagging noise and lurched sideways. We rushed to him. Was this the end? Was he in pain? A nurse came and smoothed him back into a peaceful coma.

'Not yet.' She smiled and went.

It was time for my aunt to go.

My father didn't move again for another sixteen hours until his face changed, the flesh sinking into the hollows of the skull underneath. His breathing grew slower and harsher. It stopped, started again, and then stopped forever.

Earlier in the week my aunt had told my mother to appoint a firm of funeral directors; she herself had already ordered a large leg of lamb for the wake.

I was appalled. 'He might recover.'

'I know.' My mother was uncomfortable. She had just picked me up from the airport and we were driving to Tralee General together. Her major concern was finding somewhere that sold hospital equipment. 'A high bed, the adjustable kind, will cost about a thousand I should think,' she told me. 'But I'll need it to nurse him when he comes home.' She couldn't imagine Jimmy Malone dead. All the same, she had followed Kathleen's instructions and made a phone call to a firm in a neighbouring village.

'Of course, we'll come when you need us,' she was told. 'The O'Connors of Firies have always buried the O'Sullivans of Farran.'

'Just as well I rang,' my mother half smiled when she came off the phone. 'Because I'd never heard of that before.'

She made a second call shortly after my father's death and three hours later an O'Connor was on her doorstep. Only two things were needed from her: clothes to bury him in and the exact wording of the announcement to be broadcast on Kerry Radio and published in The *Irish Independent*. Everything else was done: the church booked, the priest engaged and the burial plot acquired. They were especially pleased that my father would have a grand view of the mountains. There was no talk about choosing a coffin. A coffin's a coffin: why wouldn't he have the same as everyone else?

The first of the Mass cards arrived. Brightly printed with saccharine images of Christ, they recorded that a Mass would be said in such a church, on such a date, in my father's name and we knew that soon dozens more would come from the next village, and from across the Atlantic. That evening I started to sort through the family photographs to find a portrait of my father that could be printed onto laminated mortuary cards that we, in our turn, would send to anyone who had made contact. It was a difficult task. We had a generation of pictures to choose from, but in some he was too young and too handsome, in others he was laughing too much, and in nearly all there was a child clambering over his back, sleeping in his arms, or pulling his nose. As I looked at the snaps of my sister and myself on his knee, of the photographs of our own children hugging Grandad, the best of all playmates, I could feel the rough bristle of his chin and hear the nonsense rhyme he would sing.

'The Lord save us, said Bobby Davies.

Lather us twice before you shave us.'

My father died on a Thursday morning and on Friday evening his body was taken from the funeral parlour to lie overnight in the parish church. It was not a journey he had to make on his own. Twenty of our closest relatives gathered in a semicircle around the open coffin two hours before the advertised 'removal of the remains'. As we waited the rosary was again recited and very soon it was my turn to lead. This time, however, my mother and I were prepared. Just as my neighbour's Amens faded away, I bowed my head and covered my face with a hand. My mother patted my shoulder and whispered to the person sitting on my left.

'She's too upset. You take over.'

Shortly afterwards we were able to put our rosary beads away, as the first mourner arrived. A whisper went around the group.

'Who's that? Who's that?'

We discovered that he was the brother of the man in the next bed to my father's at the hospital and, as he shook hands with all twenty in the semicircle, he said what everyone else was to say that evening.

'I'm sorry for your trouble.'

He knelt briefly by the coffin, blessed himself and went. We never saw him again.

They came in ones or twos, then in tens and twenties, forming an orderly queue to shake each hand.

'I'm sorry for your trouble. I'm sorry for your trouble.'

My mother's hairdresser came and my father's chiropodist. Neighbours came and men he had drank with in the pub; distant cousins of my grandparents turned up when it became known that an O'Sullivan was bereaved, and people who had never met my parents who, until that moment were only dimly aware of their existence, arrived because they knew the husband of a sister-in-law. Bereavement rippled out beyond my mother, my sister and myself, beyond our families. He had been more than a husband and a father, a grandad and father-in-law: he had also been an uncle by blood and marriage; a great-uncle; a first, second and third cousin; a brother-in-law; a whiskey companion; a long-ago whist partner in a draughty community hall; a man sat next to at church or nodded to when met in town, and each side of Jimmy Malone was acknowledged.

That night my mother left money behind the bar at both village pubs. Whoever happened to come in was to have a drink on Jimmy. 'It's the last round he'll buy,' she explained.

The next day when the Requiem Mass drew to an end my husband and five other men shouldered the coffin and began their slow, careful procession down the church aisle. A large mannish hand rose from the milling congregation. It belonged to my godmother Hannah and it smacked the veneered lid with a thud. The coffin swayed from shoulder to shoulder.

'A good man gone,' she bellowed.

THE VISITOR

by Sarah Manley

Frank Boyd stood at the kitchen window watching his wife, Louise, pitch tomatoes. He loved the elegant way she repeatedly dipped her long brown arm into the vegetable patch, withdrew blackened tomato after blackened tomato, and knuckleballed the spoiled Beefsteaks into the trash. After ten weeks without any rain to speak of, the tomatoes, so promising and lush on their vines in June, were now fit only for compost. Frank prayed they would be the farm's only casualties, but he wasn't hopeful. In the west field the soybeans hung on barely, barely, but their entire crop of Sugar Beauty sweetcorn had been reduced to a whispering mass of yellow stalks, tender young ears turned to charcoal by the sun.

He looked past the garden and over the field where the green tufts of soybean plants baked in the heat. The flat horizon of soybeans edged into a slab of blue sky, a long stretch of Illinois farmland troubled only by the presence of the occasional pale grain elevator. Out there, it was an hour's drive to his nearest neighbor, nothing to see but yellow signs identifying the variety of corn growing in the fields: DeKalb, Sugar Beauty, Sullivan. No sound but the whine of insects, the distant flash and murmur of semi trucks rolling south on the interstate, the screech of a hawk dipping here and there to spear its dinner.

'These damn things are all ruined,' Louise shouted to him, producing a shriveled bell pepper for evidence. 'What a waste,' she said, chucking it into the growing pile on the compost heap.

'Too bad,' Frank shook his head, and Louise turned back to the garden. He crossed the room and opened the refrigerator to find something to cook for supper. They still had a few steaks in the freezer and good potatoes in the cellar. Onions. Carrots. He could make a nice dinner out of that, something Louise would want to eat. He'd baked a loaf of fresh bread that morning, cleaned the kitchen, put a red-checkered cloth on the table, made cherry pie, new coffee. It was the driest summer on record, but they'd get through. They always did, somehow. No point acting like a spell of weather was the end of the world.

'I got two decent peppers and a small tomato,' Louise announced, trundling into the kitchen, the scorched vegetables between her fingers like billiard balls. Her work boots scuffed over the floor, and she smelled of sweat and earth, the knees of her jeans blackened with dirt. 'If it don't rain soon . . .' she said, glaring at the peppers.

'Now, sugarpop, it could be worse,' Frank said, defrosting the steaks in the microwave. 'A *lot* worse. We just gotta think positive.'

Louise glared at him. Thinking positive was for children. Neither of them was young with it all ahead of them, nor did they look it. Louise was still narrow as a fence post and bold as brass in her trim cowboy shirts. Frank's butt had filled out a little from long hours riding a desk chair, but he knew Louise didn't mind the extra padding or his habit of wearing the long neckties he favored from his accountancy days. 'You can't force a man to be country,' he told her once in his smooth city accent. 'A man is what he is.'

Frank sliced potatoes and put them and the onions onto the hot griddle. Louise ran a hand through her sunburned hair. 'Gonna be a hundred'n five tomorrow,' she said, staring out the window. The land appeared to her as nothing but empty ground. Flat. A flock of squawking crows like black confetti in the air. Cicadas sawing in the trees behind the house. She glanced with weary eyes over her desiccated cornfield, tallying up figures in her head. 'God-*dammit*,' she said, a catch in her voice. Over the field of wilted soybeans, the heat shimmered wetly.

'Don't get too down, butter bean,' said Frank, turning the potatoes with a fork. 'Can't make the rain come by worrying about it. Maybe we ought to say a little prayer.' He put the steaks on and watched them smoke. There was nothing else to say.

Louise folded her hands and bowed her head, eyes screwed in concentration.

The next morning, Frank got up early to make breakfast and do the laundry before the heat settled in. Even at dawn the air was so thick with haze it was hard for him to see the thing moving and groaning out in the yard. A hand over his eye like a visor, he stared out into the yard, noticing a visitor had taken up residence at the foot of the silver birch tree. He put on his boots, straightened his tie and went out with a baseball bat to investigate.

Down at the bottom of the lawn sat something that looked like a man but had four arms and an elephant's head. It wore a crown of many jewels in the shape of a Siamese temple, and baggy trousers made from a sumptuous, marigold-colored fabric. Around its delicate wrists and ankles were jeweled bangles that tinkled when it moved, and the flowered garland around its neck rested on the glossy curve of a rotund belly. Frank swallowed hard, holding up his baseball bat menacingly.

'What's going on here?' he shouted. 'This some kinda joke?'

The elephant-man intruder pulled himself up to a sitting position with a great deal of complaint. One of its long ivory tusks was broken, and its back was injured so that he couldn't move without difficulty. As he struggled in the dust, the bracelets on his wrists flashed and glinted in the sun.

'I'll mess you up good 'less you tell me what's going on here. That you Larry? Dave? You makin' fun of me?' Frank shouted, keeping his distance. There were plenty in town who would play a joke on him, poker buddies who owed him a good kick in the pants. He shook his head to clear the sleep out of his eyes. It could have been any of them in a Halloween costume. But that head sure did look real. The trunk moved. The cheap plastic masks from the K-Mart didn't usually come so equipped, he thought. Frank raised his bat to striking position, afraid to take a swing.

The thing waggled its head from side to side, and said something in an incomprehensible language. It put its many hands up defensively and attempted to stand, but collapsed back into the dirt under the weight of a stiff back.

Louise came out of the house and stood on the back porch in her nightdress. 'Frank! What are you shouting about!' she hollered. 'It's six o'clock in the morning!' She narrowed her eyes at Frank, who hovered over something sitting at the foot of her favorite tree. 'What the heck . . .'

'Louise!' Frank shouted. 'Keep back! I don't know what's goin' on here, but this thing might be dangerous! It might bite you!' He advanced towards the injured elephant-head man, who waved its hands and protested. 'All right,' Frank addressed it cautiously. 'I want you to tell me what you think you're doing in my backyard.'

'Frank!' Louise shouted after him. 'Why don't you let it alone and phone the police?'

Frank dropped his bat. Louise, in such matters, always had the upper hand. He gave the thing a look and walked back to the house in a huff.

By the time the county sheriff turned up at their door, wide-brimmed hat cocked back on his sweaty forehead, Frank and Louise had been staring at the thing so long it no longer seemed worthy of police intervention.

'Louise, Frank,' the sheriff said as he huffed up the stairs to their porch, one hand on the gun in his holster.

'Hey there Spud,' Frank replied and led him out back to where their curiosity was napping in the sun. The sheriff crouched down before it and scratched his head. He looked the elephant-headed man up and down, took in its trunk and broad flat ears, studied the creature's golden jewelry carefully to make sure it wasn't wearing stolen goods. 'Well, I've never seen anything like it,' the sheriff declared, flatly. 'Kinda exotic looking, if you know what I mean. Why's it favoring that back?'

'I don't know,' Frank said. 'Looks like he fell a long way on it.'

'Hmm. Interesting,' the sheriff said, turning over a thought in his mind. 'Say, you two been doin' much praying these days?'

Louise and Frank looked at each other, their sunburned faces wary. 'Well, uh, only for the usual thing,' Louise said. 'Health and goodwill and what have you. Prayin' for a little *rain,* a course.'

The sheriff stood up, righted his hat, and checked under his arms for sweat. 'I don't wanna jump to any conclusions Frank, but I suspect whatcha got here is an angel.'

'A what?' Frank squealed. He had never been a churchgoer, and didn't know what he or Louise had done to warrant a personal visit from an angel.

'Now, don't get excited,' said the sheriff. 'I'm no expert, but I'm pretty sure that thing's, uh, supernatural. Don't know what else it'd be. You say a prayer or two, thing comes out of nowhere, case closed. I betcha he hurt his back fallin' from heaven.' The sheriff said, goggle-eyed. Putting a finger to his lips, he stared into the sky. 'If I remember right, a couple in Centralia had an angel about twenty-five years ago. Glory a God shone bright about him, harp and that. They made a TV movie out of it, Peter Falk was the angel,' the sheriff said, looking at Frank and Louise like they should be impressed. 'I tell you what, Frank,' he said, scratching his neck. 'If it's not an angel, you're lookin' at a spaceman.'

Louise scoffed and waved her hand in the air. 'You gotta be joking. That ain't no angel. It doesn't even look like one.'

Frank put his hand on her shoulder. 'Now Lou, we never saw an angel before, so how do we know?'

The sheriff nodded his assent, and put his hand on Louise's shoulder. 'He's right, ma'am. Maybe you wanna consider callin' in the authorities. A man of the cloth'll set you straight.' He tipped his hat to Louise and made his way back to the squad car. 'Let us know if that thing starts actin' funny, Frank,' he shouted over his shoulder. 'We got stun guns and stuff that'll take care of it in a jiff.'

Frank and Louise both eyed the creature suspiciously. 'I just want to remind you that this was your idea,' Louise said to Frank without blinking.

'My idea!' Frank hollered, throwing up his hands. He peered at the thing and shook his head. The elephant-head man yawned and waggled his trunk. 'I just wanted a little bit of rain, I didn't think God would send an angel!'

Word soon got out that Frank and Louise had a bona fide messenger of God in their backyard, and by mid-morning, everyone in the county knew about their captive phenomenon. People trickled in from neighboring towns and stared at the angel as if he was a circus act. Little kids threw bottle caps at it and poked it with sticks, trying to get it to do something interesting. Men with crossed arms stood wondering what to make of it, their bristled jaws working great wads of chewing gum. Local women marveled at the sight of his spectacular golden jewelry, admiring the way the diamonds and rubies flashed in the bright August sun, and the bravest of them reached out to shake one of its hands.

'Isn't that something,' a woman said to Louise. 'A real, live *angel.*'

The angel wobbled his elephant head and spoke to the assembled crowd in a language that sounded like sweet water bubbling over smooth creek stones, but didn't make sense to anybody. He sat calmly in the dust, surrounded on all sides by curious stares, and even the most skeptical of onlookers was soon won over by his polite manner and charming smile.

Frank and Louise realized the angel had no intention of leaving anytime soon, so they gave it a cushion for its injured back and decided to bring it out a plate of food. Frank cooked up a stew of leftover beef with dumplings made out of flour and egg, and placed it on a tray with a cold can of Schlitz beer. When he set this lavish feast in front of the angel, the elephant-headed man shrieked and scrambled away from it, clutching at its stomach as though Frank had given him a plate of chicken-fried cobra.

'But this is good food! You gotta eat somethin'!' Frank shouted, angry that his delicious meal should go to waste. 'This is nice *beef!* The least you could do is taste it!' He stood in front of the angel, defiantly, as the thing jabbered at him, flapping its hands in the air. 'Look, now, I can't understand what you're saying. You gotta talk *s-l-o-w-l-y*. Don't you speak English?' The angel's golden bracelets and glittering headdress winked in the sun, its four palms pressed together as if praying. Frank bent down to pick up the untouched tray. 'All right, all right. How about if I bring you a few pieces of bread and we'll go from there?' The angel bobbed its head from side to side, and lifted its trunk in a gesture Frank took to be gratitude.

By evening, a whole crowd had gathered on Frank and Louise's lawn from towns as far away as Normal and Cairo. Some brought cameras, others bibles, and one or two even held out vials of holy water and sacred totems for the angel to bless. Penitents crawled across the lawn on their knees to pay homage to it, and a few shuddered and fainted clean away as the power of God coursed through them. Nobody seemed at all bothered by the angel's mysterious costume or language; supposing merely that he was a survivor of some strange celestial conspiracy they did not have the heart to question a creature of heaven.

A television reporter in a candy-pink suit and a lacquered blonde hairdo arrived from Peoria to interview the angel, but when she shoved a microphone in his face and asked him a few questions, she wasn't able to understand his reply. Instead, she interviewed the assembled crowd, all of whom were eager to offer an opinion.

'That ain't no angel. Angels got wings and harps. That's just, uh, somethin' else.'

'That angel's got an elephant head!'

'At last, God has answered our prayers and sent us a sign.'

'So,' the television reporter said earnestly to the camera. 'As you can see, God works in mysterious ways. Mysterious? Or deceptive?' She cocked an eyebrow and looked meaningfully at the lens. 'This is Susie Cunningham reporting from the Boyd's farm. Back to you in the news room, Chip.'

'What are we supposed to do about these people?' Louise asked Frank. 'They're trampling on the flowers, and I bet they all want to be fed. We don't have enough food for a crowd.'

Frank peered out the kitchen window at the mass of people in his yard. 'Let's see if the angel will provide us with a few loaves and fishes.'

The next morning dawned bright and hot, and with it Father Ambrose, the church expert on holy apparitions arrived from Chicago. Over the course of his long career, he had been called out to investigate a number of potato chips and damp patches that appeared in the shape of Jesus, and once had been summoned by the Archbishop himself to ascertain the legitimacy of a vision of the Blessed Virgin Mary that materialized suddenly on the side of a split-level ranch house in La Grange. However, Father Ambrose had never been sent far into the middle of the state for the sake of an actual, corporeal, celestial being, and he was giddy with the possibility.

He emerged from the air-conditioned darkness of his Mercedes sedan and walked around the back of the Boyd's farmhouse. A huge crowd had gathered for the second day to gawp at the angel, and the farmyard had the air of a carnival. He was surprised to see Mennonite women in long dresses and lacy caps praying fervently before it, and to hear a choir from the First Evangelical Christian Church in Petonk singing hymns in four-part harmony. Placards bobbed above the crowd with messages for the angel and names of people who required immediate attention from the Almighty. A hat being passed around fluttered with dollar bills. The angel himself seemed to be enjoying the attention immensely. His back propped against the silver birch, he waved to the crowd and kept time with snapping fingers.

Louise and Frank sat on their porch drinking coffee, already tired of the hoopla. Father Ambrose approached them and introduced himself. 'I've never seen anything like it,' he said. 'How extraordinary. Does it speak? Will it eat?' he asked Louise elegantly.

'It speaks some foreign gobbledy-gook, and we tried to get it to eat something but it won't touch nothing but bread.' She said, crossing her arms in front of her chest. 'We can't make head nor tail of it, but it sure is pretty.'

'It is most unusual,' he said. 'I shall try to converse with it.'

Father Ambrose strode over to the angel and tentatively held out a hand in greeting. The angel pressed its palms together and bowed its elephant head majestically. Father Ambrose said a few words to it in Latin, but the angel only looked back at him blankly. Father Ambrose scrutinized it, perplexed, suspecting that any angel who did not understand the language of the church might be an impostor. He narrowed his eyes and peered critically at the stacks of jewelry on its arms and the ornate crown on its elephant's head. The angel certainly did not appear to be of the customary order, and Father Ambrose wondered if it might not be too worldly to indeed be a messenger of God.

As he puzzled over the being, a child spoke up from the fray. 'If that's a real angel, he should perform some miracles, right?'

'Well, yes, I should think so,' Father Ambrose replied. 'Is there anyone in need of a miracle?'

There was much murmuring amongst the crowd. Finally, a blind woman was rustled up and brought forth.

As the blind woman felt her way bravely forward, the angel sat up straight, his crossed feet resting comfortably on his knees. When the blind woman and the angel were almost nose to trunk, Frank, Louise and the rest of the assembly leaned close to witness an honest-to-God miracle. The blind woman knelt down before the angel, and he put his hands on her face. Not a moment had passed before a large lotus flower sprouted from her navel and blossomed.

A gasp rose from the crowd. 'It's a miracle!' they cried.

'It ain't no miracle!' the blind woman shouted. 'I can't see for shit!'

Father Ambrose sighed and approached the angel, whose hand still lingered on the woman's forehead, and shook his head sadly. 'No miracle was performed here today,' he declared. The disappointed crowd groaned and muttered. He turned his attention again towards the angel, studying its costume and manners carefully, when his eyebrows shot up with sudden recognition.

'I suspect,' Father Ambrose announced to the gathering, 'that the angel may be of foreign origin.'

An audible hush fell over the crowd. 'Foreign . . .' somebody muttered. Suddenly the pilgrims erupted in chatter. 'Foreigner . . .' they mumbled. 'Cheat! Sneak! Impostor!' A great outcry arose, for the farmers and country-folk of the region were more willing to accept a supernatural being than a foreign visitor, and this was more than their overtaxed imaginations could bear. As the sun climbed higher in the sky, the disgruntled crowd began to disperse.

The next morning, Frank and Louise scanned the horizon for rain clouds. The angel had been in their vegetable garden for three days and still the soybeans withered in the field, the remaining blistered tomatoes split and dropped from the vine, the singed cornhusks flaked off the cobs and blew away in the breeze.

Father Ambrose had set up a tent under the birch tree so he could be near the angel at all times, and performed experiments on it. He questioned the angel about philosophy, philology, and theology in Hebrew, Aramaic and Greek, but the angel only replied by wobbling its head good-naturedly, and placing large marigold blossoms into the priest's hand. By now the angel's back, injured by his fall from heaven, had healed enough for him to walk around the backyard, and he toddled about scaring Louise's chickens, the dogs and the few remaining onlookers who didn't care much about either miracles or foreigners but had come to gape at the curiosity anyway. He was gracious enough to do a few household chores, the mending, the ironing, a little light bookkeeping, so that Frank and Louise could be freed up to tend to the farm. On the whole, it was an agreeable arrangement for everyone.

Father Ambrose, after days with his nose buried in weighty texts, had finally discovered that their angel was not an angel at all, but a Hindu god. 'The god of good fortune,' he declared. 'Its name is 'Ganesha.' But I've no idea why it's come. Hindu gods almost never make appearances except in extraordinary circumstances. Surely,' he intoned to the nervous Boyds who had no problem playing host to an angel but were embarrassed at the idea of opening their shabby home to a real Hindu god. 'Surely there is a reasonable answer,' he said, tapping a pencil against his teeth and retreating back to his books.

Louise put on her work boots and went outside to make the yard more presentable for their guest. She didn't know if she believed it was a Hindu god or an angel or merely some quack in an elaborate get-up, but whatever it was she hated the idea that he should be sitting in an unkempt garden. When she passed the angel she dipped into a deep, albeit awkward curtsey, for lack of any other response. The angel bowed its head and pressed its hands together, settling itself for a snooze in the soft grass under the tree.

'Everything alright?' Louise called to him as she trimmed the hedges and raked the grass. 'Got everything you need?'

The angel waggled its trunk and closed its long-lashed eyes.

'Well,' Louise called, 'you just holler if you need anything.'

In the meantime, Father Ambrose had invited scholars from the university to investigate the phenomenon. The scholars, by and large a thin and rapacious bunch, spent their afternoons quoting Heidegger and studying the angel. They attempted to discover if the angel used the toilet, preferred blueberries to sour cherries, or could crack pecans with his trunk. When they were done questioning it for the day, they plowed through the bakery Frank offered them, fantastic feasts of light sponge, fruitcake and buttermilk biscuits with strawberry jam, gallons upon gallons of his strong coffee. Of all the people who had visited the farm to see the angel, Frank disliked the scholars more than anyone. They lounged around all day thinking, books and papers strewn hither and thither over the lawn, and refused to answer questions in a straightforward way.

'Do you want ham sandwiches for lunch?' he asked.

'Ah, good sir, the glorious sandwich, named of course, after the Earl of Sandwich . . .' came the reply, igniting an argument between the scholars about luncheon, history, and existential philosophy.

'Fine. Go hungry then,' Frank muttered, stomping back into the house.

A week after its arrival, the angel had taken to lounging extravagantly beneath the waving branches of the silver birch, fanning itself with a rhubarb leaf. Occasionally, he would traipse through the vegetable patch and conjure up a lotus flower or two from the cracked soil, but they withered almost as soon as they blossomed, so unless you were paying very close attention there was nothing to see. Frank shuttled trays of the cumin-scented flat bread the angel liked best and jugs of cool water back and forth across the yard, making more coffee and cakes for the scholars and skirting Father Ambrose's various long-distance calls to the Vatican. The farm had become more like a fairground, and nobody seemed in any urgency to be on his way. The pilgrims who still came to venerate the angel were happy to take up residence in the far field – forced to remain at a fifty-foot distance by court order – Father Ambrose hinted that he might be more comfortable in Frank and Louise's guest room, the scholars moved into the barn and the angel himself was content to stay put where he was under the tree in the back yard.

Louise decided to get back to work. All the angel business was merely a distraction. She had a farm to run. It was clear that the angel, or whatever it was, wasn't going to bring any rain, and she had wasted enough time with this nonsense. She drove her big John Deere tractor out of the barn and waved back when the angel waggled its trunk as she passed. The soybeans were dwindling in the sun-slaked field. Another day or two without rain and they would be finished. Her tractor rolled through the beans, carefully bypassing the weakest plants. It would be the first time in her family's history that the entire crop had failed. Her father would be so disappointed. All he had worked for was gone. She and Frank had no more credit to extend anywhere. They could sell the tractor, the car, but that would only by them a little time. If the crop didn't deliver, they would have to sell the farm. It was more than she could bear. Louise steered the tractor carefully through the soybean field and pretended to herself that it was only the dust stinging her eyes.

The sun rose higher and higher in the sky until it was night, and the crowds of shouters, leaflet-passers, prayers and starers made their way home to their own beds to dream of elephant-headed angels and a bright and unforgiving sun.

Well after midnight, Louise tiptoed out of the house and made her way across the trampled grass to where the angel was sleeping. As she approached, he opened his benign and sensitive elephant eyes and inclined his head curiously.

In her hand, she held a few blossoms snipped from the marigold plant beside the back porch, and a plate of sugarcoated donuts, which she presented to the angel.

'Here you go. I thought you might want something to eat,' she said, sitting down on the grass beside him. 'Frank made donuts for breakfast, but he won't miss a couple.' The angel pressed his four palms together and bowed his head, gratefully accepting the offering, which he held in his lap but did not eat.

Louise gazed at the stars shining brightly in the night sky. 'Clear,' she said, matter-of-factly. 'It's never going to rain. I guess my soybeans are done for.' She tucked her knees into her chest and folded the hem of her nightdress under her toes. 'I don't know where you came from, or why you're here, or even if you are an angel, but I think you came to us for a reason. I suppose you know things are pretty bad for Frank and me. If we don't get some rain soon we're done for,' she said, looking distractedly over the cornfield. 'This place was originally my granddad's. You probably didn't know that. Course, in those days he only grew corn. It was my dad who put in the soybeans. Yeah, it's a good old farm. I've been here all my life. Never even seen the ocean, if you can believe it.' She looked at the angel, who curled and uncurled his elephant's trunk and encouraged her to continue. 'Look, I don't really know what I'm doing out here in the middle of the night talking to a spaceman from God-knows-where, but if there's anything you can do to help us, anything at all, we'd sure be grateful.'

The angel calmly put his hand on Louise's shoulder, jeweled bracelets tinkling slightly in the evening breeze. As he did, she was filled with the greatest sense of peace and serenity, which made her very, very tired. Her eyelids drooped and she couldn't hold her head on her neck any longer, so she rolled up in the circle of the angel's arms and went to sleep.

She was awakened by something cold and wet on her cheek. With a start, Louise jerked upright. It was dawn. She had slept in the yard all night. Louise turned her head and looked at the angel. He was holding his big elephant's head in hands and weeping. Fat tears rolled down his kind face, dripped from his trunk and broken tusk, and collected in pools on the ground.

'Hey now,' she said. 'No need to get all worked up. I know you're homesick but I'm sure you'll be moving on soon. Your back's much better, there's nothing keeping you here. Don't cry now,' she said, patting the angel's knee, trying to reassure him, but he continued sobbing. As he wept, teardrops splashed on his hands, on his magnificent jewelry, on Louise's hair and the baked ground around him. He bawled uncontrollably, and it seemed like his tears came from the silver birch, and the marigolds and the chestnut tree. Drops of water splashed on the ground, creating little puffs of dust where they hit the parched earth. The angel's shoulders heaved, and a great thunderous sob shook the air around him.

Thunder.

Louise stood up and ran to the middle of the yard just as the sky darkened and cracked open, and at long last came the rain. She stood with her arms held out to the clouds, the warm droplets soaking through her nightdress and coursing down her body, rainwater collecting in her ears, nostrils and open mouth. She cheered, 'Woo hoo!' and kicked up a puddle. The rain poured hard, pounding on the hankering soybeans, drenching the steaming vegetable garden and the wilted flowers on the porch. A sharp smell rose up from the earth as dust turned to mud and the plants and flowers drank thirstily from the sky above. Louise had never been so happy to see thunderheads piling up in the sky. It seemed like the prosperity that had eluded them all summer had finally come to pass. Certainly it was the angel's doing, and she spun around to thank him. She wanted to run and embrace him, to kiss his elephant's head and dance with him in the rain, do great reeling cartwheels across the rain-splattered lawn. But when she turned, he was gone.

Blinking water from her eyelashes, she looked this way and that, but the angel was nowhere to be seen. She hardly noticed the lotus flowers blooming in the vegetable patch, or the marigolds sprouting in the chicken coop drinking up the long awaited rain. She peered at to the soybean fields, around the barn where the scholars slept, towards the house where Frank was just walking out onto the porch, rubbing sleep from his eyes.

Louise whirled around to search for the angel over the cornfield, and that's where she saw him catch a breeze and float up towards the sky surrounded by a bubble of golden pink light. He raised a palm and bowed his elephant's head, a compassionate smile playing about his mouth. Louise bowed deeply in great thanks, and righting herself, waved joyously. 'Ha ha!' she hollered, watching as the elephant-headed man became smaller and smaller in the distance, retreating against the clouds until he was no longer visible. Wiping rain away from her eyes with the heel of her hand, she stood staring at the spot in the sky where she had last seen their visitor, no longer a mysterious curiosity but now only an imaginary golden dot over the horizon of the plain.

LABOURS
by Wes White

Chapter 3

The Hind of Ceryneia

"Noli me tangere, for Caesar's I am,
And wild for to hold, though I seem tame."
– Sir Thomas Wyatt, *Whoso List to Hunt*

1

run. run like a hurricane, run like superman, run so fast and so hard and so long that the running takes over and you're no more than a shell for it. run ninety-nine times as fast as you ever ran before in your life, and once you get that fast, start putting some effort into it. don't let the speed drop over mountains or through swamps; and even so you'll always be the runner-up: you'll always be behind the hind.

2

once glimpsed, the hind becomes an irresistible magnet to her witnesses – her ivory hide between trees, the glint of her hooves and antlers in sunlight. she runs to keep them chasing – there are lions in her wake hunting a meal to end all meals, birds and beetles who don't know why they sprint, and stags who do. the lucky ones lose sight of her – less fortunate followers have fallen dead from exhaustion. they speak her name with their final breath.

3

does a horned hind sound unique to you? and if not, if those horns are made of gold? and if not, if the beast is sacred to artemis, goddess of wild things? maybe so. but however it might seem, she's not a one-of-a-kind hind. she had four sisters just the same, so fleet of foot that the five of them were judged fit to draw their divine mistress's chariot. this one got away: her huntress goddess couldn't hunt her down.

4

whatever happens, don't hurt her. it's against the rules. she's as precious as she is intangible, as fragile as she's treasured. leave a mark on her and what will all that running, all that desperation have been for? at the end of the day, damaged goods. this isn't a test of your destructive powers: it's a test of your humility. you prove yourself here by determination and gentleness. kill that other monster, beat that other beast. let this beauty be.

5

artemis once became the hind herself: chased by giant twins, she took the form of the only one among her subjects ever proven faster than her. elusive? hunting artemis is as much about who to chase as how. some thought her found in eileithyia (olympian midwife), selene (the moon) or hecate (nights without it). artemis was cynthia (the mountain of her birth), delia (the island), phoebe and pythia too. in oinoe, they called her oinatis. it brought her no closer.

6

she's a stream: liquid where you are solid. she's flowing downhill, away from you, and you're going as hard as you can to keep up with her, catch up with her, follow her, go where she's been, move like she's moving. but you're just a rock at the top of the hill, watching her catch the light, watching her carve out her future, and knowing that she'll always stream away from you like this, making your sprinting look like stillness.

7

it is said, as it is of certain other creatures, that the hind laid waste to fields. a bearing of false witness? artemis would have held in low regard bad farmers who blamed their failings on her most sacred beasts. she may even have sent a particular boar in retribution: realised their wolf-cry. or it might be that fields, which cannot chase, wither and die when the hind has been so close – and in an instant is so far away.

8

by way of a body of evidence for those beetles who don't know why they sprint: there is a moth whose ancestors were so profoundly affected by her momentary proximity that they (the descendents) now bear her mark. a moment, and now thousands of years later – who knows how many? – charaeas graminis, noctuid moth (a moth of the night), wears antlers on its wings in honour of her precious antennae, its larvae leave pastures ragged in confusion of her intent.

9

some of the earliest experiments with motion photography demonstrated that when horses run, their feet touch and leave the ground in a particular order, over and over and over. the same equipment used to capture the incapturable cerynian hind would reveal, in black, white, gold and bronze: four hooves in a particular position, all clear of the ground, followed by four hooves in a different position, clear of the ground, and every frame thereafter clear, and never hoof touching ground.

10

look into her eyes. you could do, if only you could put yourself in front of her for long enough, which you could do if only you got close to her, which you could do if only she would stop. they are the wildest eyes that ever darted frantically from one thing to another: you understand nothing in them, from your all-too-thinking vantage point, and she understands nothing in you but that one essential element, your will to chase her.

11

one thing you can be sure of when it comes to speed is that of light. nothing goes faster, and light does not slow, and does not accelerate. but that shine like the sun between branches, the light which meets your eye after bouncing from the metal horns and toes of the hind, you can be sure was glad of its speed on its way to the beast, and sorry to keep it as it travelled thereafter to your retina.

12

be be hind the hind. be be hind the hind. be be be be be; hind the hind the hind; be the hind. (taygete). be the hind. taygete was told she must become the hind when she took the love of zeus upon herself, which was together to have been her punishment and her salvation (a cruelness to be kind). no-one ever documented how the hind felt about this, and in any case, she'd first have had to catch it.

13

while it is thought that the speed of the cerynian deer is such that her gallop would be more aptly named a flight, and certainly no hoof marks have ever been identified, it is also true that the earth over which she runs desires her as much as any pursuant, and stretches up in vain hope of giving the hind leverage. she sprints therefore always over a swell in the ground, and where others would leave footsteps, trails broken soil.

14

the hind's mistress artemis (if the two can so brazenly be said to be distinct) was not the only one to go by pseudonyms. as well as cerynian, the hind was called arcadian – an adjective indicative of the presence of paradise. is that what tugs at those she tows behind her? the little piece of heaven that might be found within her? and, when those who were tugged collapse, breathless, say her name – have they then obtained it?

15

there are many third parties lining the path of the hind who will never know she passed, because they blinked and they missed it. they are simultaneously the least fortunate people she ever ran past, because more beauty than they will see in a lifetime has been before them in an instant, and there will not be another chance – and the most, because they will not long forever for that chance, like those whose eyes were open in that moment.

16

according to the precise position of the hind, at any given moment, and because of the desire held for her by even inanimate constituents of the world, at any given moment, by imperceptible degrees, the movement of the tides, the orbit of the moon and planets, the tendency of compasses to north, the currents of the wind and the leaning of trees will each in their way be microscopically affected, be drawn a fraction's fraction of an inch towards her.

17

there is (although because of the effect she had on lodestones carried by those near, it was hard to be sure at the time) evidence to suggest that on one particular run, she led her pursuants (and you among them) a long way north of the greek soil from which she started. in sweden, where it might be the endless run ended, there live the only deer on earth of which the female half are horned. she was the precedent.

18

she will have passed, to reach those snowy climes, through teutonic nations: that land, germania: through middle europe. there, too, she is remembered. the german stories see antlers on stags, and in this a sign of spiritual sensitivity. they echo in so seeing a fast doe passing through, who wore horns like a stag, and was all spirit. the word antler once meant only the first branch in deerhorn. so, their spiritual resonance was once attributed only to one deer.

19

she's a stream: what stream then? she is called cerynian from the river cerynites, arcadian from the region from which the cerynites flowed. later her being this river was to come to her aid, when beneath a tree whose fruits camouflaged her horns, the deer-shaped restlessness rested, and was protected by another river-creature wrapped around the tree. deer and dragon knew each other wholly, instantly, having in common a goldenness, the fact of being strange, and embodiment of moving water.

20

out of luck, breath and the furthest borders of anything you might call home, you throw yourself – as if to catch the moon – at the haunting white blur that is forever beyond your grasp, mocking yourself as you do so in that moment for imagining the horizon (and her) within your range. expecting bruises and exhaustion on the ground below, you cover half the distance, and then half of the remaining distance, and then half of the remaining distance, and

21

in a moment in the past which has only ever been that way, only ever remembered after the event, never in the present tense, never – happening, never on the verge of happening, never anything but known and waiting to be known once more; four exquisite white legs ending in brass hooves, whose owner defies their weight each time they're lifted, are tethered by a thick white rope – and learn for the first time what it is to be held still.

Chapter 6

The Cretan Bull

TWOhundred hundred hundred hundred hundred and ten hundred and ten hundred and ten do I hear TWOhundred and twenty twenty twenty thank you two twenty. Two twenty. Two twenty. Do I hear thirty thirty thirty thirty thirty. Thirty? Thirty. Two hundred and thirty pounds. Two forty? Two forty. Two fifty? Two fifty. Two sixty? Two sixty. Two eighty? Two eighty. I have two eighty and I have THREEhundred hundred hundred hundred do I have twenty do I have twenty I have THREEhundred hundred hundred do I have twenty do I have ten. Ten. Ten? No. Going for THREE hundred hundred hundred and going and going and

It came up lowing. It came up lowing. A swell in the water that swelled again, obscenely, and became a cascade off the back

GONE for three hundred pounds to the man at the front in the flat cap and padded jacket.

That could be any of them. The last one who nodded looks pleased with himself. Can't say I know why. Looked like your everyday cud-chewing bovine hunk of meat to me. But I'm not a farmer, I'm just a herdsman, and to tell you the truth I'm here for a very particular animal.

Which, I think, is going to be presented to us soon, so I move forward out of the small crowd. The sun finds a chink in the overcast sky up above us and straight away there are sharp shadows everywhere and already some of the farmers are unzipping their jackets and stuffing their caps in their pockets and wiping their brows as if it's been beating down on them all day.

Anyway it's not the next one. This is just another grass-guzzler. A haver of hay. The fat man who was just shouting numbers gives us a run down. He's stood in the same space as the beef, in that fenced-off ring, and it's a good thing he doesn't count his calories or he'd be more than dwarfed by the big tamed beast beside him.

Just another grass-guzzler, but all the same, it's incredible, looking at it. Muscles the size of your torso, still, unflinching. Like it was bound and muzzled, but it's not. Doesn't it know it could take the lot of them? Doesn't it know it doesn't need to be enslaved? Maybe it's here in atonement for something. Maybe in wilder times this bull or one of its ancestors committed some monstrous crime that meant it was honour-bound to serve these people even if its feet aren't tethered with thick white rope.

Bulls have been known to rape before, did you know that?

Maybe not.

and the front and the sides of the lowing creature beneath it.

Did you ever see a horse clad for jousting or a ritual? Picture the material trailing to the ground. For a moment, the bull (for bull the lowing creature was) wore the ocean in a shroud like that, a hidden beast with horns, and then, the cascade completed, the salt-white bull stood on saltwater, and lowed again. A sound like thunder heard beneath waves issued from the creature's

The page this one appears on in the lot sheet looks like this:

BULLS

LOT

92. RAVENSWELL LLOYD GEORGE'S MARVELLOUS MEDICINE 27269, (RVN-S19)

Sire Ditchwater Disgraced Doctor 31121

Dam *209329 Millhill Harold Lloyd Fetish Hour CM, GM, MM (2), dam of lot 16

Ravenswell Lloyd George's Marvellous Medicine is maternal brother to the 5-and-a-half tonne 6.58% (4.11) Millhill Silent Slapstick Dream, Lot 16, to the 5,016kg 7.09% (4.19) Millhill Monotone Movie Machine, Lot 25, to the 4,645kg 6.20% (3.66) heifer Ravenswell Stuntman Pioneer, Lot 37, to the 4,713kg 5.76% (3.75) heifer Millhill Charlie's Chalky Chaplain CM, dam of lot 32, and to Ravenswell Yearlong Shameful Fixation (Pin+£42)

*Millhill Harold Lloyd Fetish Hour CM, GM, MM (2), See Lot 16, produced over 50 tonnes of milk. She gave-

2.	3/4	5,205	305	6.07	(4.15)	6.	7/3	6,700	305	6.03	(3.92)
3.	4/4	5,588	305	5.80	(4.20)	7.	8/4	6,922	305	5.98	(3.87)
4.	5/4	5,348	305	6.04	(4.05)	8.	9/8	6,632	299	5.55	(3.87)

Her dam was the 6,599kg 5.72% (3.72) Danish Midnight Voodoo Totem GM; gd gave 5,193kg 6.97% (3.94); 3d gave 6,143 6.98%, and 2 other lactations over 7.00% Butterfat.

LOT

93. UNBEARABLY GREAT POSEIDON ADVENTURE* 31114, (RVN-S19)

Sire *Fertile Seabed Equine Earthshaker 29181

Dam not known

*Fertile Seabed Equine Earthshaker also sired the 5,321kg Stunning Equine Aeronautic, the 6,107kg Fertile Dangerous Golden Swordsman (both by Stunning Dangerous Gorgonzola); the 6,110kg Massive Arid Seabed Menace and 6,019kg Massive Earthmoving Mountain Havoc (both by Busty Massive Ocean Hunger), as well as several other promising studs and a female calf (by Agriculturally Significant Earth Mother) whose name we are not permitted to print here.

throat and echoed off the skies, and it stamped its front right foot on the surface of the sea and, having announced its presence to the spaces above and below with its mouth and its hoof, cast about for other observers.

The bull's white eyes fixed on the sun, and it paused for a moment as if weighing up its position relative to the shining ball of light.

The pause, and then the bull bowed its head and curled the hoof it stamped

So there you are. I know it looks confusing if you haven't seen this sort of thing before. All those figures on the first one are to do with its mother's and its sisters' milk production, so that the farmers standing around and about see how much milk (and how creamy) its daughters might be putting out once it's gone forth and multiplied with half their herd.

Now if you ask me, there are better ways of telling how things are going to work out in the future than by looking at how they worked out for a different person (or even animal) in a different situation in the past. Many better ways of working out the future. But, more than that, cattle produce has a lot more to do with what you do with them than who their aunts are. Give me any other cow from any other herd and I'll double what it puts out for you within a year. Which will make those numbers look somewhat irrelevant.

Hey, I said I was just a herdsman, I didn't say I wasn't a very good one.

Still, like I said, I'm waiting for the next one. The other people at the front seem keen though and bidding starts in earnest. THREEfifty fifty fifty threehundredandfifty pounds and so on. After the chance bids are priced out, it seems to come down to three main contenders. Let me tell you about them.

There's a well-tanned man (honey roasted) with wrinkles on his face so deep and thin I imagine they'd be a task to wash out, who bids by pushing his lot sheet a couple of inches up through the air and back again. He gives a big slow nod at the same time as he does this, as if to confirm that he's doing it deliberately, which makes the first action redundant, but he seems settled.

Resigned might be a better word than settled. The bidder a few men round to his left (we've a distinct shortage of women at this assembly) really is looking settled, like he sees the whole thing as a big joke. I like him, because the whole thing *is* a big joke. He's

before and drew it back in a line, kicking drops of sea up in a spray. It snorted two small jets of flame from its nostrils in the direction of the star, and turned to march inland over the water, throat still moaning.

I am here.

…'bull SHIT!'

That was Simon talking. Simon was usually the first to take an argument to a more animalistic level like this. For once, however, the talk was already animal related.

the oldest of the three bidding and the shortest and the only one with white hair. And he has a stick which, at moments seemingly almost randomly interspersed with the constant joking with and muttering at the people around him, he points out horizontally as if at the eye of the animal. That's how he bids, although he does it so casually it could look as if he simply wasn't aware it was happening.

'Telling you straight, Sigh, it had hooves. At least one foot was a hoof. And patches of fur all over. It was still mostly boy, but it was definitely partly bovine. Bovine boy, haha.'

The third farmer is much younger (thirty?) and much less interesting (not that I have anything against young men generally, you understand) and seems to treat the auction (and I imagine many other things) as a Very Important Thing and to see himself as above the kind of joking exhibited by his white-haired competitor.

As if anyone could be above laughter. This bull is Beyond A Joke. I think not. What is? Still, I've got a feeling he'll get it.

Simon asked how it was that Seth knew this, since the premise he was putting forward was that this boy had been holed up in the walls of the palace for all the years he lived, and you could see something Seth was saying was bothering him, like he suspected its

That's the way I see them anyway. I've always thought I was a pretty good judge of character.

Eventually it goes to the arrogant young man I had the hunch about because the gruff one I told you about first apparently decides the cost is too high and the mirthful one with the stick seems to forget at some point that he was interested in the first place and looks puzzled when the auctioneer looks to him for a bid.

So this Ravenswell Lloyd George's Marvellous Medicine joins a herd which will be collectively struck by lightning while stood under a large oak tree in a fierce May storm. Don't ask me how I know that.

What it means is that that very particular animal I mentioned to you earlier is up for sale now. Some people move back, some people move forward. I already got to the front to watch the goings-on I just described to you going on, but just opposite me emerging from the huddle of buyers there is a figure who rather stands out.

The first two things I always notice about her are her eyes. Which is strange, because they're not eyes you'd expect to notice on anybody else. They're not the emerald green or sapphire-blue eyes of fantasy women in fantasy tales; not the bloodshot or yellow eyes of a person who's put their body through too much or the intense staring eyes of the mad.

They are cool and grey. Grey like stone. There are stories about things that turn people to stone when looked upon, and the colour there in her eyes is as if she gazed at one of those things, but then there was something in her that stopped any more than her irises from turning.

People actually freeze around her as she steps forward, though I'm not sure they're aware of it. She remains as cool as her eyes.

This is her then. She wants it too. All fun and games.

Athene and I, you could say we go back a long way. There have been a lot of places where our interests have overlapped, let's say. And lot number 93 appears to be another.

Lot 93 is being allowed out into the ring.

And this one has muscles the size of your torso too, but these ones aren't still, and they aren't unflinching. It's pretty clear that every effort has been made to *keep* them still, and *stop* them flinching, but its huge leather harness and the chains that hold the parts of it together are like pleas to the waves to stop crashing in. Within moments the auctioneer is the same side of the fence as us, all comic reliefs ever, washed up by the earthquake of a bull he'll soon be selling us.

truth but didn't want to accept it, or it touched a nerve, or it was a secret he shared too and he didn't want to let on.

And Seth put his hand on the bar then, and leaned in close to Sigh, and right in close. And you could see Simon smelling the beer on his breath, and Seth enjoying Sigh's discomfort, and them both knowing what was going to be said but its having to be said anyway because the whole point was that the imparting of the

It bucks and bucks, a roll travelling through its body from hind-hoof to forefoot again and again, scrapes its tethered hooves along the ground and, when it snorts against its muzzle, flames lick around its nose.

If not for the restraints there would be dead people here.

If not for the bull there would be more than three staying, but rage in a pale leather skin and salt crystal horns clear farmers from a market faster than free drink would.

Athene's at its right flank, and I'm at its left, and the round auctioneer is looking like he's thinking of leaving, sweat beads on his brow, but she fixes him with a gaze made of the greyness of her eyes and that fixes him harder and faster than the harness holds the bull.

It doesn't. Stop bucking.

We bid things the auctioneer doesn't understand, doesn't know the value of: a certain large number of sunrays bid against the knowledge of particular as-yet undiscovered crafts, enlightenment for a specific number of so-far unborn children versus the awareness of the potential consequences of certain paths. And the auctioneer understands nothing of this, not why we want the bull, not who will profit from our purchase, not how it ends, who gets the ocean-in-leather in the end.

Even when it finishes he doesn't know who won.

It doesn't always pay to see the way things end. Just know that there was a bull that was an earthquake, know that it knew it didn't need to be enslaved, and know that your gain was its sacrifice.

information made it true, because it was its not having been said for so long that had kept it from being true, kept it just being a story, an urban legend, a myth, a whisper.

And Seth said in the smell of beer:

"I'm the one they got to kill it, Sigh."

LENNY BRUCE'S THING

Lenny Bruce used to do this sketch about what's jewish and what's goyish.

It was not literal.

Dizzy Gillespie, for example, was
jewish.
While the widely respected charity and social organisation B'Nai Brith was,
while technically jewish
by Bruce's definition, being so starched stiff-collar WASP-aspirational,
as goyish as a southern state restricted golf club.
You begin to get the idea.

Here: try a few.
DIY? And cookery? The mountains? And the beach? Clinton? And Dubya?
Irony?
And Poetry?

On the drugs front, coke was of course v. jewish,
So was marijuana, jews fringe players on pre-pop Lenny Bruce's modern
jazz scene.
Booze: well, jews don't drink.
As for heroin: you might dabble, at a pinch, a squeeze, ingest a line or
even nudge a
needle just to mix it up.
But jews are survivors.
They, we, don't go in for that Charlie Parker total self-destruction scene.

They found Bruce.
Puke-smeared bathroom tiles. Dartboard arms. The whole yellow rag
downtown LA
scene.
What happened?
Heroin's for those who can't handle the pain.
The ones who aren't born for this world.
But jews – jews thrive on pain. That's our thing.

Lenny – you should've stayed true to the jew.

THE LORD ABOVE

Dad remembered
shortly after Kristalnacht
days before they left everything behind
he saw
an elderly neighbour dragged out by the neighbours in their black shirts.
They literally pulled him along by his beard,
his chest scraping the ground, at least
eighty, all the way his finger
wagged wildly, Dad said, and he cried out
'By whose authority?
I recognise no authority but that of
the Lord above.'

I heard this
and cringed.
The stubborn stupidity.
Jews.

NASTY JEWS

There are so many different kinds of jews.
The crumpled jews, bruised, put-upon, cowered
beneath the shadows of chimneys and smoke.
The jews who ran like rats into the cities,
broadnecked, wide smiles, schmoozers, go-getters.
Owe them respect.
The slick, smooth straight dealers, clean-shaven with
neatly parted hair.
The bold-ass kikes, the Nasty Jews with power-jew hair. Mailer. Jacobson.
Lou Reed. These are the ones I admire the most.

And then there was the
schlump who reeked of gefilte fish, he invaded the shivah. I sat on the
    low chair and
he asked
'You married?'
'No.'
'That must have been a source of great distress to your father.'
I wanted to do a Nasty Jew kike bad-ass stomp all over his face.
Crumpled. Bruised. Cowering.

MY GOD IS BIGGER THAN YOUR GOD

My god he is bigger than your god.
My god he is espresso. He is double espresso.
Your god, your god he is hot chocolate.
My god he is more angry than your god.

My god he wears tights shirts, my god he is packed with comic
book muscles.
My god he will arm wrestle any of you and win.
My god my god.

My god he is a dab hand in the kitchen.
His chicken flambé is a sight to behold.
And my god his salmon en croute is something special,
the pastry flakes perfectly.
My god he is my god.

My god, in the evening my god mixes a mean Martini.
He slips on a disc from his incomparable collection.
Exile On Main Street, Trojan, alt country, Bitch's Brew.
Everything is cool. My god. My god.

My god, at night in bed my god he is a master. His tongue threads
needles. My god
has movie sex. Hours. Really. That is my god.

My god has your god for breakfast.
He says your god can take his wafer and wine, mix them up and stick
them up his
crucified arse.
My god he doesn't even believe in your god.

RAVING MAD

by Claire Wyburn

Me feet is in bits. 'Is shoes 'e bought me been slysin' fru me soles all night.

Nevvah mind, jus' a few moah steps to our fron' doah.

I still cahn't believe we live in 'is total palace in Finsbury Park, even though we been 'ere six monfs. We got an upstairs an' a hooj basement wiv a jacuzzi an' all. The jacuzzi was what swung it foh Ray.

'We is goin' to be like Tom Cruise an' Nicole Kidman when we move in 'ere,' 'e says aftah 'e signed the papers.

'E meant when they was togevvah, Tom an' Nikki. They 'ad problems, but blokes don't keep up wiv stuff like 'at, do they?

I mean, marriage to Ray ain't exac'lee been fluffy clouds since 'e started DJ'in' rahnd the world wiv the big league names like Oakie an' The Judge. 'E was jus a little raver when I met 'im at the Helter Skelters. Fin as a pin an' dealin' up wicked party pills in between pickin' up 'is dole check.

The girls in me office fink I'm stupid cos Ray got me the job. Fing is, I make Pedro money. You don't get to my age an' not know where you stand in the big scheme ov fings.

I'm a looka, plain an' simple.

I just 'ave to put on one ov me tight skirts an' a low cut top an' wham! I've sol' fousans ov pahnds worf ov choons ovah one boozy lunch. The uvah girls don't like 'at.

Yesterday, I ovah heard Louise imitatin' me laugh when I was on me way to the kitchen foh me aftahnoon caffiend 'it. She finks I'm a flirt.

S'cuse me.

I seen 'er lashes flutterin' like some tropical butterfly whenevah Ray pops 'is 'ead in.

It don't bovvah me if the uvah girls take the rise outah me behind me back, cos I got the last laugh. Me nose is sweetah, me mouf is fullah, me legs is longah, me 'air is blondah an' me tits is biggah 'an all the rest ov 'em put togevvah.

It's why I landed the dream bloke an' not 'em, innit?

Oooo, it's a relief to sit me arse dahn an' peel 'is shoes off me feet.

I love this kitchen wiv its French windows 'at show off our hooj back garden. Weepin' willow looks jus' like the feather boa I used to weah to Ministry of Sound yeahs ago, wiv the slee-pee sun's crimson fingahs combin' fru it.

Me toes is all stuck togevvah in a point, like 'is shoes. They is like summink the Wicked Witch ov the West wood weah. Not really me fing, but I faught I would make the effort, seein' as 'e goes on abaht how expensive they is.

'E bought 'em when 'e was ovah in Miami foh the music festie. I wanted to go wiv 'im, but 'e says I'd jus' get bored while 'e was schmoozin'.

Not as bored as I was stuck at 'ome.

Spent me nights in watchin' these gardenin' channels on cable. Faught I might as well learn abaht 'ow to keep 'em plants an' flowahs growin' in 'at garden, cos the last ownahs propah looked aftah 'em. It'd be a shame to see 'em die fru me own ignorance.

Bless 'im. 'E means well, me Ray. 'E always brings me back a pressie aftah 'e's been on one ov 'is longah tours an' there's been loads ov 'em, layt'lee. I don't 'ave the 'art to tell 'im I cahn't stan' 'at bitch off ov *Sex in the City* cos 'e 's on a mission to get me wearin' the sawt ov gear she's into. 'E reckons she's propah sophisticated. It's funny, cos I was just in me usual trackies an' traynahs when 'e proposed to me at Helter Skelter's '97 summah festie.

We was at the top ov the big wheel
face-to-face wiv a bling, bling sky
Ray stood up, the carriage rawked
we was sailin' fru the atmosfeah
'im steerin' past 'em stars shynin'

'How abaht 'at one comin' up, baybee?' 'E goes. 'If I jump high enuff I can pluck it right aht the sky foh you.'

I grabbed 'is legs an' started screamin' cos I was sure 'e was goin' to fall aht ov our carriage an' hit the ground wiv a splattah.

'E was 'at nutted.

'It's just outta reach, baybee,' 'e says aftah I dragged 'im back dahn onto the seat. 'Ave to make do wiv one ov 'em cheapo rocks from Dalston's jewellery shop, 'till I get moah sets. You sweet wiv 'at?'

'You proposin' to me, Ray?'

'E 'rapped 'is ahms rahnd me, oooo it was like slippin' on a mink coat, 'e was 'at soft an' warm.

'If you'll 'ave me.'

'E put 'is tremblin' fingahs on me cheeks. The stars was reflectin' in 'is marmite eyes.

'I must be the luckiest geeze in the world to 'ave someone so beautiful foh me soul mate,' 'e says.

I wish we could ov stayed on
top ov 'at big wheel fohevvah
snoggin' each uvah's faces off
comin' up on 'em wicked doves
wiv all 'em stars winkin' at us
felt like the 'hole world was in love.

I'm still wearin' the ring we picked togevvah. Yeah, 'e's offered to buy me one wiv a biggah diamond in it. Fing is, it wouldn't be me engagement ring 'en, wood it? Jus' lookin' at it now reminds me ov how fings were back 'en. I loved 'im an' 'e loved me an' nuffink else mattered.

Where is 'e?

Must be givin' 'is life story to that poah cabbie. 'E's on a high aftah getting' back from Oz, 'e went dahn so well aht there, 'e's got loads moah gigs in Sydney an' Adelaide. Means I won't get to see 'im much ovah the summah.

'E kept interferin' wiv Lee's set tonight, didn't 'e? Mandy was givin' me what foh in the laydees, tellin' me I should give 'im a few 'ome troofs.

Ray's not perfick, I know 'at.

Who is?

Take me, foh example. Me 'air is jus' this shitty dishwawer collah wivaht a little chemical assistance. Ray 'as 'is chemical help an' aow, that's how I see it. If Mandy an' Lee was into the snow, they wouldn't notice it so much. 'At's what I noticed aftah Mandy tawked me in to havin' a sneaky E. I needed it cos ov me feet. Wivaht it, I would nevah 'ave showed me support an' danced to Lee's set.

This hooj blistah popped 'alfway fru *Fix My Sink*. Honest to God, it felt like me wawers was breakin'. 'Sept it was in me foot cos I'm not preggers or anyfink. Got free spare bedrooms in this gaff, though, an' some fings are worf puttin' up wiv a little bit ov pain foh, yeah?

God, I've a hooj laddah up me tights an aow. I hope no one noticed 'at dahn Plastic People.

Time foh a mirrah check.

Tawk abaht dustbin lid pupils, an' 'at's 'im slammin' the fron' doah. 'E'd kill me if 'e sussed I'd swallowed a pill.

'What you sittin' in the dark in the kichen foh, Opal?'

Me man swerves past the bin
almost, 'e don't manage it
'E falls right in. Gets up
gives me one ov 'em looks
like 'e finks it was me did it.

'Jew not fink our willow looks beautiful wiv 'at purple light comin' fru it? Be a few minutes an' the sun'll be streamin' in.'

'Fuck the sun.' 'E goes ovah to the French windows an' shuts 'em blinds. 'Sun'll bring us dahn an' we ain't even started to 'ave a good time yet.' 'E switches on 'is Pammy Anderson light in the cawnah.

I watch the two bulbs in 'er boobs flickah on.

'What the fuckin' 'ell was Mandy an' Lee's problem?' 'E scratches a chair away from the table, plonks 'imself on it, digs 'is 'rap aht ov 'is jeans pocket, an' chops up two lines wiv 'is credit card. 'Is mouf is goin' like a washin' machine on a spin set.

'I cahn't believe they wouldn't come back foh a drink. Some fuckin' anniversary celebration this 'as turned aht to be, wiv yoh chief bridesmaid givin' me stinkahs aow night. Who does 'at ugly cow fink she is?'

'It was jus' a substance clash, Ray. Forget abaht it.'

'Don't give me 'at bullshit. They is only on the E cos they cahn't affawd the snow an' 'e 's too proud to 'ave some ov ours.'

'E bangs 'is fist on the table, puts his face next to it an' blows 'is breaf across it. 'Is snow scattahs aow ovah the place.

Smells like diarrhoea, 'at beer 'e's drinkin' these days.

'Let the kitchen 'ave their allocation! I ain't no penny pinchin' fuckah like Lee. They is jealous of us, so fuckin' jealous they spited 'emselves by not comin' back foh a dip in our jacuzzi. Tellin' me they'd ravvah be stuck in 'at matchbox flat ov theirs. Total idiots, ain't they?'

Ray nevah used to be into beer.
When 'e start swallowin' 'at stuff?
I cahn't remember an' I won't heah
'Is shit bringin' badness into love.

'At Lee finks 'e's bettah 'an me cos 'e DJs credible shit. It might make you look good, but it don't bring the quids in. 'At's why e's workin' in 'at poxy record shop. 'E's been there a decade now, innit? Tell you summink, Opal, 'e ain't evah gunnah be treatin' Mandy to wintah holidays in the Caribbean. 'E'll be lucky to get aht ov 'at towah block, rate 'e's goin'.'

'You was a bit rude to 'im, though, Ray. I don't fink you should ov stood behind 'im all the time 'e was on 'em decks, tellin' 'im why the choons 'e was playin' wood nevvah make it big. 'At was 'is set tonight an' 'e'd been lookin' fohward to it.'

'Since when jew get so precious abaht 'im? You fuckin' 'im behind me back?'

'Don't be so stupid.'

'Wouldn't put it past you. C'mon Opal, admit it. You only 'ang abaht wiv 'at Mandy cos she's a dog an' it makes you look good when you stand nex' to 'er.'

I'm comin' dahn off ov 'at E. Musn't be a propah one. Ain't like Mandy, she's an E connoisseur, got the best pills in London. Fing is, I've got lock jaw an' me 'ead hurts an' I'm startin' to get these horrible palpitations. A drink wood ease 'em up.

'I fink we should change the subjeck.' I get off me chair an' 'ead foh the fridge.

'Suits me, jus' so long as you get it into yoah fick skull 'at we're fru wiv 'em two.'

I make two strong Jack Daniels in our new crystal wine glasses, put a splash ov coke in.

'Why cahn't we jus' accept they is different to us an' still be their mates?'

I hand Ray 'is drink.

'E gives me a look 'at makes me shuddah.

'Don't fuckin' tell me you've been neckin' E wiv 'em pair?'

'No.'

I keep me eyes locked dahn on 'em kitchen tiles. The floah is covahed in mud. I was doin' a bit of gardenin' yesterday aftahnoon while 'e was dahn the basement wiv a couple of 'is new DJ mates, frowin' 'is snow arahnd.

'E scrapes 'is chair back like fundah an' comes right foh me, clampin' 'is fingahs rahnd me cheeks an' pullin' me face towards 'im.

'Yeah you 'ave. Speakin' to someone who knows, remembah.'

'Ray, 'at hurts.'

'E tightens 'is grip. Me lips hit me nose.

'Let me see yoah eyes, Opal.'

I meet 'is eyes, bloodshot an' swollen.

'E pushes me away an' turns back to the table.

'Pilled up cow. How many times 'ave I told you 'at E's a kids' drug? I won't 'ave you on it, showin' me up in front ov the uvah DJs. They is grown outah that shit.'

'Fing is, we wasn't wiv 'em, was we babes? We was wiv our two oldest rave mates.'

'Who cares! Life ain't one long *Telly Tubbies,* is it?' 'E poahs some moah snow on the table an' hammers 'is credit card fru it.

'Snort 'at, Opal. 'At's big enuff to get rid ov 'at pill nonsense.'

'E hands me a rolled up note. 'Go on, it'll make you feel bettah,' 'e says. 'Meet you dahn the basement. It's time foh some propah party music aftah aow 'at Lee's shit.'

I listen to 'is feat clatterin' dahn 'em stairs.

Then I follow 'is example, put me mouf to the table an' blow aow 'is snow away.

It settles like dust into the fah cawnah ov the kitchen.

It's a Marie Celeste fast food shop dahn 'ere. 'Is DJ mates 'ave abandoned the place an' lef' their chicken bones rollin' abaht the floah.

Gree-zee newspapers are stickin' to me toes like they is slugs.

I bend dahn an' peel this bit ov chicken skin off ov me foot.

It wouldn't be so bad if there was some windows I could open an' give the place some breaf.

This basement's 'is pride an' joy. 'E spent monfs rippin' the old ownahs' gym aht so 'e could put 'is club an' studio set up in. It's amazin' 'e didn't go spare wiv whoevah crushed all 'em chips on 'is leopard skin sofa. It's fake, yeah, but it cost 'im a fortune. I brush ash off ov its left cushion an' perch on the edge ov it.

'You finally made it, baybee,' 'e says from behind 'is decks.

I cahn only see 'is blonde spikes shynin' beneaf 'at red an' blue fibre optic light 'e got in Las Vegas. It looks like some horrible sea monster tentacle fing 'at's eatin' 'is face off. Still, 'is voice sounds happy enuff.

'You not dancin'?'

'E puts on some new mix of *Let Me Be Your Fantasy.*

I prefer the original. Who'd mess wiv a classic like 'at?

'It's wicked, innit? Me an' Shiver made it foh 'em Ozzies. They is at leas' five yeahs behind us wiv the house music.'

E comes ovah an' sits right dahn on 'at pile ov mushed up chips.

'They is behind us in most fings, though, ain't they baybee?' 'E gives me a nudge.

I cahn't be bovvahed to laugh at 'is joke.

'You is in a big cream puff wiv me cos you fink I forgot yoah anniversary pressie, ain't you?'

I give 'im a shrug.

He leans ovah an' brings a bottle of champagne aht of 'is beer fridge.

'Wait till you heah this.'

'E takes me glass an' chucks the remains of me drink into a plastic cup 'at's filled wiv coke an' fag butts.

'From nex' Monday, it's official. You is goin' to be a laydee of leisure.' 'E pops the cork, clinks our two glasses togevvah. 'Cristal wiv crystal, innit?' 'e says.

'What jew mean?'

'Pedro took some convincin', but when I pointed aht you an' me wanted kids, 'e soon changed 'is choon.'

'I've worked there foh years, Ray. 'E 'as to give me maternity leave.'

'I faught you'd be well pleased, you is always complaining abaht 'em shitty wages 'e pays you.'

'Fing is – '

'Opal, you is firty, you still look gorgeous to me, but music PR is a young girl's game. Pedro's gunnah get rid ov you as soon as you stop gettin' bevvied wiv 'is clients, an' you ain't gunnah be doin' 'at wiv a kid in yoah belly, is you?'

'I'll go stir crazy alone in this place.'

'You can be me PA. I'll make you a nice office in one ov 'em upstairs rooms. They'll be no moah hour long commutes on freezin' wintah mornins. Fuckin' 'ell, what you cryin' foh?'

E rubs black blobs ov mascara off me cheeks wiv fingahs as gentle as the ones 'e proposed wiv.

'I'm sorry, 'at E's makin' me act silly.'

'E puts me hair behind me ears an' moves in foh a kiss.

It feels like I've taken a gulp ov 'at coke an' fag butt potion.

'Anuvvah line'll get rid ov the last traces ov 'at E shit. Stuff's 'at strong, I cahn't believe the first line didn't do it.'

'E picks up a record sleeve lyin' by me feet.

When did 'em purple veins pop up?

There's two huge forks juttin' aht ov me hands an all.

Layt'lee when I put on me eyeshadow, I've noticed it won't do smoov, it just 'eads foh 'em crinkles that's appeared across me lids.

'... amazin'? Hardcore 'as moved in to Moscow an' I been rummaging fru our old rave choons. We got *We Are Eie, Party People* an' *Injected With A Poison* – '

Mandy tol' me while we was in the laydees swallowin' 'at cheeky E that she was ready to 'ave kids, only, 'er an' Lee saw someone get shot aht ov their living-room window las' week. Jus' a boy, really, Mandy says. She reckons she 'as to wait a bit longah, till 'er an'Lee can scrape a mortgage foh a flat in some moah safer estate. It's a shame cos Mandy's like me – we always wanted to 'ave kids in our twenties. We got sidetracked by the ravin', it's amazin' how a decade rushes by.

'... Russia's at 'at honeymoon stage on the E an' 'at means I'll be gettin' loads moah gigs – '

I wish Ray could tawk abaht summink uvah than 'imself. Oh well, 'e ain't gunnah change now. At least 'e's out the country foh most ov the summah. I cahn invite Mandy an' Lee ovah.

'... soak in our jacuzzi, looks like 'em luncheon meat feet you got need it.'

'E hoovers up a long white line.

I could do a little bit of gardenin' every aftahnoon, go to the gym or me beautician. Me Ray's right, Pedro's only goin' to frow me in the bin.

Ray passes me 'is rolled up fifty. 'Go on, it'll make you feel bettah, baybee.'

I wipe me runny nose wiv the back ov me hand an' shove 'is grubby note up it.

'E's right, me Ray is, I'm feelin' bettah already.

WHERE THEY WERE MISSED*

by Lucy Caldwell

One morning, Mammy pours orange juice over our Shreddies. There's no milk been delivered, she says. There's no milk deliveries because there's no more milk bottles to put the milk in, I tell Daisy. We saw the news, after Children's BBC, and they showed wee boys chucking milk bottles and bricks at a row of Army vans. There were cars burning in the background, and big piles of wooden crates and fencing and barbed wire. Mammy came in and turned the television off. That's quite enough TV for one day, she said. But we didn't complain because then she did a jigsaw puzzle with us, a proper grown-up one, spreading the pieces all over the living-room floor. She showed us how to start with the ground and the sky, finding all of the pieces with a flat edge. It was Daisy's job to find all the pieces with a bit of blue sky on them, and Mammy and I fitted them together. The jigsaw was a jungle scene, with tigers and monkeys and parrots, and she let us leave it on the floor so that Daddy could see it when he came in.

Me and Daisy like it that there's no more milk because orange juice on Shreddies is more fun, but Mammy doesn't like it because you can't put orange juice in coffee. Is it too much to ask, she says, to have a wee drop of milk for your coffee? Is it too much to ask?

When we walk to the shops to buy milk, we see where they burned a car at the bottom of our street a few nights ago. Twisted black bones are all that is left of the car. The ground is smooth and shiny all around, where the road melted in the heat of the flames.

Daddy says that for the foreseeable future, while there's cars being burned and milk bottles being thrown, Mammy is not to take us across town to visit the Antoney-oney-o's and their ice cream parlour. He says that if Mammy wants to see her friends they can come to our house. He isn't cross when he says it. He says In Light Of Circ-um-stances. Me and Daisy aren't sure what Circ-um-stances are. I think he means the two of us. Mammy gets cross. And she doesn't like it when Daddy calls them the Antoney-oney-o's.

---

*Published with the permission of Viking

- It's not funny. In fact, it's downright bigotry so it is. You're just a pig-headed bigot.

- Jesus, woman! Catch yourself on! It's only my wee joke.

- A wee joke is it? Well do you see me laughing? Some joke! I don't think it's a joke, snaps Mammy. Then she adds, I think it's just damn rude.

Daddy doesn't like being called Damn Rude.

- Oho, well, talking of damn rude, it seems to me that those so-called friends of yours are damn rude. Explain to me again why it is that it's always you trailing the girls over there to visit them? What kind of friends will never come round to our house ey?

- You know fine rightly why they won't come over this side of town.

- Well, in that case you'll understand fine rightly why I won't have you taking the girls over that side of town. Not until things calm down.

Mammy rolls her eyes but she doesn't say anything, like that's the end of it. But she still takes us to visit the Antoney-oney-o's (only I'm not allowed to call them that or I'll get a slap across the back of the legs) but it's a Secret we're not to tell Daddy. I'm glad we don't have to stop our visits to the ice cream parlour. We have to get two buses to get there, a bus into town that takes us to the City Hall and then we have to walk round the back of Leisureworld and get another bus up the Falls. The bus that goes up the Falls has metal mesh across the windows, just in case anyone throws a stone, Mammy says. Daisy and I press our noses right up against the glass to try and see out of the metal mesh. Sometimes you can only see mesh, and then your eyes pop and you can see outside until they pop again and you can't see past the metal. The ice cream parlour is called An-to-ni-ni's Ices. That's how you say their name properly: An-to-ni-ni. Mr An-to-ni-ni – Grandpa Tony, he tells us to call him – makes me a special ice cream in a tall glass, with vanilla *and* strawberry ice cream and chocolate sauce *and* marshmallows and whippy cream and he never forgets to put a bright red cherry on top that I save til last. Sometimes he sticks a little paper umbrella in the whippy cream, and I lick the stick and fold it down and put it carefully in the pocket of my pinafore. I keep the paper umbrellas in the ballerina box with my other treasures. When Grandpa Tony sets the ice cream sundae on the counter in front of me, Mammy opens her eyes wide and says, Heavens above, and aren't you the lucky girl? Have you said thank you to Mr Antonini?

- Ah, it's Grandpa Tony, he says, and he does a little bow and presents me with a long silver spoon.

- Da-dah! There you are, my *principessa.*

He turns to Mammy, shaking his head and pretending to be angry.

- And your Mama, we need to feed her up, eh? Too skinny, you hear me? You're too skinny, he tells her.

Mammy smiles a tight little smile and turns away.

- I'm just a wee bit tired these days, she goes.

Mammy and Isabella, Mammy's best friend, drink little cups of coffee like dolls' cups. Me and Daisy sit on stools up at the shiny counter and eat our ice creams with our spoons that have long handles so you can reach right into the bottom of the glass. Isabella's baby Andrea is strapped in a high chair beside us. Andrea is a baby boy. There's two girls in my class at school called Andrea. But Mammy says that in Italy, Andrea is a boy's name. Baby Andrea is fat, with squashy cheeks and lots of curly black hair. Sometimes, if we go to Isabella's house instead of the ice cream parlour, me and Daisy have to play with Baby Andrea. Isabella gives us crayons and a colouring-in book, but if Andrea scribbles over our pictures or snaps a wax crayon in half we mustn't say anything because he's not my brother and we're guests in Isabella's house. Mammy tells me to be a good girl and play nicely with Andrea, and Isabella says to Andrea we're his Irish sisters, and I can't say that me and Daisy don't want to play with the baby. And to make things even worse Isabella's house doesn't have a garden to play in. The front door opens right onto the pavement, and we're not allowed to play in the street even though there's always other children playing in the street. I said to Mammy why can't Isabella and Andrea come over and play in our house that has a garden, but Mammy says that Isabella is scared to come to our part of town because she's from a foreign family and some people in some parts of Belfast don't like people from other countries. When she says that I think of Baps and Wee Man and sometimes the girls on our street yelling, Away back to yer own country ya Taig! and, Tell your ma she's not welcome here! But I don't tell Mammy that.

The An-to-ni-nis come from a little village in the mountains called Cassylahteeko.

- Cassylahteeko! goes Grandpa Tony.

- Cassy-LAH-teeko! I say, and he laughs, and makes his happy-clown face.

Grandpa Tony has pictures of Cassylahteeko on the walls of the ice cream parlour, and sometimes he points out his house. It's small and white, with a roof made out of tiles, and a pig and a chicken sitting outside. Cassylahteeko is in Italy. Mammy showed me Italy in the map of the world in our encyclopaedia.

But we couldn't find Cassylahteeko. I told Grandpa Tony that, and his face went all droopy.

- All the people leave, he said. All the people want better life.

- Why'd'ye come to Ireland then? I said. Grandpa Tony's always going on about how beautiful Italy is and how sunny Italy is. Italy sounds far better. In Ireland it just rains all the time and when it is hot the people get mad.

- When you grow up, *principessa,* you leave this country and you go to live with my family, *capisci?* Marry a nice Italian boy, no? You're gonna be a heart-breaker, *bellissima* just like your mama, and I tell you all the Italian boys gonna be falling over themselves to marry you!

Grandpa Tony has started teaching me some Italian words for when I go to his house in Italy and marry an Italian boy. But I'm not sure if I want to go to Italy because even if it is better than Ireland and even if I could have a proper big Italian ice cream every day like he says I'd miss Mummy and Daddy and Daisy. I whisper that in Mammy's ear and she kisses me and says, not to worry, he's just Home-Sick and it makes him feel better talking about Italy.

Home-Sick is a special kind of sick you get when you're away from your home. It's not like a tummy-bug because you get it by just thinking about people or places and the only cure is to go back home.

- Why doesn't he go back home then?

Mammy sighs.

Perhaps he'll turn to dust, I think, the minute his foot touches the soil.

- A long time ago, before you were born, *céadsearc,* there was a War, and lots of people left Italy to come to Ireland. Grandpa Tony was one of those people, and his home is here, now.

- Well why does he get Home-Sick then? I interrupt.

- Oh, Sha. Isabella – Grandpa Tony's her daddy – she was born here, and she grew up here and married a man from here, and wee babby Andrea will grow up here, and they're Grandpa Tony's family. But sometimes, Grandpa Tony gets sad about everything he left behind.

I still don't understand why he can't go home just for a little bit, just until the Home-Sick wears off, but Mammy says that even if he went back, nothing would be how he remembered it, and maybe the home he left all those years ago wouldn't be there any more.

Mammy goes quiet and her eyes go all shiny.

- Why are you crying, Mammy? I whisper.

- I'm not crying, she goes, and she turns away. But I saw a tear slide down her cheek and drip off the end of her chin and she didn't even brush it away.

The air is thick with heat and sweat and me and Daisy are bored playing in the back garden. My hair is damp across my forehead and my skin is all crawly and itchy. The girl across the road has a paddling pool in her front garden and some other girls from our street are playing in it, but Mammy's said we're to stay away from them after the dog turd mud. I don't want to play with them anyway. *Yer eyes are too close thegether,* they've started shouting when they see me and Daisy. My eyes don't look too close together to me. But it's hard to tell. I look at Daisy's eyes; hers don't either. But I can't tell how close is too close.

Daisy and I want an ice cream. We ask Daddy if we can go to the shop at the bottom of the road. Daddy was working all last night so he's sitting in a chair in the garden, snoring, with the *East Belfast Newsletter* over his head. We take it in turns to poke him until he wakes up with a jolt. He says he doesn't want us going to the shop. Please Daddy! we go, but he still says no. Please will you come with us, we say, but he says he's dead beat and will we ever give his head peace. In the end he gets us each an Ice Pop from the freezer but there's only the blue ones left and we don't like the blue ones. They have a funny taste. I like the red ones and the green ones and Daisy likes the yellow ones and the orange ones, and we both like the pink ones, but neither of us likes the blue ones. Daisy throws her blue Ice Pop on the kitchen floor and Daddy shouts.

- Daisy! Pick it up this instant!

- No! I want a proper ice cream! Like Grandpa Tony makes! I want to go to Grandpa Tony's!

We're not supposed to mention one word about going to see Grandpa Tony because it's a Secret. Daisy remembers as soon as she's said it and she goes quiet and looks at me all big eyed.

- Has your mother been taking you to that ice cream parlour?

Daisy looks at me and I look at Daisy and then I look down at my sandals and fit my feet along the cracks in the kitchen tiles. Daisy's blue Ice Pop is melting on the floor. Mine is melting too and it's dripping down my hand. My hand is cold where I'm holding the Ice Pop. There's a different sort of cold, as well, in the middle of my tummy.

- Sunshine? Answer me.

I still don't say anything. The cold patch in my tummy is getting bigger.

- Sunshine! Look at me when I'm talking to you!

Daddy's guldering. A bit of spit goes on my cheek. I wipe it off with my gooey blue hand and leave a sticky cold smear on my cheek.

- Sunshine! he roars. I'm your father! If I ask you a question you're to answer!

- Yes Daddy, I whisper.

- What do you mean, yes daddy? Has your mother been taking you to that ice cream place?

- Yes Daddy, I say again.

Mammy's in bed with one of her sore heads but it doesn't stop Daddy storming up the stairs and shouting at the top of his voice.

- Daddy's ragin', I say to Daisy. That's your fault, so it is.

- No, she says, scared.

- It is, I go.

We don't get to go to the ice cream parlour again. One day, Mammy puts down the phone white as a sheet, and she pushes me away when I try and hug her, and she says that Isabella and Baby Andrea and Grandpa Tony are going back to Italy for good. We take two taxis to Isabella's house in the Falls, one normal taxi and one big black taxi, because the big black taxis are the only ones will go up the Falls. Isabella's tiny wee house is full of people, and more and more people are coming and going all the time, bringing casserole dishes of food and making tea and smoking and crying and talking in angry whispers, and I watch behind the blinds as a big van with BBC on it films the house and the street until a woman in a padded pink coat with rollers in her hair still comes up and tugs the blinds back down and pulls me away and says, It's a disgrace, so it is, coming to juke at us like we're animals in a zoo, they've no respect, so they haven't, no respect at all.

So then I sit in a corner, cross-legged and quiet, shushing Daisy when she starts to play too noisily. Mammy starts to cry, and she and Isabella hug each other, and Mammy seizes Baby Andrea onto her lap and kisses him again and again and says, You poor wee thing, you poor, poor wee thing, until Andrea starts gurning too.

Later on that evening, crouching on the little landing halfway up the stairs and pressing my face in the gap between two of the banisters, I can see a slice of the living room and hear Mammy and Daddy talking about what happened to Isabella's husband Frankie.

- He's sitting at the bar, Mammy goes, just sitting having a quiet wee drink, after work, like. Just sitting on his tod having a quiet wee drink.

- Aye, I know, says Daddy. Terrible shame, so it is.

- *A shame?* Is that what you call it? Jesus, a shame?

- Look, love, Daddy interrupts, this isn't helping anything.

But Mammy will not be talked down.

- Them two loyalist gunmen burst out of the bogs with their ballyclavas and their machine guns, burst out and start shooting all around them –

- Calm down love –

- And you call it a *shame?*

- Love -

- Jesus.

- There's no need for this! You're getting yourself worked up. There's nothing to be done.

Mammy ignores him and raises her voice again.

- Frankie's his back to them. And do you know what?

Daddy's shoulders slump and he sits down.

- *Do you know what?*

Mammy's voice is shrill and her face is twisted so it doesn't look like Mammy any more. I want to go back to bed. I want to go back to bed and climb in with Daisy. But I can't even stop looking.

- What, love.

- They said his neck was almost completely blown away. His head was barely attached to his body. Isabella had to, had to identify him and his head was barely attached to his . . . And Isabella's had to hear all the details again and again from the police and on the telly and on the radio and – what kind of country are we living in, can you tell me that? Jesus, what kind of life is this? Why did I ever come up North? What possessed me, for crying out loud?

Daddy's got up and he's grabbing her wrists and she's shrieking. I cover my ears with my hands. But I can't move from where I'm crouched down on the stairs looking through the banisters. When I take my hands from my ears, I hear Daddy saying how the brother of one of the gunmen was in the Forces and how that brother and that brother's wife were blown up by a bomb planted underneath their car, blown up in front of their six-year-old daughter and the babysitter, who were waving bye-bye from the front room.

- Sunshine's age! That wee girl was no older than our Sunshine.

- Are you – are you *justifying* what those men done?

- I'm not justifying. Jesus! I'm not – justifying, I'm only saying.

- I cannot believe I'm hearing this. No, get off of me! I cannot believe you're justifying what those men done. Think of that wee baby boy with no father. Think of –

Daddy's shouting over her now.

- What I think of, is I think of that wee girl who saw her mummy and daddy killed – blown up – in front of her. That the wee girl is the exact same age as my Sunshine.

- You're disgusting, so you are. Bringing my children into this to use against me.

- That's not what I'm doing, I'm only saying –

- So what are you saying?

- What I'm saying, is –

- What you're saying is, that it's alright for men to go into a pub and kill innocent men like Frankie? That revenge is alright so long as it's revenging something terrible enough?

- Jesus, that's not what I'm saying. I'm just saying – there's always more to it. That's what I'm saying. Catholic men shot dead in pub by Loyalist Paramilitaries, the headlines go. But the story behind it -

Mammy's gone all quiet and starey.

- I don't believe I know you, so I don't.

- Come on, love. All I'm saying is that it fucking terrifies me, what goes on.

He reaches out to touch her hair.

- Don't! Don't you dare touch me!

Mammy's crying and gulping and shaking. What's become of us, she says, over and over again. What's become of us. What have we done.

I creep upstairs to bed, and get into Daisy's bed. Daisy is milky-warm and smells of sleep, but I am shivering and my ears are ringing with the harsh sound of Bombs and Guns and Ballyclavas and whenever I close my eyes I see floating in front of me that little girl my age's face as she waves from the front room window.

The next morning, when me and Daisy go downstairs, Daddy is sleeping on the sofa.

- Sha-sha, why does Daddy like sleeping on the sofa? Daisy asks.

I tell her to shush. But Daddy wakes up.

- What are you girls doing up so early? he says.

- It's not early, Daddy, it's breakfast time, Daisy goes.

- Breakfast time, already? Daddy goes, pretending to be shocked. Sure, it wasn't that long ago I went to bed, it can't be *breakfast* time!

There's purple under Daddy's eyes that looks like me or Daisy crayoned it in with colouring pencil, and his eyes are small and pink and puffy like the eyes of the school rabbit when it got sick. Daddy looks at me with a funny look on his face. Then he yawns and stretches and does his monkey impression. Daisy giggles.

- Come on, girls, he goes, and Daisy jumps onto his lap. I slide in beside him on the sofa, and he puts an arm round me.

- Listen to me carefully, he goes. I don't know what you may have heard people saying the past couple of days, but you're not to be scared and you're to remember that your daddy will always protect you, d'ye hear me? Ey?

He's gripping my arm, and he looks fierce. I nod. Daisy nods too, wide-eyed.

- Never you forget that it's your daddy's job to protect people, and to catch the bad people and make sure they go to jail. Understand? So long as I'm here, nothing will hurt you. Ey? You with me? Nothing will hurt you. You girls remember that, now.

- OK Daddy, I whisper.

- Give me a kiss. Now let's get up and dressed and get some breakfast in the both of youse.

AUTHOR BIOGRAPHIES

JENNIFER BARKER was born in Paddington (not the station) and lives and works in Northampton. She attended Goldsmiths College from 2003 to 2004. She says that her influences are J. G. Ballard, Anna Kavan, Janet Frame and Robert Lowell, along with any old nonsense with a bright cover. This piece, 'Diplodocus', is part of a longer work, which she will finish very soon. Or possibly not.

LUCY CALDWELL was born in Belfast in 1981 and now lives in East London. She read English at Queens' College, Cambridge, and completed the Masters in Creative and Life Writing at Goldsmiths in 2004. *Where They Were Missed,* to be published by Viking in February 2006, is Lucy's first novel.

CATHERINE CASALE is interested in the questions life writing raises about the relationship between subjective private history and 'objective' public history, individual and cultural identity, memory, truth and fiction. An American by birth, she has lived most of her adult life in London and Tokyo where she worked in academic publishing. Prior to Goldsmiths, she earned a bachelors in history at Tufts University and a masters in South East Asian area studies at the University of London's School of Oriental and African Studies. Her essay 'A Patchwork Life' appeared in a collected anthology, *Swaying: Essays on Intercultural Love.*

ANGELA CLELAND was born in Inverness, Scotland in 1977. She graduated from Glasgow University in 1999 and completed her Masters at Goldsmiths in 2003, which she says was one of the most enjoyable and productive years of her life yet. Her work has been published in print and online magazines, including *Brittle Star, The Frogmore Papers* and *The Rialto,* and she regularly performs her poetry at open-mike and arranged readings in London, where she now lives and works. A selection of her poetry is featured on her website at *www.angelacleland.com.*

ELLEN CRANITCH read English at Cambridge and medicine at The Royal Free Hospital, London. She has worked as an arts journalist for, amongst others, *The Times, The Independent, The Irish Times* and *Vogue* and as a drama script editor at Granada Television.

GETHAN DICK works as a creative educator for the British Library and the Arts Council, collaborating with other artists to design and deliver workshops. She publishes *Sisters*, themed collections of work by her and her sisters, every summer. She teaches creative writing at an adult education college. She contributes to Wes White's zine, *Attack!!!!* She writes mostly short things (currently a collection called *Things Go Bodily Wrong)* and sporadically works on a long thing about a girl who sleeps for a living. She wrote 'Green' and 'Purple' – two of a set of seven monologues called *Sing A Rainbow* – in 2001, which she says feels like a long time ago.

MIRANDA DOYLE'S short story 'The Cardboard Coffin' was shortlisted in 2001 for the Fish Prize and 'A Double Bake' was broadcast on radio in 2003. She was selected for The Royal Literary Fund and Arts Council funded Writers' Pool in 2004.

PATRICK EARLY is a member of the London Poetry School and a Masters graduate of Goldsmiths' Creative and Life Writing programme. He has lived and worked for extended periods in a series of beautiful and sometimes dangerous cities, in the former Yugoslavia, the Arab world, Argentina and Brazil. He has published poetry and criticism in a wide variety of journals in Ireland, Spain, Serbia and the UK. He is a strong supporter of the Centre for Poetry in Translation at the School of Oriental and African Studies, London, which is dedicated to translating less well-known work from non-European languages.

LARA EASTMAN is 24 and lives with her family in Stapleford Abbotts, a little village in Essex, which nobody has ever heard of. She has travelled several different career paths already, but currently works in science publishing. She is now thinking of becoming an English teacher. She likes sunshine, running and buying new clothes. She dislikes unkind words and swimming costumes.

BEN FELSENBURG is a Goldsmiths three-timer: undergrad, Masters (Creative and Life Writing 2003) and now working his way towards a doctorate. An Aquarian and life-long Arsenal fan, he also enjoys Sesame Snaps, finding it especially hard to choose between coconut-flavoured and chocolate-coated. He has voted Labour at every election since 1987 but is open to offers.

LARA FRANKENA now has a Masters in Creative and Life Writing from Goldsmiths College in addition to a Masters in fine arts. She has occasionally shown her video, installation and photography work. Her poems were published in *Reactions* in 2005.

IRENE GARROW was born and grew up in Scotland but now lives in London. In another life, she made short documentary films for television, which taught her about telling stories in pictures, and the importance of editing. She now works with a smaller, more reflective lens, the inner eye, but the same rules apply. Capture the image and edit the text until it works, and always remember the reader/viewer. She loves the short story form and the process of writing which is part séance; part dream; but mainly intense, concentrated labour. 'Gala Day' is from a collection of short stories called *Voyage*.

AMY HANSON is a 26-year-old Londoner. The main theme in her writing is family. She has almost finished a childhood memoir about growing up in the 80s and having a father accused of murder. For the last three years, she has worked as a children's Story Builder. Until recently she has cared for her elderly grandma at home. 'Grandma Clarice' is a piece of life writing, dealing with a family member dying, remembering that person before death took hold and the conflicting feelings this evokes. It is dedicated to her memory. At present Amy is in Nepal and is keeping a tally of the number of monkeys she sees.

JANE HARRIS was born in the United States, grew up in Italy and has lived in Britain on and off since 1975. She has written and published poetry and completed a novel. Among the writers she most admires and who she looks to for instruction are Shakespeare, Chekov, Alice Munro and Jane Austen. She lives in London with her husband and two teenage sons. She is currently working on a novella.

JILL HARRISON completed the Goldsmiths Masters in 2003. Her submission was made entirely of poems. She writes very short pieces, like this one, and slightly longer, imagist/narrative poems – some of which form linked groups. Sometimes, she writes about dreams but more often about members of her family, people she meets or events, which trigger moments of tight emotional focus. She lives in a village on the edge of East Anglia with two cats and two sons.

KAREN HERMAN, born in Philadelphia, Pennsylvania, received her Bachelors in journalism from Boston University and a Masters in Creative and Life Writing from Goldsmiths College. She has written for newspapers in the United States and South Africa. Her work has appeared in literary journals in Paris and in an anthology published in the United States this year. She is completing a novel about rivers.

PATRICK HOBBS was born in South America and studied history at Bristol University. He has worked in various fields, including social work, managing a bar, curating an art gallery and making furniture, as well as making bread in a monastery. His poems have twice won the Jack Clemo Memorial Prize, been performed on BBC Radio 4 and featured in the anthology series *Reactions* and various magazines. His first poetry collection *Paper Hands* was published in 2001. He took the Masters in Creative and Life Writing at Goldsmiths College, gaining a distinction in 2004. The extract in this anthology is the opening chapter of his first novel.

PENNY HODGKINSON lives in Suffolk with her family; she works as a speech and language therapist for children and adults with learning disabilities. Working with people to find their voice – literally and metaphorically. This piece is an extract from a longer work dedicated to her late father-in-law who died in 2004. His legacy has been the opportunity to write and study at Goldsmiths. Penny is working on several short stories and an idea for a novel about an institution and its many voices – patients, nurses, gardeners, cleaners and cooks who lived there.

KELLIE JACKSON was born in Newcastle, Australia where she grew up. She has lived in Sydney, Hong Kong, New York and now, South London. She has an English degree from Goldsmiths and is working on a collection of short stories. Her story, 'Isola Bella' was recently shortlisted for the 2005 Asham Award.

ALEX JOSEPHY lives in the East End of London, works in Holloway as a teacher trainer, and often thinks of ideas for poems while cycling home along the Regents Canal. She enjoys performing her poetry at venues such as Speakeasy in Hackney and the Bug Bar in Brixton.

SARA LANGHAM was born in 1973 in London. After completing her first degree in Russian and English at Leeds University, she worked in the television industry for seven years before completing her Masters in Creative and Life Writing at Goldsmiths in 2004. In 2004 she won a Jerwood/Arvon Young Writer's Apprenticeship award, one of the nine young writers selected. As part of the scheme she worked for six months under the mentorship of the writer Andrew Cowan on her novel, *How It Ends,* which she is currently in the process of completing.

GREGORY LEADBETTER was born in Stourbridge in 1975. He studied Law at Trinity College, Cambridge and practised law for five years before leaving to concentrate on writing. In September 2004, he completed the Masters in Creative and Life Writing at Goldsmiths College with distinction. His poetry was commended in the Arvon International Poetry Competition 2004. In 2005, he was shortlisted for the Strokestown International Poetry Prize and placed second in the Kent and Sussex Poetry Competition. His poems have appeared in *Agenda, Raw Edge, The New Writer* and *Poetry London.* In October 2005, he began a research studentship at Oxford Brookes University. Greg writes for the BBC radio drama *Silver Street.*

TOM LEE'S stories have appeared in *Zoetrope All-Story* in the United States, *The Dublin Review* in Ireland and *Zembla* Magazine in the UK as well as being broadcast on BBC Radio 4. In 2004 he toured with the Tell Tales short story project. At the beginning of 2005, he received an Arts Council grant to complete a collection of short fiction.

This very short story covers a number of **TOM LEVINE'S** writing obsessions – the role of leisure in modern life, the surreal in the everyday, the search for intimacy. It is typically quick, light and comedic. At Goldsmiths and in his writing life before the Masters, he has looked to stretch his writing range, experimenting with autobiography and a collection of poems. His heart, however, is in fiction, and, having completed a number of short stories, he is now working on his first novel – *The Book of Good Skills* – which he hopes will be ready soon.

SARAH MANLEY is a graduate of Illinois State University, where she received a Bachelors in theatre and music, and of Goldsmiths College, where she received a Masters in Creative and Life Writing. Her work has appeared in a number of American journals, and her story 'The Visitor' was long-listed for the 2003 Fish Short Story prize. A Chicago native, she is married and lives in London.

B THEO MAZUMDAR completed his Masters in Creative and Life Writing from Goldsmiths College in 2002. He is currently at work on his first novel, along with a collection of short stories loosely based on the absurd side of life in Texas. He lives in the New York City area.

JOEL MELLOU, born in France, originally studied fine art at Goldsmiths and completed a Masters in 2003.

ALEX MITCHELL lives in North London and is close to finishing his first novel, *Broken Orange Pekoe,* set in Sri Lanka at the turn of the 20th century. He also writes short stories, nonfiction and completed the Masters in Creative and Life Writing in September 2005.

A trained toolmaker, **MAX MUELLER** left his native Germany in 1990 after refusing national service. He now lives in London. His previous writing includes 'Mars Flight' (2004, with Alasdair Mangham) for BBC Radio 4.

JULIA NAPIER was born in 1974 in Madison, Wisconsin. After studying English and French literature at Haverford and Bryn Mawr Colleges, she moved to Argentina. Eschewing all literary concerns, she ran her own shoe company in Buenos Aires for several years. Argentina's 2001 collapse forced her back to writing and somehow on to London. This chapter is an excerpt from her novel-in-progress *Exit Arcadia,* the story of a kidnapping in contemporary Argentina. Her home is in Buenos Aires.

ALEX PHEBY was born in Basildon. In his twenties, he studied art history and went on to work and study critical theory in Manchester throughout the nineties. He currently lives in London with his wife and son and completed the Masters in Creative and Life Writing at Goldsmiths in 2004. His first story, 'The Man Who Drank Bleach', was published by Comma Press in their *Manchester Stories 7* anthology in 2004. He is currently working on his first novel.

AMY PRIOR is a writer based in London. She has edited critically-acclaimed anthologies which have been published in the United Kingdom and the United States: *Retro Retro, Strictly Casual* – published in the United States as *Inappropriate Random* and *Lost On Purpose* – an international collection of stories from cities – to which she contributed her own London story. She has published her fiction in the UK journal *Pretext* and has stories forthcoming in some US journals. She recently completed a book tour in the US for *Lost On Purpose.* She has also read her work at a number of UK venues. She has a Masters in Creative and Life Writing from Goldsmiths, and is completing a linked collection of London stories for which she recently received an individual grant for writing from Arts Council England.

ROSS RAISIN is nearing the end of the first draft of his novel – *Fothergill* (working title). He has been working on it since March 2004. He graduated from Kings College London in 2002, with a First in English, then managed a wine bar for red-cheeked lawyers in the City, and completed the Masters in Creative and Life Writing at Goldsmiths in 2004. He is twenty-five. He has also written a number of short stories, poems and a story for children.

YINKA SUNMONU is one of the first graduates from Goldsmiths' Masters in Creative and Life Writing. In 2003, she published *Cherish* (Mango Publishing) – a novel about private fostering that inspired a conference and led to the 'Cherish the child campaign', a national survey to raise awareness of this issue. In 2004, she founded Ebony Reads, the black and Asian literature website. Yinka has made guest appearances on Radio 4's Open Book and Woman's Hour. In October 2005, she launched Greeoh, the children and young person's website of diverse literature. She is working on her second novel with a working title of *The Stop Gap Café*.

A freelance writer, **BRIDGET WHELAN** has been an agony aunt, a researcher for investigative journalist and socialist campaigner Paul Foot, and contributor to Miriam Stoppard's *Daily Mirror* column. Born within walking distance of Fleet Street, she left school at sixteen and later studied for a degree in Irish history in evening class while her family was growing up. Winning $4,000 in an international short story competition gave her the confidence to apply to Goldsmiths and work on a period novel set in the London Irish community. She now lives on the south coast with an encouraging husband, two handsome sons and a fat cat.

WES WHITE lives in an Arcadian landscape alongside extraordinary creatures comparable to the Bull and Hind of the pieces he contributed to this anthology. His beauty, strength and wisdom are renowned among those fortunate to have met him. In the last ten minutes alone he has wooed a fairytale princess, built a monument to his love for her with his bare hands, and released a small red butterfly found trapped in his bedchamber out into the picturesque landscape of his homestead. Just one of these things happened, but all reflect his nature, so believe any and you won't be led astray.

JENNIFER WINTERS was born in Ireland where she grew up. She studied English at Trinity College Dublin. Her poetry has been published in various publications in the United Kingdom and Ireland. She lives in London where she works as a teacher.

CLAIRE WYBURN is working on her first novel, called *Losin' It,* which is about life after rave culture. A dedicated hardcore raver throughout the 1990s, Claire was editor of various underground house music publications, spending most of her time at Glasgow's *M8,* then Brixton's *Wax.* As well as spending her days immersed in the world of fiction, Claire freelances for various soul, urban and house music magazines and is contributing editor of *MOBO* (Music of Black Origin annual).

EVIE WYLD was born in 1980. She studied creative writing and art at Bath Spa before joining the Masters course at Goldsmiths. She lives in South-east London and won the 'poetry plate' at school – an award that was made up – which consisted of a dinner plate to be returned to the kitchen after the ceremony. This covers her triumphs to date.